DUBAI AMPLIFIED

To Núria

Dubai Amplified

The Engineering of a Port Geography

STEPHEN J. RAMOS
Harvard University, USA

Routledge
Taylor & Francis Group
LONDON AND NEW YORK

First published 2010 by Ashgate Publishing

Published 2016 by Routledge
2 Park Square, Milton Park, Abingdon, Oxfordshire OX14 4RN
711 Third Avenue, New York, NY 10017, USA

First issued in paperback 2016

Routledge is an imprint of the Taylor & Francis Group, an informa business

British Library Cataloguing in Publication Data
Ramos, Stephen J.
Dubai amplified : the engineering of a port geography. --
(Design and the built environment series)
1. Urbanization--United Arab Emirates--Dubayy (Emirate)
2. City planning--United Arab Emirates--Dubayy (Emirate)
3. Free ports and zones--United Arab Emirates--Dubayy
(Emirate) 4. Economic development projects--United Arab
Emirates--Dubayy (Emirate) 5. Infrastructure (Economics)--
United Arab Emirates--Dubayy (Emirate) 6. Dubayy (United
Arab Emirates : Emirate)--Economic conditions.
I. Title II. Series
307.1'416'095357-dc22

Library of Congress Cataloging-in-Publication Data
Ramos, Stephen J.
Dubai amplified : the engineering of a port geography / by Stephen J. Ramos.
p. cm. -- (Design and the built environment)
Includes bibliographical references and index.
ISBN 978-1-4094-0822-2 (hbk) 1. Harbors--United Arab
Emirates--Dubayy (Emirate) 2. Infrastructure (Economics)--United Arab Emirates--Dubayy
(Emirate) I. Title.
HE560.D76R36 2010
387.1095357--dc22

2010020552

ISBN 13: 978-1-138-25339-1 (pbk)
ISBN 13: 978-1-4094-0822-2 (hbk)

Contents

List of Figures and Tables

Figures

Tables

Preface

In writing this book, I reviewed the historic planning documents and literature on Dubai's urban development, in which I identified important moments of this history that were missing from the extant literature. I conducted interviews over three trips to Dubai between February 2006 and April 2009 with those involved in this history, which also included trips to the archives of the Halcrow Group at their London and Swindon offices to conduct primary research. Halcrow has been involved with Dubai's city building since its first engineering project of dredging the creek during the late 1950s, and continues to be an important player in its planning and development scenario.

The dearth of specific digital cartographic material and general socio-economic data was a challenge during the research, but one not uncommon to the region. As I explore in greater detail in Chapter Four, the Balkanization of planning in Dubai has created a series of semi-public regulatory agencies that now compete with one another, and in this competition, information becomes an important and protected resource. Many have discussed the challenges within the public sector of how to increase information sharing through information technology and trust (Salem and Jarrar 2009). Needless to say, if the challenge of information sharing occurs within agencies of the same public sector, acquiring such information as an external researcher becomes all the more problematic. The result has meant that the book was pushed toward a more qualitative methodology rather than an argument that relies heavily on quantitative information. The objective is that the arguments stand as a conceptual framework; sturdy and convincing enough to a point where additional quantitative and cartographic information would fit well and potentially reinforce it.

During the writing of this book, the international financial crisis greatly impacted and altered the development pace in Dubai. *CityScapes,* Dubai's real-estate trade show where it had grown accustomed to announcing its next grandiose project, as if to lay pioneering claims on the future, was noticeably calmer in 2009. Dubai's pre-eminent real-estate developers, Nakheel and Emaar, even considered skipping the event altogether, which marked a clear change from previous years where they were billed as the main event.

As such, *Dubai Amplified* now becomes a way not only to understand its business and territorial development strategies over the past decade, but also how these strategies played a role in leading up to the present financial challenges. The enormous amount of online built environment in the buildings that line Sheikh Zayed Road are now orphaned until further notice. With the continued beneficence of Abu Dhabi, its capital neighbor, Dubai will resume its development, though likely in a more humbled, deferential fashion, at least for a while. The present moment offers an opportunity to look back at those elements, patterns, and infrastructural components that Dubai produced and that produced Dubai. Exactly what the future holds is particularly hard to predict, because such a demure Dubai is hard to imagine, as the confidence that anchored its previous borrowing and building have been significantly shaken. Dubai's resilience to international economic downturn helped it through the 1980s, with the added benefit of luck of location. Conflict in the northern Gulf and Lebanon brought trade and business to its safer harbors, which happened to be located strategically along the route connecting Southeast Asian production with European markets. Many projects were then shelved that are only now being completed, including the new Al-Maktoum International Airport. It is possible that those projects announced so boldly at previous *CityScapes* but are now on hold may also return—potentially in altered, more amplified iterations (see Dubai Metro). I will visit this issue more in the Conclusion, and I suggest readers be mindful of questions concerning Dubai's future as they go exploring through its past.

Stephen J. Ramos
Cambridge, MA
September 30, 2010

Acknowledgments

This book was written with the help and input of more people than it is possible to thank here.

I would like to thank the members of my doctoral committee, Hashim Sarkis, Peter G. Rowe, Joan Busquets, and Roger Owen for their continued guidance, support, and advice, and for the many conversations that we've had over the past five years.

I would also like to thank Dean Tarik M. Yousef, the Dubai School of Government, and the Dubai Initiative at the Belfer Center for Science and International Affairs at the John F. Kennedy School of Government for their support.

Thanks to Melissa Vaughn, Carola Hein, James Onley, Mark Harris, Rodney Carran, Chris Fleming, Chris Cooch, Valerie Rose, Carolyn Court, Adam Guppy, Greg Harris, Yasser El-Sheshtawi, Joan Alemany Llovera, Todd Reisz, Nick Matthews, Tony Walker, Sarah Horsley, Andrew Trimbee, Khaled Alawadi, Richard Marshall, Teo Ah Khing, Stephen Brannon, Tarek Coury, Fadi Salem, Paul Dyer, Somaya Farid, Minas Abdulrahman Bin Dakhan, Ahmed Kanna, George Katodrytis, James Linton, Tariq Al Hassan, Saud Sharaf, Marco Sacchi, Adrian Lim, Maha Khalil, Tariq Yousif Al Janahi, Khaled Ahmed, Mahmood Albastaki, James Robinson, Kathleen Cusack, Sean O'Neil, Rami Khouri, Naseem Khuri, Ashraf Hegazy, Adnan Al Abaar, Mohamed Zafine, Gareth Doherty, Neyran Turan, Rania Ghosn, El Hadi Jazairy, Antonio Petrov, Henry S. Marcus, Daniel Schodek, Bjarke Ingels, Rosa Rodrigo Sanz, Amina Baar-Baarenfels, Santiago Campos, Salvador Borrell, and Maria Buhigas.

Many thanks also go to my family, including Peter, Diane, and my beautiful nephew Simon, my father Emilio and my mother Jane for their love and support.

Finally, I thank my daughter Gala, and my wife Núria, to whom I dedicate this work.

Introduction

On September 9, 2009, the trains of the newly-inaugurated Dubai Metro began service for the public. The $7.6 billion metro system was the first of its kind to open in the Gulf States, and its publicity sought to place Dubai among the great cities of the world that also enjoy metro systems: New York, London, Tokyo, etc. Ten of the projected 29 stations opened along a 41 kilometer stretch for the inauguration, but a significant portion of the system was still unfinished (Salama and Hall 2009). An elevated monorail system was projected for the Jebel Ali New Town in the late 1970s (Peddle et al. 1977: E1), but the new Dubai Metro expanded the scope and scale of the project by promising emirate-wide service throughout Dubai's territory. As the September 15 anniversary of the Lehman Brothers' collapse approached—which had a devastating effect on Dubai's boom economy—the planned event was clearly aimed at renewing international investment confidence in Dubai and to demonstrate the ability of its leadership to complete projects. In July 2009 it was reported that over 400 United Arab Emirates (UAE) projects worth approximately $300 billion (many of which were planned for Dubai) had been put on hold (Salama and Hall 2009). Also on September 9, Dubai ruler Sheikh Mohammed Bin Rashid Al-Maktoum gave press interviews to placate worries over the emirate's financial situation in which he called for calm. "I assure you we are alright, the UAE is alright, and we are not worried … We'll be more careful now" (Hamade and Sharif 2009). The inaugural event, as political ribbon-cutting events for new infrastructure historically do, brought out the political elite to congratulate itself, in this case, for a job half-finished.

Infrastructure has always been essential to the projects and discourses of development and modernity, and contemporary conditions of rapid urbanization in Southeast Asia, the Gulf, and Africa would suggest a return to these interdependent discourses, albeit expressed spatially in alternate forms and manners (Campanella 2008, Bouman et al. 2007, Burdett et al. 2007, Rowe 2005). Infrastructure has occupied a central role in Dubai's modernization project over the past half century as a monument to the progress it promises. In his book *Risk Society*, Ulrich Beck proposes the idea of reflexive modernization as "a *systemic way of dealing with hazards and insecurities induced and introduced by modernization itself* (Beck 1992: 21, italics from original text)." For Beck, reflexive modernization represents a new phase where the consequences of modernization catch up with its aspirations and pretentions. In this regard, we can understand the Metro as response to the international criticism Dubai has received for the environmental impacts of its development model. We can further think about the Metro project as an attempt to regain the confidence of the international lending community by investing in low-risk infrastructure to counterbalance a decade's worth of speculative real estate investment with money borrowed from that community. Thus the infrastructure project takes on more layered meaning, in addition to its primary transportation function. The Dubai Metro also demonstrates that Beck's reflexive modernization can occur concurrently with traditional modernization processes, and that infrastructure can occupy multiple roles within specific urban political circumstances. Indeed, Sheikh Mohammed's statement—both projecting stability and reflexively stating that Dubai will "be more careful"—convey exactly this developmental simultaneity.

Dubai Amplified explores the multiple roles and meanings infrastructure assumes within rapidly urbanizing circumstances, looking specifically at the case of Dubai as global port geography. The theme of infrastructure is used in the book as both an heuristic mechanism to establish a narrative of metropolitan spatial development resulting from international production and trade flows, and as a lens to guide exploration of rapid urbanization processes. As communication and transportation technologies have progressed and intensified, the protagonism of "circuitries" that house, communicate or facilitate flows of goods, services and/or information has come more directly to the fore (Shannon and Smets 2010, Erie 2004, Hanley 2004, Altshuler and Luberoff 2003, Hoete 2003, Sassen 2002, Graham and Marvin 2001, Kasarda 2000, Meyer 1999). These kinds of infrastructure require a scale of investment and political expediency that spur local public/private collaboration, resulting often in a blurring of these two sectors wherein citizen welfare is overlooked in favor of an urban economic imperative.

Nevertheless, historical precedent demonstrates that it has been precisely the response of citizen action groups to these fast-track projects that have helped to forge a more open relationship of governance. Social movements to save urban environmental quality were an important part of Japanese politics in the 1970s, after an infrastructural and larger economic push had led its government's actions since 1945 (Hasegawa 2004, Sorensen 2002). In Latin America, popular urban social movements were mobilized around informal neighborhood settlements struggles for public infrastructure as a means to create new political spaces throughout the continent's post-war urbanization boom (Castells 1983). In the United States, the debates around issues of infrastructure, urban quality, and social complexity were personified in the political battles between Jane Jacobs and Robert Moses in New York City during the first part of the twentieth-century. Recent exhibitions and publications on the work of Robert Moses have served as an overdue reevaluation of his work, and part of a broader acceptance of the necessary role of infrastructure for the functioning of large cities, and not exclusively as the bane of neighborhood or community planning (Ballon and Jackson 2007, Berman 1982, Caro 1974, Jacobs 1961). This reconsideration has intensified with the present international financial crisis, as infrastructure has been identified as an important opportunity for strategic public investment, and an attractive asset for private equity (Josselyn et al. 2009). These debates also occur in the broader context of the social, spatial, and economic consequences of globalization in cities around the world.

Globalization and the City

Beginning in the 1980s, the internationalization of finance and the intensification of transnational flows of goods and services as a result of technological innovation in transportation and communications were identified as processes of "globalization," and this lead to an extensive literature on "global" or "world" cities. While the term "world cities" is credited to Patrick Geddes as far back as 1915, economic conditions in the late twentieth-century appeared to consolidate a central global function for cities. Perhaps it was a certain *fin de siècle* spirit, or the long shadow of Marxist thought which still insisted on an economic "sub-structure" determining the "superstructure" of urbanism, but as the century drew to a close, there seemed to be a new kind of city called forth to accompany a new global connectivity and communication, now possible at an unprecedented speed.

Saskia Sassen's seminal book *The Global City* (1991) argues that global financial flows bestow new command center roles on certain cities and revitalize those urban districts that are connected to global transaction networks. Her research on New York, London, and Tokyo demonstrates how these cities have become leaders in a global economy that places new emphasis on what she calls the F.I.R.E. sectors (Finance, Insurance and Real Estate), as well as the ancillary support services for these sectors, which she groups together as "producer services." Sassen's book countered claims that new communication and transport technology would eventually signify the "end of geography," and by extension, the end of cities, as some envisioned. Techno-centric research believed that innovations in technology would allow people to work from anywhere in the world ("on top of a mountain" was often cited), and thus render unnecessary our need to live in cities (Mitchell 1995). This, of course, echoed similar calls for the end of the nineteenth-century city when transportation networks were envisioned in the 1920s, and even before then in Ebenezer Howard's Garden City proposal. But the insistence of people to congregate in person proves relentless, and Sassen points out that geography will not only remain alive in the global age, but its strategic importance will become all the more decisive in attracting and concentrating global capital, talent, producer services and amenities. Thus, with globalization, the intensification of infrastructural systems magnifies the strategic importance of cities in a dialectical relationship.

Sassen's book provoked a series of responses in a broad range of disciplines, from the social sciences to public policy, but for our purposes, it opened a whole body of literature on how globalization would impact the shape of cities. This literature, in many ways, simply picked up on post-industrial urban literature and gave it a new packaging. Sassen's identification of a revitalized urban center had, in fact, been going on since the late 1970s. The gas crisis of 1973, along with increasing calls for more sustainable urban management and no growth/smart growth alternatives to the post-World War II "endless resource" mentality brought new concern for the sprawling growth of city-regions (Scott 2001, Duany et al. 2000, Garreau 1991). The international wave of fiscal tightening during conservative political regimes pushed cities to encourage more entrepreneurial strategies for their centers, and public and private ventures formed to help recover this strategic urban area. Baltimore's Harbor Place experience with the Rouse Company was repeated in many cities throughout the world as a useful strategy to commercially repopulate outdated waterfront port and industrial facilities that had fallen into disuse and decline (Ward 2006, Marshall 2001). Similar techniques were also used for ex-industrial areas in other parts of the city, under the classification of "brownfield reconversion." The urban renaissance brought new investment into city centers and began to reimbue them with civic, symbolic, and functional values that they had been lacking for decades.

Urban renaissance brought investment back to downtown areas, while at the same time, a metropolitan landscape had been firmly established which gave "city-regions" poli-nucleated mosaic settlement patterns that blurred distinctions between the urban and the rural. Along with post-war highway infrastructure, this ex-urban push into the hinterland was also the result of airport and port facilities locating outside the urban core in search of cheaper and more abundant land that could accommodate the increasing spatial requirements of these large-scale trade infrastructures. The "middle landscape" emerged, usually outside inner-ring suburbs, and much of the literature on cities focused on the difficulties in containing urban conurbations out of concerns for both planning jurisdiction and the environment (Scott 2001, Soja 2000, Gordon and Richardson 1997, Barnett 1995, Rusk 1993, Rowe 1991, Garreau 1991).

The metropolitan push and the regional focus was by no means a new phenomenon, which is why it was termed "new regionalism," to distinguish itself from Ebenezer Howard, Lewis Mumford, and other predecessors. Echoing above-mentioned economic-based literature, more than anything, the "new regionalism" was a call for cooperation among metropolitan and regional municipalities to collaborate on regional strategies to attract global investment, talent, and resources. Many of these same municipalities had historically been at odds over local investment in a kind of "beggar thy neighbor" zero-sum gain for local wealth. The new regionalism proposed that in the wake of the fiscal tightening and a general move toward political decentralization, global competitiveness would increasingly depend on the ability of regions to pool their resources and produce strategic, complementary profiles (Calthorpe and Fulton 2001, Frug 1999, Lovering 1999, Cisneros 1995). Nevertheless, competitive histories do not disappear easily, and simultaneous, complex combinations of collaboration and competition among neighboring, cities, regions, emirates, and countries is a more accurate description of how these regional issues play out (Feiocke 2004).

Part and parcel of both the renaissance of urban centers and the push toward the metropolitan scale were the increasing divisions between rich and poor communities, and the exacerbation of spatial segregation. Rich enclaves had become the exceptional and isolated spaces, in contrast to the poorer ghettos of the industrial past, thus tearing apart the social cohesion and public function of the city, as envisioned by Louis Wirth in the early twentieth-century (1925). In the literature on the spatialization of globalization and its impact on urban landscapes, issues of socio-spatial segregation, along with the metropolitan scale mentioned above, occupy most of the discussion. Terms such as "dual cities," "quartered cities," and various socio-economic partitionings of metropolitan regions echo this contemporary threat to civic and spatial unity in urban areas throughout the world (Marcuse and van Kempen 2000). Indeed, Dubai's real estate development marketing over the past decade has incorporated a multiple "cities within the city" strategy to underscore the autonomous, isolated, and exclusive nature of new residential communities as a primary selling point (Sarkis and Abulhasan 2005).

Finally, as mentioned, the technological changes and spatial demands of transportation infrastructures were among the multitude of factors that pushed cities into their metropolitan hinterlands. Until recently, trade platforms and facilities were often bypassed in urban research as processing "black boxes," existing outside the *civitas* realm of the city. However, there is now a growing literature focusing on the importance of trade infrastructure facilities as important nodes that impact and shape metropolitan geographies. After an initial infatuation with the somewhat abstracted processes of globalized flows, urbanists are now harkening back to the more tangible, physical impacts these flows have on specific localities, and how these infrastructures and facilities are increasingly important in contemporary urban development and regional competition. Airport development and strategic economic corridors between city centers and airports, transshipment centers and multi-modal trade platforms (sea-land-air), public transport and metropolitan connectivity, and digital infrastructure for telecommunication capacity are all topics that have approached what may be considered either new or more intensively-used infrastructural elements of the urban landscape (Shannon and Smets 2010, Waldheim 2006, Erie 2004, Pinder and Slack 2004, Mostafavi and Najle 2003, Kasarda 1999, 2000, Cevero 1998, Mitchell 1995).

Process and Artifact

If globalization research was overzealous in its abstract deduction, particularly in terms of the assumed changes to the urban form as a consequence of transnational flows, it is important now to closely interrogate specific localities to begin to understand if indeed global connectivity has formally impacted cities—and if so, how. If no city is untouched by processes of globalization, can we begin to identify common physical characteristics and idiosyncrasies in different cities across the globe? Is there an *ipso facto* physical form for the global city emerging? If so, what exactly are these formal manifestations? Within specific urban landscapes in different metropolitan regions in different cultures across the globe, *how* are global influences affecting the urban form?

The initial questions of this book sought to pursue these themes by combining the literature on globalization and its urban impacts with the methodologies incorporated in urban morphology research to inductively explore if and how, in fact, globalization was impacting and/or replacing the growth logic of cities. Though there are several different groupings and subgroupings of morphological research, Manuel de Solá-Morales's definition underscores the essential element of time and change within the field: "... measuring time with space. As in dance, where one discovers rings and distances in space as forms through which we represent rhythm and musical time, urban theory also needs to dare to measure time in space" (1997: 19). The research would need to accept the possible outcome that transnational flows have *no influence* on a city's physical form. Much of globalization's technological revolution is concentrated in telematic flows that may stream invisibly through cities without any noticeable impact (Mitchell 1995). This could be particularly true of urban environments with strong and diverse character that are unfazed by new forms; cities where this kind of heterogeneous cacophony is a *modus operandi*, and new architectural and urban forms arrive critically unnoticed. Conversely, the impact of globalization could have a great influence on urban form—one imagines this to be the case particularly for newer cities like Dubai, where development has either avoided an urban industrial phase, or simply moved contemporary city building to new areas of the metropolitan region. In between these two extremes lie other intermediate possibilities, where the impact of globalization may be visible but not wholly determinant.

The debates engendered in the architecture field around "regional" architecture tended to limit what could have been nuanced discussions around the internationalization of architecture into nostalgic and essentialized dead-ends.[1] Though an inductive comparative study perhaps could have avoided a similar fate, as the research continued, I came to realize that within discussions of globalization and the city, research has moved away from the agency of physical elements of city. Much of the "networked city" literature presupposes that with global connectivity, international flows will enter cities unidirectionally and reconfigure their spatial logics (Albrechts and Mandelbaum 2005, Castells 1989). This research misses the equally-important point that urban form, facilities, character, and policy can be precisely the decisive elements that attract global activities to a particularly city. There has been a more recent push-back against "networked city" research that recalls the morphological interest to understand the city as urban artifact. The literature expresses greater interest in projects not merely as the reflection of global processes, but also as agents of catharsis and change, which themselves can influence local and international processes from the inside outward (Ramos and Turan 2009, Aureli 2008). In the interest of considering these themes more profoundly in one specific place rather than potentially more superficial research of several case studies, *Dubai Amplified* looks at the case of the emirate, and intentionally studies those infrastructural projects that transformed both its geomorphology and its international standing.

1 Particularly the debates that came out of Kenneth Frampton's (1983) work on critical regionalism.

Dubai

Dubai has grown dramatically over the past 50 years, moving beyond its original walled settlement around the mouth of its creek to become an aspiring global city, of the kind that Saskia Sassen described and others rank (Stanley 2001). As an international *entrepôt*, Dubai combines a tradition of merchant-friendly policies and investment in trade infrastructure with a monarchical, *dirigisme* political structure. The hybrid of both an outward-looking, entrepreneurial state for commerce, and an internal welfare state that provides extensive social services for its citizens (who make up small percentage of the overall population), offer an optimum context to explore the spatial expressions of these globalization debates. The protagonism and territorial impact of Dubai's large-scale trade infrastructure on its metropolitan landscape have been both foundational and definitive. Curiously, however, this infrastructure is also removed from Dubai's inhabitants; surrounded largely by prohibitive free trade zone compound fences. It was this contradiction that drew me to study the emirate's urbanism to explore some of the larger questions about globalization and the city. The city's "newness" seemed to contain the contradicting multitude of twenty-first century city building and the strange spatial manifestations of an international financial system gone haywire. The extreme contrast between the attitudes of developmental invincibility and success that surrounded Dubai during its boom decade, and the precipitous fall to humility that the recent financial crises have brought on, suggest that the emirate can serve as a kind of pulse to measure the state of international cities heavily tied to global trade, finance, and investment. Dubai's development has occurred within a very specific political, economic, and historic context, and for this reason it is important to both describe these particularities, and subsequently consider how larger lessons can be drawn from this specific case study in the lower Gulf.[2]

Dubai is an emirate that, along with six others, formed the federation of the United Arab Emirates in 1971. Before 1971, Dubai was part of a larger British protectorate system known as the "Trucial States," based on the British backing of certain ruling families with the understanding that British interests would be supported in the region. Throughout the nineteenth and early twentieth centuries these interests were mainly focused on the peaceful passage of trade routes, which traveled back and forth between Britain and its colonies in India and East Asia. Oil discovery in Persia and Saudi Arabia at the beginning of the twentieth-century, and shortly thereafter in Kuwait and Bahrain, brought a more specific and intentional interest from the British to the region. Soon afterward, oil exploration was carried out in all of its Gulf protectorates, and the port town of Aden was declared a crown colony where the British built their principal

2 The region referred to as the "Gulf" is alternatively called either the "Persian Gulf" or the "Arabian Gulf" by different sectors. I am aware of this debate, but it is not central to my research. As such, throughout the book, I use the term "Gulf" to refer to this region and this body of water.

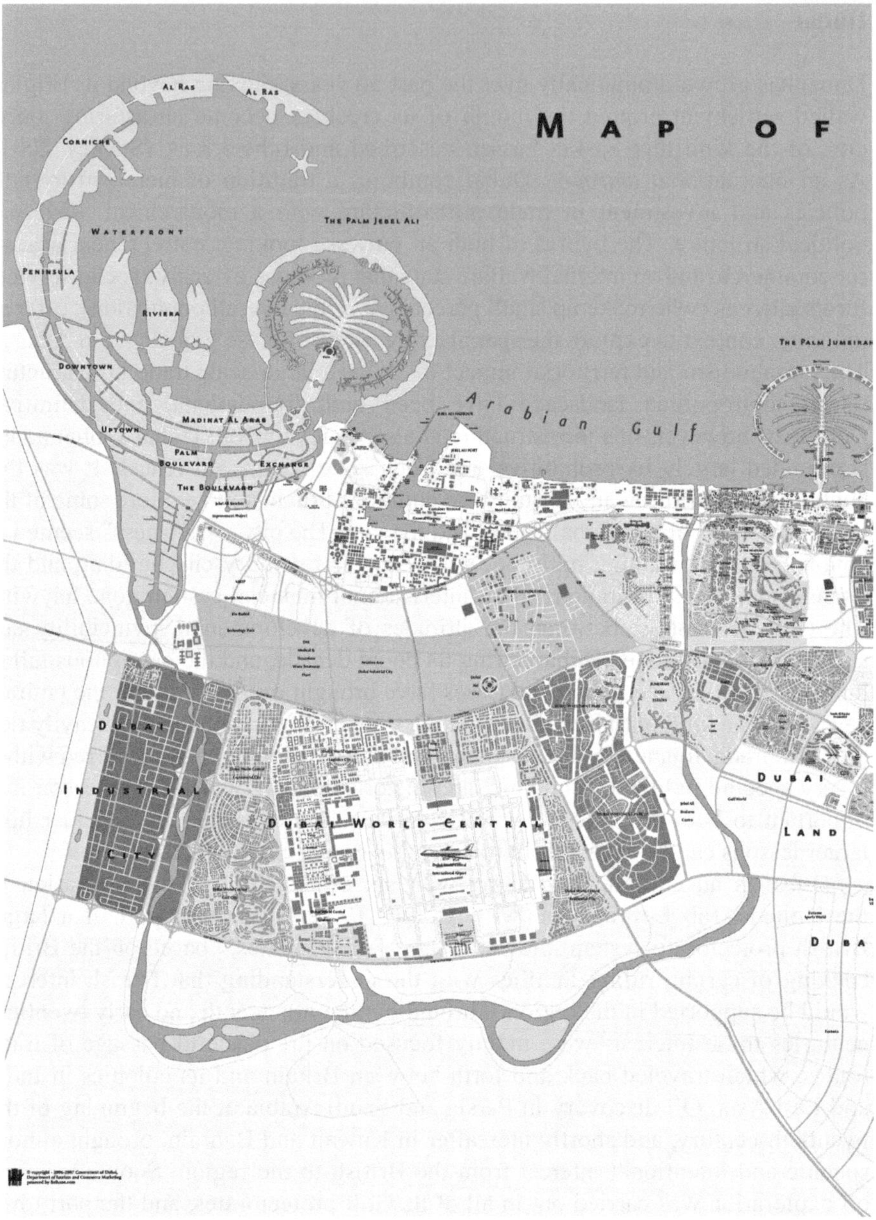

Figure 0.1 Map of Dubai from 2008 that includes many planned projects, particularly in the southwestern sector, that have since been put on hold

Source: © Government of Dubai

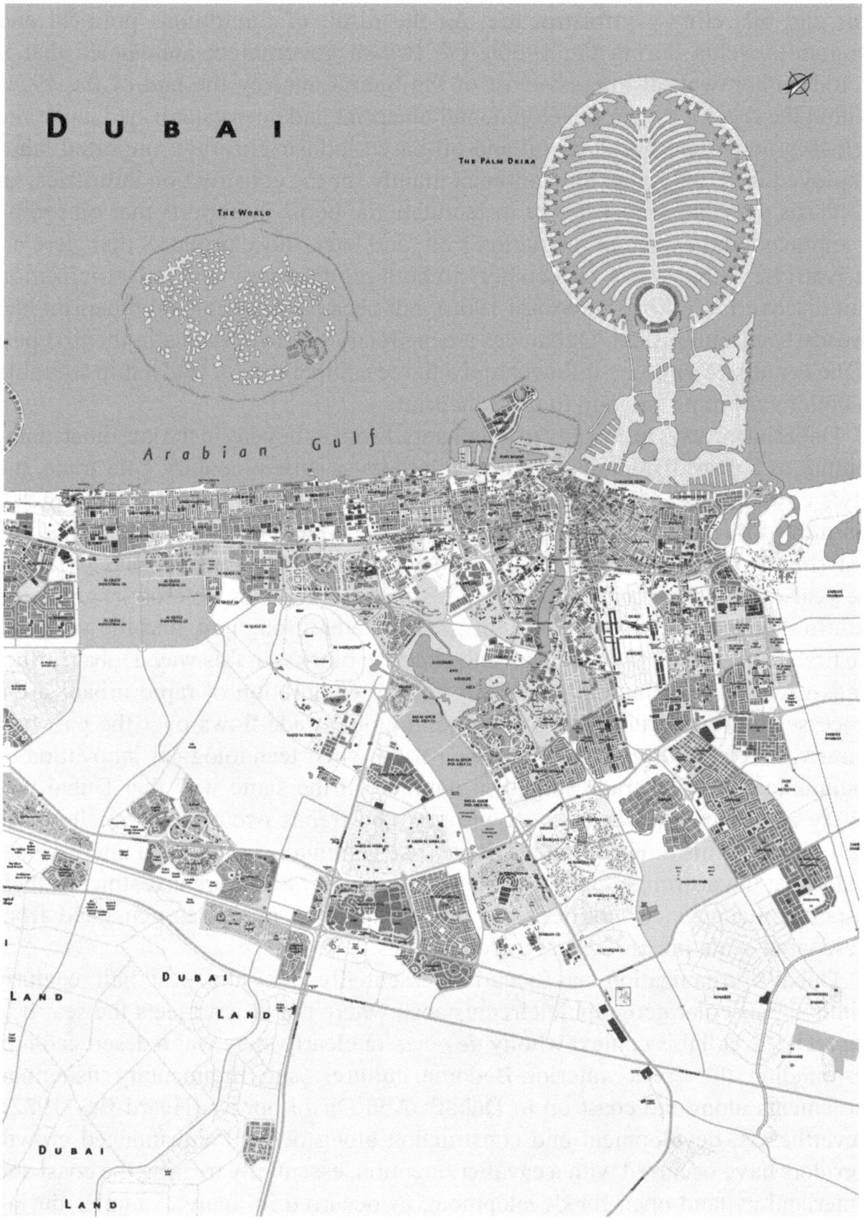
DUBAI
THE PALM DEIRA
THE WORLD
Arabian Gulf
DUBAI
LAND
LAND
DUBAI
LAND

port and oil refinery infrastructure. As the result of tumultuous political and economic events during the 1960s, the British government announced that it would withdrawal all interests east of the Suez Canal by the end of the 1971. Within the region, a clear developmental blueprint had been established under the British protectorate based on oil and oil-based industrialization: imported labor employed from the Asian Subcontinent mainly for the construction industries, an emphasis on trade infrastructure to facilitate the boost in imports that oil profits precipitated, the export of the region's oil, and later, those products that were oil derivatives. Dubai was a "latecomer" to both oil discovery and industrialization (not discovering oil offshore until 1966), but because this regional blueprint had already been established, Dubai was a beneficiary of those events in the first part of the century. As a close follower and a fierce competitor, its leadership was able to both incorporate and add to this blueprint.

Dubai has always been a city of merchants. From its heyday in the late nineteenth-century as a pearl fishing and trading hub to its twentieth-century gold trade, the city's cosmopolitan vitality has its origins in the creek and the trade activity that has moved through it. In 1956, trucking mogul Malcolm McLean launched the first shipping container voyage from Newark to Houston, which was precisely the year when Dubai commissioned the British Sir William Halcrow engineering firm to dredge the creek to allow for greater trade throughput, and the year that the first house was built in Dubai using concrete blocks. In this way, Dubai further lends itself as a fascinating case study for the exploration of rapid urbanization processes, infrastructure development, and global trade flows over the past half century, precisely during the post-war period when technological innovation in communications and trade surged in parallel. In the same way that Dubai was a very attentive follower of those projects and trends occurring throughout the Gulf region at this time, since then, it has also continuously followed international trends that have strongly influenced its own trade infrastructure investments, their associate management entities, and the urbanization processes generated from these large-scale infrastructural trade facilities.

Dubai's urbanization has occurred essentially over the past half century, within a particular geographic circumstance where the desert meets the sea. It is imprecise to call this context wholly *de novo* for clearly there was a desert ecology surrounding the creek, interior Bedouin cultures, and rudimentary fisherman settlements along the coast up to Dubai's Abu Dhabi border (Heard-Bey 1982). Nevertheless, development and construction along defined and induced growth corridors have occurred with a cavalier intention, essentially treating the coast and hinterland as land open for development, as occurred in many examples during modern urban expansion internationally. Dubai serves as a fascinating urban laboratory, having achieved in physical urban development over 50 years what it took other cities a 100 years, and sometimes more. The element of time becomes a strong force in both Dubai's development and urbanizing narratives, because of its status as a "latecomer" that needed to catch up quickly. Dubai's urban history years serves as a way to interrogate rapid metropolitan development in the globalized moment. I will explore the infrastructural logic that has guided this development both in terms of its physical manifestations, but also how it defined the internationalization of the "Dubai Model"[3] of rapid territorial development through its Dubai World Holding Company. Each have developed incrementally and cumulatively, and grown through successive cycles and iterations.

The significance of the Dubai Model changed radically after September 15, 2008, when Lehman Brothers' bankruptcy set off a chain of events that initiated a precipitous international financial crisis. The news came as a particular shock for Dubai because it was only months earlier that the entire Gulf region was awash in petrodollars as oil prices hit record peaks in July. The complexities of Dubai's debt burden grew, and it became clear that its flamboyant projects from the previous decade were paid for through highly-leveraged debt it is now struggling to pay. In this way, *Dubai Amplified* reflects on the emirate's development at the close of a particular cyclical moment. Dubai's development pace also slowed in the 1980s when oil prices fell with the international recession at the beginning of the decade. A key difference between the two periods, however, is that now Dubai's interests have moved beyond its local and regional circumstances through the various international business components of its Dubai Holding Company conglomerate. In addition, the repercussions of the model are already manifest in the scale, iconography, speed, and international ambitions of projects in places like Kuwait, Abu Dhabi, and Qatar. The Dubai Model changed regional city-making practices, precisely in its amplification of those regional projects and typologies that it originally borrowed. As a classic *entrepôt*, Dubai processed these urban and infrastructural component imports for international re-export. *Dubai Amplified* explores this history through the lens of its trade infrastructure.

Social and Environmental Considerations

Dubai's development achieved a prominent level of international notoriety. Dubai was celebrated for its vertiginous urban growth rate over a short period of time, which many deemed as a successful regional example. It was also heavily criticized, largely by the press in Western Europe and the United States, for violating fundamental labor laws and degrading the environment with an inappropriate urbanism comprised of deleterious climate control mechanisms, excessive water use, and the destruction of the marine ecology through ambitious land reclamation projects. More recently, the same Western press has enjoyed a certain degree of *schadenfreude* at watching Dubai hit dire economic straights after enjoying a highly-publicized decade of success. While it is beyond the scope of this book to focus on this international notoriety that either celebrates or damns Dubai's development trajectory, I would like to address

3 The term "Dubai Model" is used widely. See Hvidt 2007.

from the outset some points about the social contract and environmental issues associated with the Dubai Model.

Immigration is not new to Dubai. As a merchants' city, successive waves of immigrants arrived along with the pearl trade during the nineteenth-century. Immigration spiked significantly at the turn of the century when a punitive tax regime was implemented by Tehran at the Persian Lingah port across the Straits of Hormuz, which attracted trade and merchants to the newly-declared free port in Dubai. This first wave of immigration, mostly comprised of Persians and Indians, was received and incorporated into Dubai's society, fulfilling an important role in the trade community and helping to establish a finance system to fund pearling expeditions (Al-Sayegh 1998). The second wave of immigration arrived to Dubai during the 1960s, when oil exploration and subsequent discovery spawned a booming construction industry that required labor to keep up with the developmental pace. A steady labor force had been imported to the Gulf from the Asian Subcontinent for construction in neighboring Kuwait, Bahrain, and Saudi Arabia since their oil discoveries (Seccombe and Lawless 1987), so a regional labor supply was available for work. Further labor was imported as well, which would more than triple the Dubai population from 1968 to 1975. In contrast to the first wave, however, immigrants of the second wave were not integrated into the society as citizens (Pacione 2005: 258–9). This may have been due to the increased benefits and structures of a welfare system that Dubai wanted to afford exclusively to those it defined as its citizens. As a development labor strategy, there were economic advantages in keeping labor expendable, such that technological shifts would not leave an excess labor force without work and in need of government assistance, because they could simply be deported. In addition, there were certainly concerns that the demographic changes of this boom period could significantly alter the cultural composition of Dubai, and at some point, threaten the ruling family structure if the growing immigrant population were to be given citizenship. Thus the social contract was codified with the second wave of immigrants, where the imported labor force would not have access to citizenship, nor the rights afforded to Dubaians or those citizens of the greater Gulf Cooperation Council community.

Christopher M. Davidson (2008) has pointed out that along with the basic human rights for laborers with which one may take issue regarding this social contact, in the long run, it has created a system where human resources must be imported to Dubai to carry out the work in many sectors and to undergird its society. The welfare system, described above, offers comfortable jobs to a large percentage of the local Dubaians in the public sector, where they are neither required nor motivated to achieve higher educational training. This is certainly not true for the entire Dubai population, as some do go abroad for training, but in comparison with other countries of the region, Dubai's higher educational development has lagged behind (Owen 2008). While the technology transfer of joint venture projects of the 1960s and 1970s helped to import advanced "hardware" technology, the human resource training that was supposed to accompany this was not as successful (Al-Otaiba 1977, Zahalan 1984). All of this, as Davidson points out, creates vulnerabilities, and a dependence on this imported labor force that can be a limiting factor when not available. It also creates a strong, impermeable class system based on ethnicity and place of origin, demarcating clear boundaries as to who belongs where within the society.

If we return to the element of time, one could say the speed of capital accumulation and urbanization, and Dubai's "latecomer" identity, has not yet given rise to an identifiable or effective local reform movement for labor laws. If we recall nineteenth-century labor conditions of London, New York or Paris, within a similar developmental circumstance and before such labor reform had arrived, then perhaps Dubai's social contract, within its urban development trajectory, is less surprising. However, living as we do in a global society, Dubai's labor practices appear not only outdated, but offensive from a basic human rights perspective. Above I mentioned how there is a history of large-scale infrastructural projects engendering citizen movements for more transparent and democratic governance, and one hopes that this may be the case also for Dubai in its near future. What form this will take, however, has yet to be manifest.

It should also be mentioned that within the larger theme of infrastructure and urban development, the social contract in Dubai and the larger Gulf with expatriate workers is somewhat unique. There are many examples of large-scale infrastructural investment employed as a national labor policy to raise the overall standard of living for a country within developing circumstances. In the United States during the Great Depression of the 1930s, a significant portion of the public investment in infrastructure, from the Works Progress Administration to the Tennessee Valley Authority, was launched specifically to provide work for a large, unemployed national labor force. Along with the primary objectives of a specific infrastructure project, it can also be used as a vehicle for Keynesian investment to boost national employment. In more recent circumstances, during the 1960s, Lee Kuan Yew's leadership in Singapore consciously combined an emphasis on ambitious infrastructural investment with a national labor policy to both quell potential social unrest among the large number of regional immigrants entering Singapore, and to raise their living standards (Lui and Tan 2001). In Dubai, because expatriate workers are not granted citizenship, infrastructural development does not incorporate these labor policy considerations, and this iterant group is more expendable when there is no work available for them. This point is important in understanding Dubai's development policies and circumstances as distinct from those of other regions and historical trajectories.

Concerns for the environmental consequences of Dubai's growth have also been raised by international non-governmental organizations, such as the World Wildlife Fund, which identified the larger UAE as one of the world's most harmful countries in terms of its environmental footprint (Ewing et al. 2008). The effects of Dubai's rapid development processes heavily tax its ground water supplies, rely on mechanical climate control for its ever-growing crop of glass-clad buildings, emit pollutants from its industrial parks and oil and gas harvesting, and heavily impact the coastal marine ecology though massive dredging and land reclamation projects. Both the UAE and Dubai governments have recognized these processes and have pledged to improve their development practices in terms of this heavy environmental footprint, but this will not be easy. The desire to build a contemporary urban environment within the harsh climatic environment of the desert, be it Phoenix, Las Vegas, Dubai, or the Ordos Desert in Inner Mongolia, still predominantly incorporate technology for artificial climate control and the need for extensive water resources, with an entire series of energies to run such projects. Again, within a comparative context, the environmental reforms of late capitalism have come to western countries comparatively late in their urban development processes, and were largely not around during the past two centuries of western city making. In the city of Boston, indeed as with many coastal cities, land reclamation has played an essential role in urban expansion (Krieger et al. 1999). Nevertheless, improved technology for more sensitive environmental city building is now certainly more internationally available, and is at Dubai's disposal as much as anywhere else. One hopes that neighboring projects in the region such as Masdar City in Abu Dhabi, which claims to have zero carbon emission due to carbon capture technologies, will provoke a similar competitive engineering race with those parallel races for tallest building, largest port, etc. The shelving of many projects throughout the Gulf region due to international financial conditions may offer precisely the opportunity to begin to incorporate new technologies that ameliorate the region's construction practices and limit the negative environmental impact caused by future urban development projects.

Both the labor and environmental issues of globalization have been the central points around which those who protest the internationalization of business rally, with the criticism that those geographic locations that least regulate labor and environmental (not to mention financial) conditions are those that are best rewarded in the new era. The complexity is compounded as areas like China and India aspire toward material lifestyles of the west, which many claim would outstrip the global environmental carrying capacity. Clearly these are not questions with easy answers, but as one considers these themes within Dubai's specific development context, their recurrence is certainly appropriate and even urgent. It is equally important, however, that these issues be considered within wider understandings of history, development, and justice; in short, a very specific geo-political power structure, which sometimes lies outside the frame of these discussions.

"Raising Uniformity into Monumentality"

The quote comes from Otto Wagner and his ambitions for Vienna's growth plan at the end of the nineteenth-century that were guided by the functional exigencies of circulatory infrastructure, and the elevation of this functionalism to define a new urban aesthetic for the city's expansion (Schorske 1961: 97). The new aesthetic would include fields such as engineering, and raise the infrastructural logic of uniformity to symbolically represent the modern progress that this new functionalist technology conjured. In specific contrast to the classic monumentality of Camillo Sitte, Wagner celebrated the possibility of a new urban form who's expansion, in modular uniformity, would allow for the wide possibilities of a new age to endlessly express themselves, unencumbered by the overly reflective signification and lexicon of bygone ages. For Wagner, infrastructure was both the symbolic and functional way forward for urban growth, and when looking at Dubai's development pattern, the protagism of infrastructure—and its multiple roles and layers—offers the best lens with which to understand the emirate's urbanism.

In Dubai, the "raising of uniformity," or a specific infrastructural logic, to "monumentality" has been achieved through a process of closely following regional infrastructural trends and competing with them through some form of capacity differential. Once oil revenue was available to Dubai both from its own offshore fields and access (albeit with some political intrigue) to the UAE's central coffer (funded mostly by Abu Dhabi's oil reserves), Dubai initiated a supply-side development strategy that sought first to offer the largest infrastructural facilities in the Middle East, and later to compete, in scale and capacity, with those of the entire world. Cumulative programmatic intensification and successive scalar amplification of projects guided metropolitan growth and generated a territorial organization logic that outstripped the predictive capacity of traditional master planning.

When speaking about traditional master planning, I am referring specifically to that process particular to the United States and Western Europe that seeks to extrapolate population and economic growth needs and define the spatial, infrastructural, and institutional requirements to meet those needs, within relatively short-term intervals based on demand-side data. Ambitious growth strategies, of the supply-side, developmentalist sort that Dubai employed after 1973, were certainly also present in plan form in the East, exemplified in the Singapore 1971 Concept Plan (Yuen 1998). In Dubai, however, the break with John R. Harris's master plans of 1960 and 1971, which came out of the western tradition, is clear. Harris's master planning was loosely implemented, with an ingrained flexibility in each of its iterations, so that what he projected never stood in the way of an alternative development proposal from the ruler or the *majlis* (Hamza 1968). Large-scale infrastructural projects and their ancillary facilities and services determined Dubai's territorial organization, within the regional competitive environment of the post-oil boom Gulf region. In this way, in contrast to a master plan, much of Dubai's development was *reactive* in nature. Because there was no pretense of democratic city-building that public master planning aims to provide, within Dubai monarchical system, the organization of the emirate's development was more swift and nimble. When the Dubai municipality was founded in the late 1950s, it was the engineering department that was to implement Harris's first plan. Once oil was discovered in 1966, the Halcrow firm became the de facto planning office, charged by Sheikh Rashid to engineer projects that would determine the coastal geography from Sharjah to Abu Dhabi. Thus, master planning *per se*, in the traditional Western sense, was short-lived; it is more accurate to say that the Dubai landscape was directly *engineered.*

Competitive supply-side motivation meant that during Dubai's first boom period from oil discovery through the oil recession of the early 1980s, Dubai looked to exogenous trade facilities, first within the region and then internationally, against which to measure and pace its growth aspirations. The fast series of projects during this boom period culminated in the Jebel Ali Port, Industrial Area, and Free Zone, which was to become its own template from which to structure subsequent projects, Dubai World Holdings Company's international strategy, and those associate agencies that would manage and regulate Dubai's large-scale infrastructural projects. The Jebel Ali agglomeration marks a definitive "before and after" point of inflection for Dubai, when demand-side, predictive, integral master planning gave way to supply-side, cellular, large-scale infrastructural agglomerations to serve as mechanism for territorial organization.

As a development strategy, this process settled Dubai's coast from the creek to its border with Abu Dhabi. Once the border was reached, development could both move inland, such as with the new Al-Maktoum International Airport city development, and now go back eastward and revisit those projects which had previously served as typological standards in search of new development opportunities. The process can now also move beyond the limited territorial confines of Dubai, through an international strategy that incorporates those components accumulated over time—namely, port infrastructure, free zone facilities for light manufacturing, logistics, transshipment, and real estate. The Dubai World Holding Company now has companies in all of these sectors, and their clustering within the larger conglomerate creates strategic opportunities both domestically and internationally. In this regard, the process has been both iterative and cumulative; diachronic in origin, but can now be temporally flattened and synchronically delivered as a complete package for international spatial development and a strategy to amplify Dubai locally and internationally. It is precisely the iterative nature of the Dubai experience that requires the book to be structured chronologically for a clearer reflection on the element of time and its role, which I will elaborate on in Chapter 5. Recent international financial events have challenged this clustered, agglomerated business and territorial development strategy. Retracing the evolution of this strategy can lend insight into the spatial expressions of accelerated, international capital over the past decade.

Dubai Amplified focuses on the importance of specific large-scale trade infrastructure within Dubai's development. Literature on port cities and port geography links central trade functions with spatial change in urban development and hinterland communication over time, and the cumulative nature of this growth has turned the nineteenth-century central urban ports into the "superterminals" of the twenty-first century. This move, over time, brought together propulsive industries (port infrastructure, services, operations), dependent industries (maritime industry, freight traffic), functionally linked industries (freight forward agents, ship building and repairs), and marketing industries related to the export sector (warehousing, distribution, banks, insurance companies, light manufacturing), and the ancillary services that grew around these industries (Ho 1996: 8). The programmatic intensification and scalar amplification that have occurred with port infrastructure growth over time also serve as an important template for Dubai's form of urbanism, as it too followed these requirements of the international maritime industry. As a port city that has become a port geography, the emirate spatially reproduced these same intensification and amplification processes throughout its territory.

Chapter Structure

The chapter structure of *Dubai Amplified* is organized essentially into three parts. The Introduction and Chapter 1 address some of the larger themes and fields that serve subsequently as lenses through which I explore Dubai's urban development history. Chapters 2, 3, and 4 focus specifically on this development history, from the emirate's origins, through its rapid expansion, to its international aspirations and interests and their more recent outcomes. Chapter 5 and the Conclusion then reflect on this development process, and proceed to consider the larger lessons and themes that can be drawn out of the Dubai case.

Chapter 1 begins with a review of the larger role of infrastructure during periods of urban growth. I explore specific cases to illustrate both the symbolic and functional nature of infrastructure in moments of its repetition and replication. The cases are selected intentionally to inform particular aspects of Dubai development experience. I first review the Roman gridded castrum planning and the *centuriazione* that guided and structured imperial territorial development. The rapid deployment of this replicated planning and design pattern along Roman transportation and trade corridors served as a specific military infrastructure to define and protect imperial expansion, and also as a territorial settlement pattern to imprint its vast geography. The Roman urban system serves as a precedent for complete infrastructure-led development, where the transportation armature and associate urban layouts offered a modular strategy for swift urban development along principal trade corridors. The Roman precedent also demonstrates the iterative process of city-building throughout the territory, and how this could then be packaged for more immediate city-building, as exemplified in the latter *centuriazione.* In the Gulf, a settlement pattern developed, particularly as British oil interests increased and nomadic peoples were settled, with oil towns that sprung up throughout the region, along with the replicated housing infrastructure that served the needs of those itinerant consultants and workers. These infrastructural elements were also combined over time, and the British consulting engineering design organizations offered entire portfolios of infrastructure projects for developing Gulf States to invest their new oil surplus revenue. As I will discuss in Chapters 4 and 5, this clustering of infrastructural components would also guide the Dubai World Holding Company international business strategy as its interests moved beyond Dubai's territorial confines.

I then look at Ildefonso Cerdà's *eixample* plan for Barcelona as a replicated orthogonal ground infrastructure to pragmatically and swiftly prime extramural territory for urbanization. In Dubai, John Harris's projected transportation armature and grid planned for extramural expansion in a similar replicated manner. Plot size and uniformity would not hold as the pace Dubai's southwestern urban expansion increased, but Barcelona's mid-nineteenth-century experience helps to inform Dubai's initial moves outside the dense, original three settlements. In addition, Cerdà's *eixample* helped to structure a hierarchy of primary and secondary infrastructural elements that linked hinterland production centers with the coastal port. This spatial organization of an infrastructural hierarch is particularly salient for Dubai's urbanism *vis-à-vis* its ports and trade infrastructure.

The next section explores theoretical debates around the expansion of Vienna, among Camillo Sitte and Otto Wagner, to better understand both the symbolic and functional elements of infrastructure during moments of urban growth. Wagner advocated the importance of infrastructure and technology, and its potential as a new kind of urban aesthetic to replace classical iconography. In Dubai, the development strategy favored the predominance of large-scale trade infrastructure over specific architectural or design concerns. Growth patterns were defined by the emirate's ports and airports, and in this way, punctuate metropolitan corridors with a new kind of engineered monumentality. Wagner's Vienna demonstrates a more complex, layered role for infrastructure that considers its potential aesthetic attributes, and its scalar monumentality as a signifier for progress into a new kind of city.

The section concludes with the New Town projects in England in the early twentieth-century, and looks at how these served as templates for new town and regional planning internationally, and represented a moment of "greenfield" urbanization, guided by utopian thinking, to start anew. The temporal elements of new towns, and the delivery of entire completed urban products in a compressed, synchronic time-space context, runs counter to a more organic, diachronic urban development over a longer period of time. As large-scale infrastructure, the British New Towns were modular in nature, to be replicated across the greater London region. Post-war new town planning in England also served as a training ground for many of the British planning and engineering consultants throughout Gulf urban development of the mid-century. As with the other case examples, the British New Towns help to demonstrate that Gulf urbanization, and particularly that of Dubai, had precedents, and were not planned and constructed in a developmental vacuum.

Chapter 1's next section reviews the history and literature on port cities and planning. The functional and spatial interdependence between the port and its urban context define port cities, and the section goes through the multidisciplinary fields that are incorporated in port city research. The seventeenth-century European aspirations of conjuring sea dominion through monumental port city planning and construction represented a kind of gamble with the fates. If modularity and repetition characterize the previous case examples of infrastructure-led urban and ex-urban development, the particularities of the port city expansion seem to take on an added competitive aspiration that seeks to outdo simple repetition in scalar ambition and programmatic intensification. I explore these aspirations as precursor to the port city, supply-side speculation that Dubai would engage in during the 1960s and 1970s, and the real estate speculation of the past decade. History demonstrates that there is a clear precedent for the international ambitions that waterfronts elicit, with winners and losers throughout. The section finishes by looking at contemporary port city circumstances, and the spatial and programmatic requirements of this ever-expanding trade infrastructure. Technological change is an historical constant in maritime trade, and port cities have changed spatially in accordance to these needs. This technology includes not only the engineering "hardware" for increased ship sizes and containerization, but also the associate "software" to manage and facilitate these changes; ranging from port authority and management institutions, to information technology, to the labor able to run shipping and port facilities (Mcafee et al. 2003, Jacobs et al. 2007). Within the essentially connected and competitive world of shipping, and particularly for *entrepôt* ports that lack significant hinterland markets, all of these factors comprise the elements that guide the spatial organization of global trade.

Chapter 1 finishes with a section that briefly reviews the discipline of development economics. The book demonstrates the continuous linkages between economic and spatial strategies in Dubai, as alluded to above in the section on Globalization and the City. This section elaborates more particularly on the field of development economics to better inform the discussions of development in Dubai. The role of infrastructure investment as part of larger development strategies is considered, along with the work of economist Alexander Gerschenkron, for his contribution on the advantages of being a developmental "latecomer."

Chapters 2, 3, and 4 are told specifically in a chronological sequence with the intention of underscoring the element of time and Dubai's diachronic development history. Chapter 2 reviews Dubai's history within the larger context of the Gulf trade routes, local power struggles, and the succession of European powers as they move through the region. The last of these European powers, the British, established a protectorate ruling system with lower Gulf sheikhdoms beginning in 1820, and this relationship would last until their withdrawal in 1971. The chapter explores this relationship as it frames larger historical motivations and events throughout the nineteenth-century and up to Dubai's oil discovery in 1966. Though oil discovery would prove essential to Dubai's development boom, the chapter explores how the fundamental elements of a developmental blueprint were already established before oil arrived. Creek dredging and bunding, John Harris's first master plan, and the 1960 Land Law brought together the essential components of a merchant urbanism that utilized large-scale, ambitious engineering for improved trade throughput, and also strategically linked urban expansion to this engineering for a more diversified capital accumulation and development plan. Hotels, banks, municipal services and governmental structures, along with the airport, were also established at the moment before oil discovery as infrastructures to undergird future development aspirations. In these development projects and infrastructural mechanisms, Dubai both followed and competed with its regional neighbors, and this would continue, with greater scalar ambitions and programmatic intensification, once oil discovery amplified developmental possibilities. I am particularly indebted to Christopher Davidson's 2008 work on Dubai for this section. His historical contribution helped provided information to help me make a case for the centrality of infrastructure in Dubai's urban development before oil discovery in 1966.

Chapter 3 looks at the period in Dubai following oil discovery in 1966 through Queen Elizabeth II's inauguration of infrastructural projects in 1979. Regionally, this is the time when the British withdrew their interests and closed their large oil and bunking port of Aden, which provided an opportunity that regional port competition sought to capitalize on. The formation of the UAE during this period also established a new political framework that brought together seven emirates under a federated system to be headed by Abu Dhabi. This new federation would provide access to financial backing from Abu Dhabi to help Dubai fund its ambitious projects in the 1970s, but also create a political framework against which Dubai would push to maintain autonomy from excessive political centralization from its capital neighbor. The international gas crisis in 1973 increased the region's growth and diversification aspirations as a way to absorb the large sums of oil revenue that substantial price increases brought. The chapter then looks at the individual projects of Port Rashid, the Dubai Dry Dock and Shipyard, the World Trade Center, and the National Cement Company, and how these projects responded competitively with other parallel infrastructure in the region, and provided domestic markets with (limited) import-substation production, as was the case with the cement factory. Although the period marked the official end of British regional interests, the chapter shows how those ties established during the period helped British consulting firms to acquire lucrative, large-scale commissions. The projects were some of the few available in the world at that time, in "one of the few major construction markets which [did] not impose many restrictive practices" (Zahalan 1984: 85).

Chapter 4 looks at the Jebel Ali Port, Industrial Area, and Free Zone and its multiple roles and functions as a new template for development, marking the decisive moment in Dubai's history where the mimetic replication of imported models along with self-referential, supply-side driven replication of trade infrastructure were amplified into *something else*. The chapter explores the engineering and design of the port, the industrialization strategy for Jebel Ali as a marine industrial development area (MIDA), and the original plans for an industrial town/new town project that would eventually be scaled back. Although plans were postponed for the new town and airport facilities, the territorial impact of the Jebel Ali agglomeration established a regional growth pole, and defined a growth corridor where infill development occurred in a modular, replicated form, taking the World Trade Center and the Jumeirah villas of the 1960s as their prototypes. The Jebel Ali projects completed Dubai's coastal settlement from its creek to the Abu Dhabi border, and the chapter explores how these projects have defined planning, project design, and the institutional management structure for Dubai's trade and diversified business interests. The Jebel Ali Port, Industrial Zone, and Free Port represent the maximum expression of Dubai's development aspirations, and as a superterminal serves as a microcosm for the megalopolitan, cellular, large-scale project-based urbanism that has occurred in Dubai since its completion. The chapter then jumps to more contemporary development in Dubai to explore how the Jebel Ali agglomeration helped inform large-scale projects during the more recent boom period, and in structuring the international development components of the Dubai World Holding Company.

Chapter 5 reflects on Dubai's development history laid out in the previous three chapters and proposes an analytical framework through which to understand its urbanism, focusing on competitive typological borrowing, modular replication based on certain prototypes once locational and demand were fulfilled (though these demand-side requirements would give way to supply-side competition), and moments of amplification, with scalar and programmatic intensification. As in Chapter 3, I will focus on specific projects to better illustrate this analytical framework, and then focus on Dubai's international development strategy to explore how this model functions outside its territorial boundaries and can be inserted into other developing countries. Thus, the urban model is imported, processed, and then re-exported, underscoring Dubai's central *entrepôt* trade role.

The concluding chapter will place Dubai's development narrative within larger discussions of contemporary urbanism and the multi-layered meanings and roles of infrastructure. The centrality of trade infrastructure, and the increasing autonomy of its management agencies—from the traditionally politically-opaque port authorities to the increasing importance of trade facility management privatization—point toward an increasing Balkanization of single-entity planning authority. A look at projects in Barcelona, Rotterdam, Los Angeles, and the coastal cities of China will help to consider Dubai's large-scale infrastructural development and associate urbanism within the broader interests of the field.

Living the Future and Creating the Past

If we return to the importance of the element of time in regard to Dubai's development, this book seeks to understand Dubai's specific urban trajectory, and how it has developed iteratively and cumulatively over time to better understand its present manifestations. During its boom period over the past decade, the so-called Dubai Model was imitated and aspired toward within the larger Gulf region and beyond, either specifically though international Dubai World projects or through the more general diffusion processes of development templates. The international media was one of the channels for this diffusion in which Dubai was adept at selling an image of itself as a place with one foot already in the future, as if the emirate were the world's portal to that future which Dubai would build. Within this image, Dubai assumed the self proclaimed title as the *avant garde* of globalization, where the past was only referenced to demonstrate how much has been achieved since then. It was a prehistory for the city that saw itself in an eternal present with the brightest of futures. This returns, of course, to the essence of modernization discourse, and the simultaneous urge to start anew in genesis and destroy a real past so that it can be reimagined through a contemporary discourse. The objective of this book is not to romantically or nostalgically long for some past that cannot be recovered, but to demonstrate that it can be instructive in helping to understand the defining projects, and their circumstances and consequences that comprise Dubai's urbanism and its international projection. Dubai's present limbo condition offers the opportunity to trace through its developmental strategy and projects and draw out larger lessons from this dynamic port geography.

Chapter 1
Infrastructure, Port Cities, Development

> Addressing the relation linking city, landscape, and infrastructure can be divided into two parts: a question aimed at the relation between large-scale infrastructure and local networks, and a question aimed at the relation between place and program … Monographs of port cities are a search for the conscious and unconscious cultural motives (specifically expressed or implicitly suggested) that support the way in which urban planners shape the relation between large-scale infrastructure and local networks … In short, what is the meaning of a specific function (the port) for the cultural significance of the site: the territorial characteristics inherent in the natural state of the land and water? (Meyer 1999: 60–61).

Hans Meyer's quote identifies urban elements of a port city and the complexity of their relationship at that specific point where international sea trade takes form on land. The objective of this chapter is to better understand how port cities have grown according to the specific demands of their hinterland connections, along with the demands of international trade flows and maritime technological change. By bringing together a grouping of select, decisive historical events that underscore the protagonism of infrastructure within growth circumstances, and the history of port cities as a particular urban condition that is defined by its trade infrastructure, I will reflect on how intensified trade within port cities has continually impacted their urban form. Finally, I will review literature on development economics in consideration of the role of infrastructure within larger development strategies. While each is a discrete discipline in its own right, their combined review will inform the methodology of the book, where both spatial and economic considerations strategically work together in pursuit of overarching development goals.

From historic city port planning to developmental investment choices, large-scale infrastructure construction carried out within specific local contexts, and in competition with regional cities vying for similar international business, has consistently involved an element of risk. For port cities, the gamble would seem to be inspired by the grandiosity of the sea itself, and the promise of the riches beyond the horizon. It is this infrastructure gamble that frames Dubai's urban developmental history; as its developmental ambitions grew, so did its gains and losses.

Infrastructure and Urban Expansion

Within discussions of urban development, infrastructure is generally understood as a fixed asset that requires large public capital investment to enable transportation, communication, and the multiple elements in society within an overarching strategy required for production, reproduction, and growth. The term itself, *infrastructure*, connotes the space beneath structures, but elements traditionally understood as infrastructural (roads, ports, airports, electricity grids, etc.) can also serve as the principal structuring agents in urban growth. In a broader view, institutions and activities that are required for economic sectors can also be understood as infrastructural, such as banks, schools, hospitals, and housing, particularly in newly urbanizing circumstances when a market has not yet had the chance to develop within these sectors and public investment is required to nurture their beginnings.

The nature of infrastructure within urbanizing circumstance often incorporates both repetition and replication in establishing predetermined growth patterns. Urban planning first designates a series of inter-related infrastructural systems, such as public and private transportation corridors, water, and electricity, either below ground, at grade, or above ground, to then facilitate land parcelization, land use zoning, and finally, construction (Solà-Morales i Rubió 1997).[1] The modular repetition of certain street patterns, such as the orthogonal grid, and the above-mentioned systems, establish and order development, particularly within a market economy environment, to best facilitate circulation of goods and people. Thus patterns of repetition during infrastructural implementation offer the simplest and quickest way to prime a new space for development. The references for such infrastructural systems are traditionally established in the engineering field, emphasizing functional needs over aesthetic consideration, but particularly within developing circumstances, infrastructure also assumes a symbolic importance as an ode to progress and proof that the political class is both planning for and investing in the future correctly (Gurr and King 1987). Furthermore, if there is a colonial history involved, infrastructural investment often has its origin in colonial resource extraction, wherein the colonizer would build infrastructure based on experiences from cities of central empire. Examples of this kind of symbolic manifestation of colonial infrastructure produce hybrid situations, where a Dutch port could be grafted onto an Indonesian coastal settlement, or a *damero* urban system was established in cities throughout Latin America (Aureli 2008, Sutherland 1989). Infrastructure symbolically expressed colonial relations, in addition to their functional circulatory purposes. The dual nature of infrastructural replication—both functional and symbolic—has a clear historic trajectory.

By reviewing four distinct historical examples, I hope to demonstrate the many roles and meanings of infrastructure during specific moments of urban expansion.

---

1 This process was studies extensively by the *Laboratori d'Urbanisme* in Barcelona as "urbanización, parcelación y edificación," or urbanization, parceling and construction.

Each case shares the commonality of a need—either political, economic, or both—for development beyond urban centers. The outward projection either moved cities beyond their walled circumstance into the metropolitan scale through open processes of what Cerdà termed as "urbanization," or further afield into a wider networked territory. Barcelona and Vienna are examples of this kind of urban modernization, and in a similar manner, when Dubai expanded outward from its original walled settlement nearly a century after Barcelona. Roman urban expansion, British New Towns, and British oil town construction in the Gulf all represent very different contexts and scales, but each are examples of smaller settlements, rapidly deployed as complete, infrastructure-led agglomerations. In Dubai, the Jebel Ali, Port, Industrial Area, Free Zone, and projected New Town, in origin, sought to establish a bi-polar territory, networked through transportation corridors, but functionally discrete and semi-autonomous from one another. The subsequent infill development connected the two poles, and many of the British planners and engineers who trained during the British New Town projects were those contracted to help sheikhdoms imagine the future of the region's territorial development.

Infrastructural Logic

> The Roman Empire, the product of a single expanding urban power center, was itself a vast city-building enterprise: it left the imprint of Rome on every part of Europe, Northern Africa, and Asia Minor, altering the way of life in old cities and establishing its special kind of order, from the ground up, in hundreds of new foundations, 'colonial towns,' 'free' towns, towns under Roman municipal law, 'tributary' towns: each with a different status if not with a different form (Mumford 1961: 205).

Roman imperial expansion through territorial settlement, based on its epic capacity to build cities "from Chester in West England … to Antioch and Ephesus in Asia Minor" (Mumford 1961: 208), and its ability to connect these cities through an unprecedented schema of road networks, is the canonical example of vast urban expansion through the deployment of complex infrastructural systems. The imposition of the geometric order across vast expanses of land and cultures, including aqueducts, viaducts, and paved roads, and later entire urban agglomerations, was the central Roman innovation that both created and maintained its dominion. The bedrock of Roman urban development was the castrum planning system, based on the orthogonal, symmetrical outward expansion of the foundation crossing of cardinal points. As A.E.J. Morris suggests about the foundation of the Roman seaport of Ostia—founded on an original castrum layout where the Tiber River joined the Mediterranean—it "became a busy commercial port from the third century BC when its growth and prosperity directly reflected the rise of Rome itself (1989: 53)." Rome, the city and the Empire, were illustrated and made grand precisely by the system of cities that they built throughout their territories, and the networks that joined them.

Lewis Mumford believes that in order to understand the Roman contribution to urban form and expansion, its best to look at to its Syrian and North African cities, rather than the central chaotic capital. These cities served as trading posts, manufacturing towns, or military colonization cities for retired legionnaires. In addition to their primary urban functions, they also served as "holding points for the Empire," and a "watchtower for the Roman people, a bulwark against the wild tribes" that could conspire against Rome (Mumford 1961: 207, 209). Castrum planning originated as the urban planning for military encampments, or *castra*. Military legions constructed these encampments by establishing the point where the north-south *Kardo Maximus* road intersected with the east-west *Decumanus Maximus*, and proceeded to layout an orthogonal street pattern (Filippi 2003: 132). The castrum plan functioned as a land overlay, with a strict geometry superimposed onto varying topological circumstances.

Both Morris and Mumford pay close attention to the city of Timgad (Thamugadi) in North Africa, located in present-day Algeria (Morris 1979: 54), as an important example of castrum planning because it remains true its original form as the result of limited subsequent resettlement or disturbance. Located in the Roman fertile granary region, Timgad was a legionary town, or *centuriazione*, for "time-expired veterans of the Third Legion which garrisoned the nearby fortress of Lambeisis" (Ibid.). Structured on the castrum plan, Timgad was originally built with 11 streets in each direction, with 23-yard blocks. In their work on the territorial settlement patterns of the Romagna region of Italy, Peter G. Rowe and Roberto Pasini describe the *centuriazione* thusly:

> Closely associated with these encampments [castra], and as extensions of them, *centuriazione* were also organized in order to provide land for troops furloughed from the Roman army. Essentially these *centuriazione* were a regular grid work of land parcels (*fundus*), located in a regular and orderly manner between a larger grid pattern of roads, forming blocks of land parcels, 710 meters on a side (2004: 27).

The castrum plan was replicated, as were the *centuriazione*, throughout settlements along the Empire's principal trunk roads, which were used for troop movement and the passage of goods and services (Ibid.). Their gridded forms were designed specifically for replication, with a foundational infrastructure also imbedded in their structure. The replicated model would then extend throughout Roman settlement to establish and protect territorial conquest, and benefit those legionnaires who had fought for Rome as a kind of pension. Over time, and depending on imperial necessity and/or importance, these castra could then be upgraded in status into more important nodes within the Roman network (Morris 1989: 57), but the foundation for each incorporated this organizing orthogonal geometry.

Mumford describes Timgad as an example of "the Roman planning art in its latterday graces ... the regular checkerboard layout within a rectangular boundary, the arcaded walks, the forum, the theatre, the arena, the baths, the public lavatories were standard equipment" (1961: 207–8). All urban components could be found in Timgad, and repeated in modular fashion, throughout the Empire (Ibid.) Further, "none of these facilities were new. What Rome did was to universalize them—making them 'standard equipment'" (Ibid.). Rome developed this "standard equipment," or series of urban infrastructural components, both by borrowing preexisting typologies (Hellenic, Etruscan) and iteratively through its city-building experience. With *centuriazione*, Rome could deliver entire cities as infrastructural packages, in "systematic multiplication" (Ibid.) Mumford points out that British New Town planning and construction owes a great deal to this precedent, and it was of course the Romans who brought this methodical town planning to Britain in the first place (Ibid., Morris 1989: 57).

I will further explore the British New Town experience below, but the Roman example of a diachronic city-building process, that once standardized, could be rapidly deployed and synchronically delivered for extensive territorial development, serves as an important example to help understand the rapid city-building processes in the greater Gulf region in the mid-twentieth-century. For Dubai in particular, it is an infrastructural logic that guided its territorial settlement from border to border, and became part of the larger business strategy for its international holding company.

The Theory of Urbanization

Moving from the classical context to the nineteenth-century, the intervening years see the rise of the western capitalist city, when capitalist accumulation becomes the defining engine and logic of urban expansion. Ildefonso Cerdà's *eixample* plan for Barcelona can be understood as a pure formal expression of this change, projecting urban expansion beyond the city's wall as a blanketed infrastructural system to connect hinterland production with port trade centers. Incorporating technological advances in communication, circulation, and sanitation, Cerdà implemented a rational geometry and infrastructure to fight the chaotic and unhealthy conditions of Barcelona's medieval city. With reason, science, and order, he initiated modern urban planning. "'The vast swirling ocean of persons, of things, of interests of every sort, of a thousand diverse elements' that work in permanent reciprocity and thus form a totality that is uncontainable by any previous finite territorial formation such as a city" (Aureli 2008: 97, Cerdà 1867). Cerdà's recognized this developmental expansion of the medieval city as centrifugal in nature, and that the term "city" no longer wholly applicable. His proposal was an open-ended organizing process, and as such, he coined the term "urbanization" to describe this form of spatial development (Ibid.). Cerdà was inspired by the logic that guided Roman modular infrastructural repetition of the castrum plan. An important difference, however, was that while Roman urban settlements were contained forms built for approximately 50,000 (Mumford 1961: 209), Cerdà's *eixample* could be openly repeated outward indefinitely. Thus the *eixample* plan gives spatial and formal expression to industrial capitalism and its planning and infrastructural demands.

Joan Busquets describes Cerdà's plan as the fundamental imbrication between processes of industrialization and urbanization that would inevitably lead Barcelona to its modern urban condition (2005: 99). The *eixample* plan is an isotropic grid of repeated 133x133-meter blocks that periodically placed a church at nine-block intervals, a park at every eight blocks, a market at every four blocks, and a hospital at 16 blocks (Aureli 2008: 98, Cerdà 1867), and connected the old walled city with surrounding towns to enable a wider circulation of goods and people. Busquets suggests that the essential infrastructure for this process was its "colonial infrastructure"—railways and roads—that facilitated the movement of raw materials, manufactured goods, and people and connected the disparate centers of production and consumption (2005, Solà-Morales i Rubió, Gómez Ordoñez 1977). Equally important, however, was that the infrastructure also "represented a thoroughgoing structuring of the territory that produced an almost definitive organization of principal and secondary centres, between the industrial coastline and the inland areas" (Busquets 2005: 114). The *eixample* plan uses a transportation armature and an infrastructural ground to structure territorial form and expansion beyond the city walls, into its hinterland, to expand productivity and the articulation of markets for import and export. Factories in towns outside the walled city that sprung up in the first decades of the nineteenth-century were dependent on British coal unloaded and rationed at Barcelona's port. Increased exports also meant that the port had to be expanded to accommodate the increasing activity of Catalonia's industrialization process. The heart of the regional system involved a series of infrastructural developments and arrangements, repeated over the territory, linking factories to the port, and the port to the factories. If we consider Busquets's point about the "principal and secondary centres" established through the Barcelona hinterland, we can see how the inter-related infrastructure of port, roads and railroads, factories, along with the ancillary infrastructure to house its workers (Busquets 2005, Crawford 1995), and the plots established for subsequent building construction, formed a parallel system of principal and secondary infrastructure that together constituted Cerdà's territorial plan.

Industry and trade requirements helped to define the nature of the plan and the importance of circulation through hierarchical infrastructural nodes and systems. The exquisite orthogonal ground provided flexibility for subsequent infill development once the primary transportation infrastructure was established.[2] As today, this basic infrastructure primed the territory for urbanization and increased land values over time. The *eixample* plan demonstrates a modular repetition of infrastructure to fulfill the expansionist objectives of industrial capitalism. For Dubai, John Harris's plan heavily favored the uniform grid for precisely the kind of flexible infill development seen in Barcelona. Once

2 See Koolhaas's (1978) discussion of the flexibility of the New York's grid.

the transportation system was established for circulatory purposes to move goods between the Jebel Ali Port and both the city and the airport, Harris hoped that the Jumeirah neighborhood would develop within this geometric logic. As we will see, however, another spatial logic related to another form of capital accumulation would intervene as development in the emirate moved toward its southwestern border.

Functionalist Urban Expansion

While Cerdà was engineering growth patterns for Barcelona's *eixample*, the city of Vienna was undergoing a similar process of extramural expansion. The ascension of the liberal regime to power in Vienna in the Revolution of 1848, along with military losses to France in 1859 and to Prussia in 1866, signified the beginning of what Carl E. Schorske calls the "*pax liberalis*," where military strength would be replaced by artistic sensibility as the guiding symbolism for the projects of the new regime (1961: 31). In December 1857, Emperor Franz Joseph proclaimed the need to open the walled military space that surrounded the old inner city for civilian use, and in it construct a series of universities and governmental institutions to mark the new age. The *Ringstrasse* would be the symbolic project of liberal Vienna to open it to the demands of the modern city by providing a geometry of open spaces and parks to frame the new institutions built in the large belt track. Contrary to the Baroque intuition, the *Ringstrasse* did not communicate the original inner city with those surrounding settlements outside the ring, but rather continued to sociologically isolate the inner city by excluding it from the autonomous circulatory patterns of the new ring and its new state, civic, and institutional buildings. But if the *Ringstrasse* sought to bring the backward conditions of Vienna up to the modern era with its expansion of the old inner city, the architectural styles selected for the buildings looked not to the Baroque, but to the Renaissance for inspiration, strangely eschewing those liberal values for a monumentality that bespoke the previous regime's absolutism. It was precisely this contradiction that would precipitate strong criticism by two children of the *Ringstrasse* project, Camillo Sitte and Otto Wagner, whose disagreements can be understood as a kind of precursor to the Jacobs/Moses political conflicts in New York City a century later.

Schorske cites Sitte's 1889 book *Der Städtebau* (City Building) (1909), where he argues that Sitte saw the technological requirements of modernity at odds with aesthetic beauty. Instead of the rational grid, Sitte preferred freer forms from ancient and medieval city-space, and he scoffed at the technical requirements of modern urban planning as merely "traffic, hygiene, etc." (1961: 63), as if these components were synonymous with an order of capitalism that strove to strangle beauty out from the urban environment. "City building must be not just a technical question but an aesthetic one in the highest sense," claims Sitte, and the *Ringstrasse's* inclusion of large tracts of open spaces to help facilitate transportation went against his aesthetic agenda (Ibid.). Sitte criticizes these open areas for their lack of any public meeting space; essentially lamenting the loss of *civitas* in the nineteenth-century bourgeois city. Sitte celebrated the historicism of the *Ringstrasse's* architecture, as Schorske claims, following the nineteenth-century principle of selecting the historical style associated with a buildings purpose, but missing in his view were precisely the interstitial spaces of the agora, the forum, and the marketplace to frame these buildings (Ibid.). Sitte argues that the *Ringstrasse* lacked a classical urban design sensibility to accompany its architecture, whose dissonance, in his mind, was the result of excessive deference to modern functional requirements—"traffic, hygiene, etc."

Schorske then presents Otto Wagner as Sitte's antithesis. Also educated and trained during the construction of the *Ringstrasse*, Wagner's criticism of the projects focused on their excessive historicism, rather than looking to those forms and styles which he believed should emerge precisely from the modern infrastructural requirements that Sitte so deplored. Wagner won the 1890 competition to plan for the new expansion of Vienna into its suburban developments, where he labeled his projects with the decree "*Artis sola domina necessitas* (Necessity is art's only mistress)" (1961: 73). Schorske demonstrates how Wagner's functionalist ideology for the plan was forged in his work on the Vienna railway system, where the exigencies of materials choice and engineering outweighed his initial stylistic considerations, until he realized that a new style emerged out of these functional requirements. He quotes Wagner, "The realism of our time must penetrate the work of art … No decline of art will result from that; rather it will breathe a new, pulsating life into the forms (of architecture) and conquer new areas, such as the field of engineering, which are still deprived of art" (Schorske 1961: 83, Ostwald 1948). Thus, the modern functional elements from which he learned new criteria to inform city building, what he called "the metropolis," would then also be applied to his call for a modern architecture to accompany this new city. In contrast to Sitte, and in line with Cerdà, Wagner valued the grid and its massive uniformity as the basis for both urban expansion and the urban design to frame it within a capitalist economy, thus "raising uniformity into monumentality" (Schorske 1961: 97), following the dictates of the infrastructural repetition as a central structuring element.[3]

The infrastructural logic of the Roman castrum planning, and its colonial urban settlement patterns informed the spatial characteristics of the emerging capitalist city, as exemplified in Cerdà's plan for Barcelona's expansion and Wagner's proposal to expand Vienna. Technological advances in transportation and circulation could no longer fit within the densities of inner medieval cities, such that their expansion looked to the infrastructural infill possibilities of urban expansion to better communicate these walled cities with their surrounding hinterlands. For each, the functional demands of their historical moment, particularly those of industrial capitalism and its expansionist nature, meant that infrastructural replication would be the guiding principle for extramural settlement. Wagner's addition of an aesthetic component

3 See also Choay (1997) for discussion of Sitte and Le Corbusier.

to the functional, scientific, and moral (in Latin no less!) elements of his proposal complete the modern pretense of progress through projects. The twentieth-century, as well will see, took this urban growth strategy beyond the immediate surroundings of the original urban core. A review of the British New Town movement will help to demonstrate how, within a modern circumstance, entire cities were built for this move, along with educating a group of planners and architects that would later take this experience to the Gulf region.

New Towns

New towns are by no means strictly a twentieth-century phenomenon. Their history can be traced at least as far as back as Roman settlements mentioned above, and beyond. New towns are characterized essentially as settlements that are planned and built over a relatively short period of time, usually for a specific military, economic or political purpose, in contrast to a more organic growth pattern over a longer period of time. The need to build new towns for economic reasons—from company towns in the US and England throughout the nineteenth and twentieth centuries, to towns for industrialization or resource extraction, including projects from Brazil to Iran—moved settlements outside traditional city centers to more remote, *de novo* circumstances to start anew (Rovira 2005, Crawford 1995, Holston 1989, Roberts 1979, Turner and Smulian 1974).[4] Internationally, new towns were also built as politically-motivated new capitals that were either more geographically central, or represented the opportunity to build a symbolically new capital that could spatially express the aspirations of new (or renewed) nation-building projects. An exhaustive history of new town planning and construction, even within the twentieth-century, is beyond the scope of this book. Nevertheless, a brief understanding of the new town tradition, particularly within the UK, is necessary to inform later discussions of new town development in the Gulf.

At the close of the nineteenth-century, the benefits of the industrial revolution had produced cities with dangerous sanitary and public health issues in Britain that provoked reformist fervor for improved urban conditions, similar to those projected in Cerdà's *eixample* plan. This reformist movement also drew on the urban utopian thinking of the nineteenth-century, including Charles Fourier and Peter Kropotkin, and an early Scottish environmentalist named Patrick Geddes. Ebenezer Howard, a member of this reform movement, strongly believed that urban decentralization was the solution to alleviate both environmental and social problems of his time, which he understood as mutually reinforcing. His book, entitled *Tomorrow: A Peaceful Path to Real Reform*, published in 1898, was his first attempt at describing what he called a "Garden City." The Garden City was to be structured around a central commercial core surrounded by concentric

4 See the work of International New Town Institute. Avaulable at: http://www.newtowninstitute.org/.

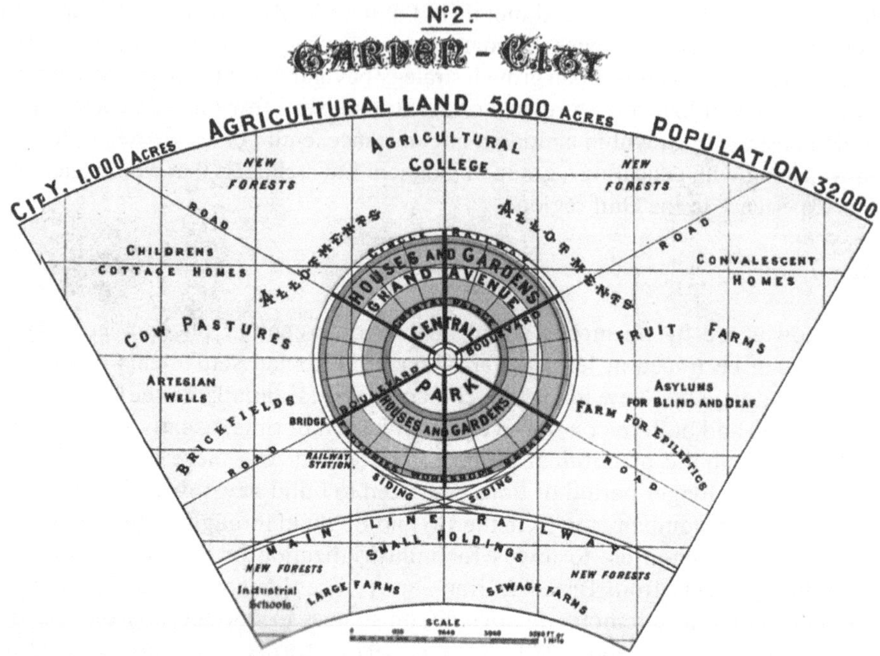

Figure 1.1 Ebenezer Howard's "Tomorrow: A Peaceful Path to Real Reform" (Swan Sonnenschein 1898)

Source: © Town and Country Planning Association

circles of intermittent natural green belts and low-density residential areas set in an Elysian environment that would only allow for a maximum of 30,000 inhabitants, in stark contrast to London's 6.5 million inhabitants at the time. The excitement around the Garden City proposal spread quickly, such that by 1899 the Garden City Association was formed, by 1903 the town of Letchworth was the first built Garden City, and by 1909, within this same reformist zeal, the Housing and Town Planning Act was passed officially giving birth to the town planning profession. Welwyn Garden City was built in 1919 with strong supervision by Howard, but the utopian aspirations were not quite fulfilled by the realities of an artificial social experiment. Nevertheless, the model of an ex-urban, low-density settlement that could be connected to a larger, central city through transportation proved to be very successful. The international economic depression, followed by World War II, halted Garden City construction, but in 1944, inspired by Howard's recommendation for urban decentralization, Sir Patrick Abercrombie presented his regional Greater London Plan, which also proposed concentric green belts and settlements. The plan essentially took the Garden City model and spread it out over a much larger region, with London at its center, and surrounding new towns proposed to alleviate population congestion from the large metropolis. The goal of full employment accompanied the new towns program, such that industrial and agricultural activities would also be decentralized to give the new towns more functional autonomy. In 1945, 20 new towns were proposed, though only 14 were started. A second round of new towns was launched in the 1960s, such that when the program ended in 1992, 30 new towns had been constructed throughout Britain (Meller 1997: 72–3).

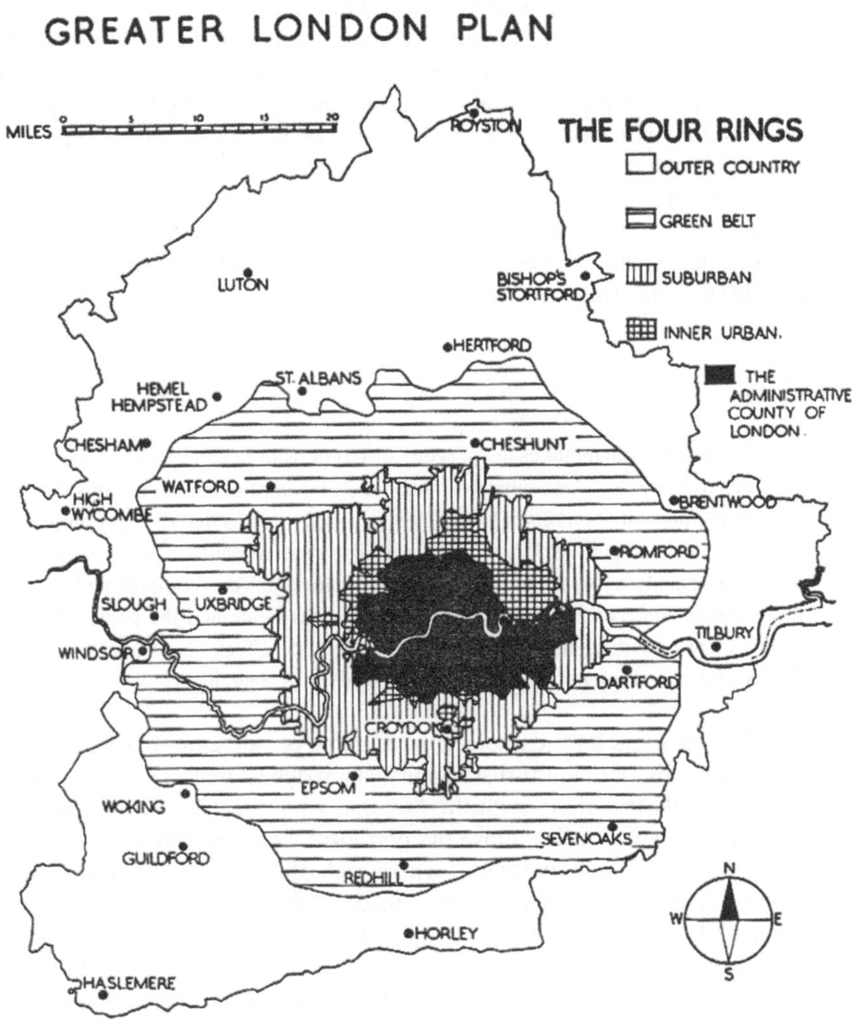

Figure 1.2 Sir Patrick Abercrombie's 1944 regional Greater London Plan
Source: © Crown Copyright

The Garden City model, Abercrombie's Greater London Plan, and the British New Town program were all widely reproduced internationally from the US, to France, to Japan (Ward 1992). The Garden Cities attracted international planners and architects who visited England to see the projects, and subsequently took the decentralized model back to their homelands as a way to address post-war population growth and urbanization pressures. The post-war new town project also served as a training ground for British planners, architects and engineers, who, particularly during the post-1973 construction boom in the Gulf, found ample consulting work on political and industrial new town projects funded by increased oil-profit liquidity ("Everything According to Plan" 1983).

The infrastructural logic of modular repetition is one of the central elements of the modern city planning, as a rational organization order that sought to reform the perceived chaos of the medieval urban settlements. In port city development, however, planning and engineering also helped to realize aspirations for epic city-building, with the hope that sea power and trade success would come naturally to reward these great visions. The gamble was not always rational. A review of the historic relationship in port cities between their trade functions and infrastructure—and their associate spatial expressions and formation—will help to understand this particular urban infrastructural typology.

Port Cities

> That it is the port which makes the port city different from other cities is, in itself, of course no more than a statement of fact, but … the explicit and conscious use of the term "port city" entails far more. It specifically means that the economic, social, political and cultural life of that city is also predominantly determined by and has to be analyzed in the light of that port function. It is that complex and all-embracing superstructure which creates both the challenge and the possibility to assess just how the port city's functional difference affects its character and identity and how it interacts with its hinterland (Broeze 1997b: 3).

As Broeze's quote suggests and implies, the research on port cities has traditionally been challenged by the multi-disciplinary approaches that necessarily cross disciplinary boundaries, along with the fact that while definitions of "port" and "city" have their own histories, those of "port cities" are less obvious. The same is true for the term "colonial port city," where each of the three terms have clearer meanings by themselves then when conjoined. Along with various disciplinary interpretations that have difficulty agreeing, causality and interrelation are often confused when researching the form and function of port cities. Does the study of the port city focus on the impact of the port on subsequent urban development and morphological change, or rather on the study of why certain ports flourish because of their urban and hinterland connectivity and the formal advantages of their location? The two, of course, share mutual causality, and while disciplines may seek to prioritize these and other elements of port city research, the fact is they must all be understood in concert. "In the beginning the harbour made the trade; but soon the trade began to make the harbour" (Hoyle and Hilling 1984: 7), mused A.J. Saregent when studying British harbor and hinterland connectivity in 1938, and of course the intimate, indivisible relationship between urban form and trade throughput is still present in the port city.

The geography of port cities presents planners with a unique set of challenges for the spatial organization of buildings, streets, and topological elements into "patterns that are derived from and recondition economic, social, and political activities and values" (Konvitz 1978: 6). Broeze's definition of port cities is helpful in that it identifies the port as the central element of "economic, social, political and cultural life," and their development. In addition, the study of port cities also focuses on the dialectic between the port and spatial change. As technology, trade, and cultural imports come through the port, all can and do serve as mechanisms for urban and regional growth, either as the result of the ever-increasing spatial requirements directly related to the port activities, or through accumulated growth whose urban germination begins with the central port function. "The port is, therefore, both a cause and a result of development" (Hoyle and Hilling 1984: 4).

Ports can be divided into either coastal ports or river ports, which then can be classified as either natural or tide gate ports, each serving to protect ships at anchor from the stronger tidal currents of the open sea. The port's primary function of protection was soon augmented by the additional needs for shelter and storage of cargoes either being loaded or unloaded. Over time this too grew, and today, customs, logistics, industrial facilities, manufacturing, and intermodal functions all agglomerate around this strategic node of sea-land interface (Rammin 1999: 2–3). Broadly, ports can be further functionally divided into two different types: the terminal port and the port-of-call. Terminal ports support a broad and diverse hinterland area, and serve as points of origin and destination, characterized by a wide range of intermodal distribution services and ship repair and overhaul facilities. The ports of Rotterdam, Los Angeles, and Shanghai are all examples of terminal ports. When traveling between terminal ports, ships may stop at intermediate ports-of-call to either unload or load cargo. The two kinds of port-of-call are either outports or *entrepôts*. Outports are located at the mouth of an estuary or smaller river to save a larger ship the costly trip of traveling upstream. These outports are usually associated with larger urban agglomerations, such as Tilbury for London, but outports can sometimes grow larger than their original inland partners. *Entrepôts* are "specialized port-of-calls serving as collective centers, where cargoes are held for collection and/or distribution" (Ho 1996: 5–6). This function is also called "transshipment" or "re-export," and free ports and free zones located just outside port customs boundaries of *entrepôts* are often established to eliminate transshipment costs or inspection. Singapore and Hong Kong are examples of port-of-call *entrepôts* (Ibid.). Dubai's history is marked by its transformation from an outport at the intersection of the creek and the Gulf that facilitated inland trading, to an international *entrepôt* with global scope.

In their book *Seaport Systems and Spatial Change*, Hoyle and Hilling incorporate systems analysis as a methodology to describe and analyze the interconnectivity of the many components, both local and international, that come together in port city research. "Systems theory comprises a set of elements with variable characteristics, a network of internal connections between the elements, and a series of external links between the system and its environment. The system may be analyzed with respect to its structure and functions but also with respect to its development" (1984: 14). Thus, for port cities, the heterogeneous elements brought together at the port include core and propulsive industries (port infrastructure, services, operations), dependent industries (maritime industry, freight traffic), functionally-linked industry (freight-forward agents, ship building and repairs), and marketing industries related to the export sector (warehousing, distribution, banks, insurance companies, light manufacturing), along with the associate ancillary activities that grow up around these core industries (Ho 1996: 8).

How these elements develop is highly dependent on technological change, ranging from coal-powered boats switching to oil after the World War II, to containerization and freight standardization replacing a large portion of the palette and bulk cargo shipping during the 1960s (Levinson 2006, Hoyle and Pinder 1981). James Bird's famous "anyport" port development model from 1963 describes five stages of port development by exploring both improved cargo throughput at the port and more efficient and complex inland transportation systems to connect port trade with hinterland markets. Building on this work, research also explored how inter-port competition exists not only within national territorial boundaries, but also at the regional scale, which is well-summarized in Robert J. McCalla's article "From 'Anyport' to 'Superterminal': Conceptual perspectives on Containerization and Port Infrastructure" (2004: 123). Using empirical research that draws on the experience of the United States eastern seaboard port system, McCalla shows how the Port Elizabeth "superterminal" in New Jersey/New York developed standardization of container technology and inland transportation, with cumulative economies of scale that rewarded it over regional port competitors. McCalla concludes, "The future for all container ports will involve big changes as they jockey to serve the sometimes fickle interests of shippers, shipping lines, and special interests groups in port cities" (2004: 140). The final element, special interests, include local constituents such as environmental and union interests in port cities that can oppose precisely the economic imperatives of physical expansion and increasing technological efficiency that drive port competition (Pinder and Slack 2004, Cau 1996). Interestingly, the political interplay these competing urban claims have each encouraged port expansion beyond urban boundaries in favor of cheaper, more abundant land for expansion, and fewer interests groups to mobilize politically and prevent port development "in their (urban) backyards."

Similar to the review of historical examples of infrastructure-led development, it is also useful to review a selective history of port city planning and morphology as a reference for subsequent discussion of port city development in the Gulf. Indeed, the review of this history underscores the point that those considerations of contemporary "globalization" and the city are certainly not wholly new (Chanda 2007).

A History of Port City Planning

In his book *Cities and the Sea: Port City Planning in Early Modern Europe*, Josef W. Konvitz looks at port city development in the seventeenth-century. Konvitz explores how the political ambition for maritime power, which had been central in both power and wealth accumulation for European countries of the sixteenth-century, expressed itself spatially in northern Europe through a prodigious round of new port city planning and construction. He begins by saying that while port city construction was an important part of the European colonial project of the sixteenth-century, Europe still relied on those ports developed in the Classical period and the Middle Ages. The importance of international maritime power launched from these port cities also increased the opinion that these cities were an influential part in gaining that power. As Konvitz writes:

> The successful extension of Europe's political, economic, and cultural power from port cities had only reinforced the impression that such cities were indispensible to sea power. Inspired by this impression, leaders in northern and western Europe began to imagine that new port cities would encourage an even more effective and expansive use of sea power ... Those who were anxious to increase sea power by developing new port cities ... were reluctant to abandon such enterprise to chance. The planning process alone, they believed, would make possible a bold and artful reconstruction of the European world (1978: 3).

Konvitz argues that developments that made the seventeenth-century port city boom possible were the ideal port city planning tradition, the practical port city planning tradition, and the migration of these two traditions northward to French and Scandinavian planners who could then learn and borrow from each in their own port city projects.

The ideal cities movement prompted European artists and engineers to visually express utopian thinking, exemplified in the Italian Renaissance by the work of Leon Batista Alberti, which included the reimagining of classical port cities as "Utopias-by-the Sea" (Konvitz 1978: 8, Choay 1997). The practical planning tradition to which he refers occurred in the Mediterranean basin during the sixteenth-century (Rammin 1999), when port city growth relied more on the correlated needs of both the port and the city. He contrasts the two traditions thusly, "In spatial terms, ideal city planners tried to relate the parts of the city to each other, whereas in actual sixteenth-century cities, the process of growth and change were unequal between the traffic and commercial networks, which shared the same city but did not grow in relation to each other" (1978: 12). When looking at seventeenth-century port city planning, Konvitz distinguishes Paris's elimination of its northern wall by Louis XIV without an accompanying master plan to lead the disorderly growth that followed, from the more ordered, rational, orthogonal expansion along Amsterdam's waterfront with the "plan of three rings" at the same time in 1607.

Though the French and Dutch examples are contrasted in terms of their levels of success, each essentially incorporated the methodology of the practical planning tradition to consider specific growth pressures and discover urban outlets to fulfill this demand. The more exaggerated example of the new European port city building as a way to call forth maritime power and its financial prosperity comes from seventeenth-century Swedish port city planning. Putting the cart before the horse, as it were, Konvitz argues that seventeenth-century Swedish new port city planning occurred at a moment of significant resource and manpower limitations, with the belief that these cities would symbolically and then effectively attract those missing resources through their scalar and formal ambitions. Beginning with Gothenburg and Jönköping in the early part of the century, Swedish planning incorporated the gridded rationality of the Dutch, but with added megalomaniacal growth projections that dramatically overshot actual needs. Konvitz argues that Swedish frustration with gridded urban expansions for Gothenburg and Jönköping, which did not fulfill this growth prophecy, prompted the Swedish to explore Italian ideal city planning for formal inspiration, which perhaps would be capable of physically calling forth the dominance and growth they aspired toward. "The Italian sources for these Swedish designs had once been part of an aesthetic, philosophical movement with roots in the Renaissance. In Sweden, however, Italian styles were not used to represent philosophical ideas in drawings, but were applied to the task of shaping actual cities. Such planning was supposed to reflect the greatness of Sweden's achievements and the will to sustain them" (1978, 53).

Surely Konvitz uses Sweden's new port city projects, particularly those he deems influenced by ideal planning forms that were never actually realized, as straw men to underscore the conflicting impacts of ideal and practical planning in seventeenth-century new port city planning, but the example highlights the exaggerated aspirations for grandeur and endless new urban possibility the promising and menacing sea invited. The prospect of maritime power in exchange for grandiose, classically-influenced urban monumentality rings also of a kind of temple building for Neptune, or in this case, Aegir, the Norse equivalent. The belief that these new port city projects could secure maritime power, particularly in competition with the neighboring Danes, ended in the complete collapse of Swedish power by 1720 when they had built beyond their economic means (1978: 61). The example calls forth a kind of mythology of Icharus, or perhaps more accurately, as Konvitz states, "In Sweden more than anywhere else, planning became a Promethean art" (1978: 45).

The Swedish port cities serve as an example for the kinds of borrowed urban strategies and the travel of particular kinds of typologies that occurred within Europe during the seventeenth-century, but of course this same kind of influence was spread throughout the world as a part of the European colonial experience of the sixteenth-century. Frank Broeze's work has explored this theme, particularly throughout Asia (Broeze 1989, 1997), although similar research focuses on colonial urban morphology of African and Latin American port cities (Knight and Liss 1991, Hoyle 1989, Hoyle and Hilling 1984). In her work on the Indonesian port town of Makassar, Heather Sutherland (1989) describes the result of Dutch colonial influence on the urban structure as an eighteenth-century "hybrid town, created by the forcible grafting of a Dutch outpost upon an Indonesian port" (1989: 97). Sutherland discusses how both the British and Dutch East Indies trading companies established "company town" outposts at the port locations of their trading interests throughout South East Asia, the result of which expressed the colonial power relationship indelibly on the ports' urban structures.[5] The residential spatial segregation in this, and most, colonial port cities were common throughout the region for both the Dutch and the British, exemplified for the British by the spatial and physical heterogeneity in their treaty port tradition in East Asia (Elder 1999). The British also brought this port city construction attribute and political administration to its oil towns, protectorates, and commissioned new towns throughout the Gulf.

There is a clear history of borrowing port city attributes, which could be traded as readily as the other international goods arriving to ports. This kind of mimetic aspiration also fed hopes that through imitation a port city could also conjure regional port city success. The ideal and functional models represent the same kind of symbolic and functional dualities in the history of port city planning, as the more general relationship between infrastructure and the city mentioned previously.

Port City and Development

Over the three centuries of world shipping and trade initiated in the late fifteenth-century, European maritime networks were forged through exploration, colonization, and trading that joined regional systems into a global network, which was further intensified by steam and iron technologies of the nineteenth-century (Williams 1997). Steam engines replacing wind power meant that ships were no longer at the mercy of capricious winds and tides, and iron (and later steel) meant that larger vessels could be built to better endure the force of the elements. The British maritime network grew in parallel with their colonial aspirations throughout the late eighteenth and nineteenth-centuries, and a good portion of trade was initiated through routes based on coal trade and the British mail system that stretched from the United States to the Far East (Harcourt 1997). Though

5 While not the same as industrial company towns, see King 1984 for some similarities in purpose and layout with the bungalow typology.

steam propulsion was introduced in the 1820s, it would not definitively overtake wind-powered boats until 1900 (Williams 1997: x), when it would soon have another form of competition. British oil extraction in the Gulf region in the early twentieth-century marked the beginning a new energy source that would reshape many sectors throughout the century, and the maritime world was no exception,. The British decision to convert its powerful naval fleet from steam to oil power, advocated primarily by a young Winston Churchill, not only helped the British Navy to dominate sea conflict during World War I, but launched another paradigm shift in the energy that fueled maritime trade, and the larger capacities that this afforded through increasingly larger ships (Longhurst 1959).

The economic crisis between the wars slowed the switch to oil-powered ships, but the economic recovery period after World War II incorporated port development, maritime industrialization, and shipping policy as an important combined strategy to help cities and nations recover from the damages of two world wars and the global economic crisis of the 1930s. The moment was framed politically by the Cold War and its associate philosophical debates regarding capitalist free-market development and more state-centered command economic development strategies of the Socialist Block. In P.J. Rimmer's analysis of port development in Japan that helped the country to achieve the post-war economic miracle, he points out that Japan's development does not fit comfortably within either narrative of the two opposing camps (Rostow 1959, Rimmer 1984). He proposes a third alternative, which he and others would refer to as a "developmentalist" state approach, which began during US occupation after World War II, but continued once they left the island. Rimmer suggests that while the US often cited Japan as a successful free-market example for other developing nations to follow, in truth, Japan involved heavy state intervention in its port and industrialization strategy, and the tacit understanding between the *zaibatsu* titans of the private sector and the government could not truly be described as a free-market environment. Maritime port construction and industrialization became a part of many national economic strategies throughout the post-war developing world. "Most African and Asian countries, especially those favored by substantial income from oil, have embarked on considerable port development as a part of their overall development policy, from a desire for independence and in some cases in pursuit of decentralization and regional economic stimulation" (Hoyle and Hilling 1984: 5). This included countries in the Gulf region in the Middle East, and the parallel success stories of East Asia, particularly Singapore, Hong Kong, and South Korea, which followed the Japanese model of a developmentalist state in pursuit of international market trade (Armstrong 2007, Wang 2005, Olds et al. 2004, Tan 2001, Ho 1996, Chiu and Chu 1984, Rimmer 1984).

Port construction and industrialization was incorporated as part of larger economic development policies not only for countries in the developing world, but also in Europe and the United States. Hoyle and Pinder's book *Cityport Industrialization and Regional Development* offers case studies of cities and regions throughout northern Europe and the Mediterranean who also invested heavily in maritime industrial development to recover from the war, and to keep up with the changing technologies that were advancing within the sector. Again, though perhaps not to the extent of Japan or its developmentalist progeny, state coordination within a larger market setting was clearly central to carry out such large capital port investment projects. The same is true with examples of post-war port development in the United States, where heavy federal spending, and the city competition for this spending, was determinant in giving certain coastal ports advantage over others. This was particularly the case for the ports of Los Angeles and Elizabeth, New Jersey (McCalla 2004, Rodrigue 2004, Erie 2004). Thus, though port and maritime industrialization required private capital and the participation of many private firms, the role of the state was central in their funding, planning and construction in the extreme cases of post-war developmentalist states, but also within the free-market states in the United States and Europe. A more elaborate review of development economics will help in understanding the role of infrastructure within larger, overarching developmental strategies.

Development Economics

The study of development economics has accompanied modern nation-building projects from the late eighteenth-century through today. Research on wealth development and accumulation at the national level to help governments plot out the best path for nascent economies to grow has long held an important place in the larger study of economics. Development economics is interested, generally, in trying to find optimal combinations of state investment and intervention with market factors for specific development scenarios. The state represents the decision-making authority for public expenditure and the market is an "organization coordinating competition among people seeking profits by impersonal means of pricing" (Hayami 1997: 7). Up through the 1930s, developmental economics was primarily interested in what are termed "factors of productions," those components within nation-states that economists believed either enabled or inhibited development, such as its natural resources, labor and capital, and how these combined with the levels of technology at a given point to increase efficiencies and output.

The focus on natural resources as a variable factor for economic growth was inspired originally from the work of Thomas Malthus. Malthus warned that increased population growth as a result of the combinations of increased fertility, decreased infant mortality, and increased life expectancies, all results of medical and societal advances, carried the associate dangers of depleting a county's natural resources as population grew. Malthus believed that populations grew exponentially while natural resources would reach their carrying capacity limits, and that this combination could only end in catastrophe. In contrast, David Ricardo (a contemporary of Malthus) was a great advocate of trade. Ricardo believed that if countries focused their production on those sectors where they had certain natural advantages and could develop specialization in these fields, then each country would be able to complete any deficiency that another may have by trading with one another. Trade could also include the transfer of technology developed in any one country's specialization, opening the possibilities for production even further. The most common recent example cited for this debate was the "green revolution" of the 1960s, where food production increased dramatically and helped to feed the post-World War II demographic boom experienced throughout the world, particularly in the Global South.

After the Great Depression in the United States, and changes in the world economic status of countries such as Argentina, who were the fifth economic power in the world at the beginning of the twentieth-century (Freiden 2006, Bulmer-Thomas 2003), much of the developmental economics field had to be revisited to consider other elements that could also influence economic growth. History had shown that this development process could go backward as well as forward. The "scarcity model" on which development economics had been based, whereby a lack of economic development in any given country could be explained by the scarcity of any one factor of production, or the appropriate technology, was no longer enough to explain new development conditions. Public interventions to help rescue failed economies through Keynesian investment programs lead economists to explore the role of institutions within a society, either public (education, rule of law, health care, etc.) or private (banks, financial mechanisms, etc.), and how their presence influenced and interacted with the factors of production and technology to either promote or inhibit development. In addition, research also began to explore the larger cultural value systems that framed economic development in any given country, exemplified by Max Weber's work on the Protestant work ethic (1958).

The role of technology also received more attention by development economists, and the work of German economist Joseph Schumpeter looked at how technological innovation was economically rewarded through efficiency and production increase, particularly in the short time differential between innovation and the general spread of the innovation to competitors, which would then stabilize prices (Clemence 1989). The increased focus on technology saw firms investing more in technological research and development, thus distinguishing "investment in tangible capital," typically associated with construction and capital creation, and "investment in intangible capital," focusing on exploring technological advances in any given sector.

Though Schumpeter's work highlighted the benefits that technological innovators reaped, in 1962 economist Alexander Gerschenkron, in his book *Economic Backwardness in Historical Perspective* (1962), argues that "latecomers" in economic development can also reap the rewards of "backwardness" by having the advantage of borrowing technologies from those other "leader" countries that have already developed them. Gerschenkron believed that the more behind any county's economy was from the world's innovative leaders, the more sustained growth they could enjoy during this catch-up period. These countries would not have to invest in research and development in new technologies because they would enjoy the benefits of those technologies they could borrow until they caught up. Gerschenkron's work focused particularly on those continental European countries that followed the British industrial revolution lead, and took advantage of Britain's example to help each sustain industrial growth during the middle and late nineteenth-century. As Moses Abramovitz puts it:

> In a "leading country" ... one may suppose that the technology embodied in each vintage of its stock was at the very frontier of technology at the time of investment. The technological age of the stock is, so to speak, the same as its chronological age. In an otherwise similar follower whose productivity level is lower, the technological age of the stock is high relative to its chronological age. The stock is obsolete even for its age. When a leader discards old stock and replaces it, the accompanying productivity increase is governed and limited by the advance of knowledge between the time when the old capital was installed and the time it is replaced. Those who are behind, however, have the potential to make a larger leap (1986: 386).

Gerschenkron also emphasized, however, that in order to successfully borrow technologies, the proper institutions needed to be in place to accompany technology for it to function successfully. In his European examples, he focused on the important roles of banks to make industrialization possible. In France, he pointed out the importance of the *Crédit Mobilier* savings banks necessary to help fund railroad development, and the German "universal banks" to provide the large quantities of investment capital required to launch the heavy equipment and chemical industries (1962, Hayami 1996: 150–51). In his book *The Strategy of Economic Development*, Albert Hirschman questions Gerschenkron on the basis that he assumes latecomers can elect the proper moment to shed their "backwardness" and enjoy the technological benefits available to them through example, which implies that not to do this is also a matter of election. Along with the necessary components mentioned above, and (to be fair to Gerschenkron) the proper institutions to accompany technological transfer, Hirschman argues that the elusive element for economic development depends more on those agents able to merge all of these component factors together properly and strategically to generate positive cycles of wealth accumulation and investment. Ambamovitz's focus on individual entrepreneurialism and the "social capability" to indentify development opportunities and capitalize on them are also challenges that are overlooked in Gerschenkron's work.

Within this framework, the combination of these various factors are weighed so as to induce positive changes toward economic development, be they technological, institutional, or within one of the factors of production. An example often given for induced technological change is in economies where there is a surplus of capital and a shortage of labor. The limitation on growth is the shortage of labor to match capital surplus, which often induces technological investment and innovation to mechanically resolve the labor shortage. Once induced, this technology then spreads to other competitive sectors to catch up with the new efficiencies generated by the new technology, which can cause problems in economies with an oversupply of labor. The gap between those who benefit from mechanical innovation and the larger group of surplus labor laid off as a result occurred during industrialization processes throughout developing world. State protectionism or other forms of public intervention accompanied some of these examples, but over time, this gap increased in size for many others. Gerschenkron's work in bank development in Europe is an example of induced institutional change.

Other factors considered in development economics are those usually included in United Nations Development reports, which are more easily quantified and tabled, such as per capita Gross National Product, changes in a country's industrial structure, investment savings and growth, external debt and inflation, and commodity prices, along with living standards such as education levels, heath care services, and crime rates, which reflect areas of public investment. Though scarcity causality is criticized in development economics as reductive in trying to explain different countries' development paths, governments are constantly faced with investment choices within limited budgetary constraints, where they must evaluate the costs and benefits of different investments to determine which will have the most efficient overall impact in both the short and long term.

In his discussion of this dilemma, Hirschman explains how governments chose between essentially two kinds of investments, which he calls Social Overhead Capital (SOC) and Directly Productive Activities (DPA). He describes criteria to define SOC activity as essentially synonymous with infrastructure: "services provided by the activity facilitate, or are in some sense basic to carrying on a greater variety of economic activities; services are provided publically in most countries, unless by a private company subject to some public control; services cannot be imported; and the investment required for the service is technically indivisible and has a high capital-output ratio" (Hirschman 1958: 83–4). He suggests that during economic developmentalist periods, governments tend to emphasize these kinds of infrastructural investments more over investments toward directly productive activities precisely because it is harder to calculate strict cost-benefit investment analysis of such infrastructure. Thus it is more politically attractive to broadly invest on faith that the infrastructure will be important for attracting future investment. Hirschman wrote his book in 1958, so surely part of his critique of what he saw as an overemphasis in developmental infrastructure investment came from the kinds of blind duplications and excessive funds directed toward what would become underutilized projects. Because of this, he believes that risking some degree of infrastructure shortage in favor of greater direct productivity attention could benefit many governmental investment decisions, of course with the caveat that a minimum requirement of infrastructural provision is a threshold that all economies must meet first before moving toward productivity investment.

The two extreme examples he then gives reflect his recommendation. First, what he calls the "cargo cult" in post-World War II New Guinea that built wharves into the sea and cleared an airstrip in the jungle, expecting that cargo flows would instantly appear, but which never did (Hirschman 1958: 94, Firth 1951: 12). Second, he gives the example of a boom city whose infrastructure shortage does not perceptibly affect its success, but only emphasizes the increase in economic activity. Hirschman also warns about the risks of overinvesting in infrastructure during boom periods only to find that when the increased capacity comes online, the growth has already subsided. The hyperbole shows a clear bias, but within a climate where these kinds of infrastructural recommendations from international development agencies were widely and almost blindly applied, Hirschman's recommendation suggests that countries balance infrastructural investment with directly productive activity. Should infrastructural shortage occur, demand will surely induce infrastructural expansion, which can perhaps even incorporate some private investment if demand is strong enough.

In contrast, more recent studies from the World Bank have demonstrated that the infrastructure differential between East Asia and Latin America has been an important developmental element leading to the economic success of the former and regional challenges for the latter over the past 30 years, in part resulting from deficient infrastructural investment. In addition, other World Bank literature also underscores the direct and indirect benefits of infrastructure for developing countries (Andrés et al. 2008, Calderón and Servén 2004, Calderón et al. 2003).

When weighing different development possibilities, another aspect of the decision as whether to invest in infrastructure or direct productivity involves the maximization of linkages that can be derived from any principal economic activity of the economy. Once a key industry has been determined and established, linkage development tries to strategically connect that central economic activity to satellite economic activities, which can either use excess output of the central activity as an input for some other activity, or develop an economic activity whose production can substitute any given input needed for the central economic sector. These linkages are classified as either *backward* or *forward*, depending on their role within the supply chain. "The proximity of customers (forward linkages) and of suppliers (backward linkages) may generate positive externalities for entrepreneurial clustering. As firms cluster (and employees too), local markets grow up. These market-size effects foster geographical concentration" (Tohmo et al. 2006). Forward linkages generally use output from a primary sector as an input for either a secondary or tertiary sector (or from secondary to tertiary), while backward linkages move tertiary outputs as inputs for either primary or secondary sectors (or secondary to primary). Thus economic investment decisions, either in infrastructure or productivity, should also strive to grow local markets though the kinds of economic clustering and linkages that connect a key industry with satellite industries. An example of this would be the linkages within oil-producing countries to connect oil extraction with a satellite fertilizer or plastics industrial production, as oil is an essential input for each of these. The Organization of the Petroleum Exporting Countries (OPEC) often limits the amount of oil that its member countries can export to fix and standardize international prices, so individual countries can use excess oil as an input for satellite industries, which many in the region have done and continue to do.

Since the 1970s, a significant portion of development economic research has turned its attention to both environmental impact concerns of economic development, as well as the need to include grassroots or community efforts ("bottom up") in larger developmental strategies to complement the governmental ("top down") policy. Social sciences have also critiqued the concept of a single development linearity, and the political institutions that have grown around what is now a powerful international "development" sector (Escobar 1995). Thus it is no longer possible to think about "development" *per se* uncritically (Rist 1997). Within the framework and focus of this book, however, those modern development economic narratives that served as the standardized guide to national economic and nation-building projects can help to explain the decisions made within the period of rapid modernization and urbanization after World War II, as has clearly been the case in Dubai.

Finally, since the late 1970s and 1980s, neo-classical economic theory took over much of the discussion within development economics, as a part of a larger political movement in the US and England. In his work on the Singapore state-driven development model, W.G. Huff writes:

> Investigation of Singapore's economic development … suggests a conclusion which might be termed "neo-structuralist," pointing to the scope for state intervention and the importance of specific country circumstances. Principal themes in the Singapore model of economic development—government intervention and planning, industrialization, labour mobilization and rapid capital accumulation—are … the core of development economics prior to a 1970s and 1980s neo-classical ascendance (1995. See also Sen 1983)

For Dubai, within the larger debates of development economics, one could draw similar conclusions. Dubai certainly followed aspects of Singapore's state *dirigisme*, particularly during the island nation's intense trade infrastructure period of the early 1960s. Each city-state leveraged their geographic locations to flourish into international trade *entrepôts* using significant state intervention to control local economic factors and measures. The book will explore the dimensions of Dubai's state intervention and "specific country circumstances," outside the neo-classical development perspectives. This theoretical framework was still accepted internationally during Dubai's nascent boom period and clearly is more appropriate in understanding its development trajectory.

Developmental Port Cities

"The port is, therefore, both a cause and a result of development," as mentioned above, and within the heterogeneous nature of this chapter, this theme underscores the dialectical, mutually-defining, contingent relationship between large-scale trade infrastructure and the city, and indeed infrastructure in general for territorial settlement. Discussions of globalization and the city comment on how global flows of capital, information, services, and labor can change the particular circumstance and form of cities (Scott 2001, Marcuse and van Kempen 2000, Simmonds and Hack 2000, Koolhaas and Mau 1995, Mitchell 1995, Castells 1989), but as the discussions of this chapter demonstrate, this misses the other side of the equation. Competition among cities and regions to attract global flows involves development strategies that seek to offer the appropriate infrastructural hardware and capacity, and rapid, efficient hinterland market connectivity. Because of the nature of this regional and international competition, development strategies are both proactive and reactive in nature, identifying internal sectors that could give one region a competitive advantage over another, and identifying opportunities in reaction to moves neighbors are making to better compete for regional business and success. Within developing circumstances, particularly those involving some type of scarcity element, this can be a gamble. There is a speculative element of infrastructural provision that invests heavily in the hopes that such infrastructure will attract the above-mentioned flows. As we have seen, East Asia was successful in this regard, particularly in comparison with Latin America, which was slower to invest in infrastructure. While Hirschman warned of the "cargo cult" phenomenon and the misled belief that infrastructure investment will always inevitably attract development, the Latin American example would seem to suggest that under-investing in infrastructure can, in fact, hinder economic growth. Historically, similar examples can be drawn from those who followed a more demand-side port growth model, like the Dutch, and the more speculative attempts by the Swedish to build ambitious port cities with the hopes that sea dominion would naturally follow. The Swedish ambition led to their early eighteenth-century economic collapse, the New Guinea cargo cult may still be waiting for trade to arrive, and the economies of East Asia have performed more successfully than their Latin American counterparts, illustrating that infrastructural investment is both essential and speculative, elemental and risky, and contingent upon competing regional development strategies and the particular nature of global flows and trade.

We can also draw examples from the chapter where both symbolic and functional motivations for infrastructure investment are repeated and replicated as a city moves outside its core into its hinterland. For Roman expansion, this involved an infrastructural logic of the castrum plan and the *centuriazione* that met both criteria; developing a settlement pattern along major trade and communication axes throughout the Empire, and symbolically inserting the geometry of this Roman imprint in these distant settlements as an ideal to be followed and obeyed. In Vienna, Sitte's historicism and symbolic assignment of building styles to fit their functions was replaced by Wagner's belief that infrastructural functionalism should be emphasized, allowing new styles to emerge from the specific technological requirements of the age. Indeed, the same kind of dual nature of infrastructure played out in those port city projects of the seventeenth-century in Northern Europe, where the template of ideal port city planning was contrasted with a more pragmatic growth model, and cities chose which model best suited their port city aspirations. As a "latecomer" to industrial capitalism, Barcelona was certainly aware of the British template, similar to Gerschenkron's point about Germany and France, but it was the functional repetition of Cerdà's grid and its programmatic components that defined its expansionist infrastructural logic. For both Barcelona and Vienna, one can argue that time has been the essential element to allow for spaces of *civitas* to emerge from the formal structures of Cerdà and Wagner. Nevertheless, during their moments of expansion, infrastructural systems were the principal guiding elements, based on the economic imperatives of industrial capitalism and spatial pragmatism. While never quite achieving the utopian aspirations of Howard's vision, the Garden City model (and the subsequent Abercrombie Plan and new town model) was also widely replicated internationally as an ideal typology to house a rapidly urbanizing world of the twentieth-century and decongest the urban core of cities to their outer peripheries. In each case, a combination of replication and repetition of forms, either self-referential or imported, were incorporated during moments of development.

Another element of the port city that is important to underscore is the cumulative nature of its development over time. As McCalla points out, the move "from 'anyport' to superteminal," demonstrated a programmatic accumulation and intensification over time, which in turn, required a scalar reconsideration, intensification and amplification, to keep up with the competitive requirements of the maritime industry. Whether to accommodate increasing ship size, the move from coal-based ship energy to oil-based, bulk cargo to containerization, or the information technology advances that transformed basic shed storage into an entirely new sector of logistics and supply-chain management, the incremental and paradigmatic technological changes in port structures would serve as a microcosm for the wider spatial changes precipitated by this central infrastructure.

In the following chapters, I will look at the development of the emirate of Dubai to illustrate how its port and ancillary trade infrastructure served as the primary structuring mechanism for territorial development, settlement, and programmatic accumulation, intensification and amplification. Dubai's development occurred within a particularly regional and historic context that provided its leadership with the competitive motivation to develop trade infrastructure and ancillary services that could outdo first those of their neighbors, and subsequently sought to outsize those of the world. The case offers an important example of the mutual causality and impact of competitive development and the multiple roles of infrastructure. In this way, the various discussions of this chapter converge within the spatial contexts of what was originally a lower Gulf port city, and has now become what I argue to be a global port geography.

Chapter 2
Blueprint

To understand the modern history of Dubai since its founding in 1833, one must go further back in time to explore the regional history that frames its foundation. European powers—beginning with the Venetians, and then subsequently with the Portuguese, the Dutch, and finally the British—were interested in the Gulf region as a means to secure trade routes to and from the Indian Subcontinent and points eastward. This meant that from the fifteenth-century through the late nineteenth-century, if trade routes could move uninterrupted through the Gulf region, European powers were not involved in the societal affairs of settlements as a traditional colonial ruling class. European merchants also avoided trade exploration within the region, believing that it required more effort than either the climate or the local economies were worth (Owen 2008). Local tribes were divided among the maritime coastal groups and those that were nomadic and land-bound, and conflict among these groups occurred in parallel to the larger European conflicts also playing out in the region. The intersection of the two came with the increase in piracy, which in very basic terms represented a kind of cultural disagreement on trade customs. Europeans felt that they were unjustly looted, and local groups believed that they were simply protecting themselves from foreign incursion and taking their rightful share. Historians still debate this issue today, but in relation to Dubai, the piracy of the times serves as an example of how looser understandings of the licit and illicit, particularly in terms of trade, could be capitalized upon as a business venture. The smuggling of gold, weapons, and other goods throughout Dubai's history may have been seen as illicit from perspectives outside Dubai's ports, but within the merchant-friendly, locally-autonomous environments trade flowed freely and without regulation.

British interest in regional affairs increased as the pearl trade sector grew, and once oil was discovered in Persia and Saudi Arabia at the beginning of the twentieth-century British firms entered the region more actively. Inspired by oil profits and the gold trade after 1947, the British government and firms behaved more paternalistically, and established a more direct protectorate relationship with trucial sheikhdoms, including Dubai. The interrelation of the British presence, resource exploration and wealth, and local aspirations for development define this period, which culminates in oil discovery in Dubai in 1966. The emphasis on infrastructural projects in Dubai marked its development pattern throughout, which would then serve as a blueprint for projects in its post-oil phase.

In this chapter, I will trace the regional history of the Gulf, along with the presence of a continuum of European powers, and then focus more closely on

Dubai's relationship with the British, and how this both influenced and determined the urban development of the emerging sheikdom through oil discovery.

Geographical History of the Gulf Region

Dubai is an emirate within the greater United Arab Emirates (UAE), located in the eastern part of the Arabian Peninsula between 22degree 50'N-26degree N and 51degree E-56 degree25'E (Peck 1986: 4). The UAE is comprised of seven emirates: Abu Dhabi, Dubai, Sharjah, Ras al-Khaima, Fujairah, Umm al-Qaiwain and Ajman, and of the total UAE land area is 83,600 square kilometers (32,270 square miles). Dubai occupies 4,114 square kilometers (1,588 square miles), and is second in size after the significantly larger Abu Dhabi (Kassar 2007).[1] This land, in section, falls into four geographic categories of coast and coastal plain, interior desert, an upland plain, and rugged interior mountains (Peck 1986: 6). Traditionally, this geographic diversity has marked two distinct cultures: coastal settlements dedicated to trade, fishing, and pearling and other socio-economic activities oriented toward the sea, and interior settlements and nomadic Bedouin communities based on agriculture and animal husbandry. In her work on the geographic and economic conditions of the lower Gulf region before oil was discovered, Dr Frauke Heard-Bey points out that tribes of the region included many subsections that were individually sea-oriented or nomadic, but intermingled with one another in tribal confederation as the basis for "the creation of a nation-state within a large and geographically very varied territory" (1982: 34). This intermingling included marriage within the different sections, and intensive trade based on seasonal pearl and date harvests. I will look further at the subsections of the regional tribes below, but it is important to recognize that these two forms of economic cultures were often collaborative. Considering the region's resource scarcity, both in terms of limited arable land and seasonal fishing possibilities, this mutual interaction and dependence was a pragmatic survival mechanism.

Though the UAE was only formed officially in 1971, the history of the region is rich, and recent discoveries are only now beginning to fill in wide gaps in the knowledge of its past. For Dubai in particular, in 1981 Iraqi scholars discovered evidence of a trading center there from 3,000 years ago, which is unsurprising, both in light of its geographic location and its subsequent maritime trade history (Peck 1986: 24). The voids in the historical knowledge of the region appear mainly between the arrival of Islam, the Prophet Muhammad and the first caliphs in the seventh century, and the encounter with the Portuguese in the late fifteenth and early sixteenth centuries (King 1997). The coastal trading settlements of Julfar (present Ras al-Khaimmah) and Dibba (present Fujairah and Sharjah) are

1 Land reclamation projects in Dubai and throughout the UAE will expand this total land area significantly, but this is the latest published data.

mentioned in Arab accounts of this period, and archeologists believe that the Al-Jumayra settlement, just west of Dubai (and now the name a Dubai neighborhood) was settled in the ninth century (King 1997: 76, Wilson 2006: 22). Historical accounts of the period are limited to speculation on the changing landscapes of local tribal settlement and power struggles. Archaeological sites have produced evidence of Chinese pottery, which corroborate the belief that Arab traders communicated with the Chinese during Admiral Cheng Ho's fourth voyage to the Gulf region in the early fifteenth-century (Rosenberg 2009).

Venetian trade within the larger Middle Eastern region, particularly in Damascus, Aleppo, and Alexandria, is also recorded in the fifteenth-century with some evidence of contact with the Gulf for pearl trading (Nyrop 1977: 21). But it was the Portuguese who were the European power able to take control of the Gulf through the maritime dominance of their powerful men-of-war fleet in the sixteenth-century. Rather than colonial imposition or re-settlement of the area, Portugal's principal objective was to control spice trade routes from the Indian Subcontinent to Europe. The sea route around the Cape of Good Hope, which they had discovered, helped the Portuguese to access the Indian Ocean, and by taking over the Island of Hormuz in the Straits of Hormuz the Portuguese could strategically control trade routes throughout the region. As a precursor to the later British experience, the Portuguese signed a treaty with the Sheikh of Hormuz to pacify local opposition to their occupancy in exchange for Portuguese support of the sheikh in controlling local matters (Nyrop 1977: 22). The maritime focus of the Portuguese period in the Gulf meant that local institutions remained essentially unchanged throughout the sixteenth-century (Peck 1986: 27).

The decline of Portuguese power in the Gulf came at the hands of both the Dutch and the British, though each would eventually enjoy power in the region at different moments. Each country established East Indies companies in the early seventeenth-century, and in line with these trade pursuits the British and Dutch helped the Persians recapture the Island of Hormuz from the Portuguese in 1622 (Ibid.). As was often the case in European political intrigue and shifting allegiances, the British and Dutch allied to defeat the Portuguese fleet in the Indian Ocean, only to then fight each other for power over regional trade supremacy. A British-Dutch war in the mid-seventeenth-century extended to the Gulf region, causing damage and losses for the British fleet (Nyrop 1977: 23). The Dutch achieved power over trade routes during the seventeenth-century, but their power slowly waned in Europe and internationally, and ended symbolically when they abandoned Bandar Abbas and Kharg Island in 1765 (Ibid.).

The British commercial interests in the region increased, particularly in India and along their East Indies Company trade routes. But with the fall of Dutch power, the rise of what was called "piracy" by Omani and Qawasim attacks on trade ships created instability for the Gulf. As Nyrop states:

> From the end of the seventeenth-century until 1778, chaos reigned in the gulf. Piracy was a long-established tradition, recorded from Assyrian times. In the

> modern period the Arabs, particularly the Omanis, were the first pirates to attain general notoriety. It is doubtful whether the word "pirate" can be used as a designation for people using the only means at hand to defend their land from foreign occupation and therefore exploitation, but such was the name given by Europeans who themselves were exceedingly active in piracy on the gulf and elsewhere (1977: 24).

Omani "piracy," or local Gulf maritime power, held sway through the first half of the eighteenth-century, but a civil war between the Hinawi and the Ghafiri factions weakened Omani power, and the Qawasim were the principal group attacking British trade ships, particularly in the lower Gulf area. The Qawasim origins are debated, but it is believed that they were the Hawala who came from central Arabia in the seventh century and migrated to lower Persia (Peck 1986: 29). Eventually crossing the Gulf to Oman, through maritime battle and taking advantage of Omani internal power struggles, the Qawasim took control of the area between present-day Ras al-Khaimah down to Sharjah. Inspired by both strategic and religious interests, the Qawasim allied with the Wahhabis and intensified their sea attacks. The British and the British-Indian fleets allied with the Omani's in retaliation against the Qawasim, but their joint expeditions between 1808 and 1819 were unsuccessful, so that by 1817 Qawasim were only 70 miles from Bombay (Peck 1986: 31). It was not until November 1819, when a group of 3,000 British and Indian forces attacked the Qawasim naval base at Ras al-Khaimah, were the British able to assume control of the region. A mixture of treaties, truces, indirect rule, and canon diplomacy would maintain this rule until their departure from the region 150 years later. In his book on the structure of British rule in "the Arabian frontier of the British Raj" during the nineteenth and twentieth-centuries, James Onley describes the policy of indirect rule as decided according to strategic economic interests, based on the principle of "informal control if possible, formal control when necessary." As he states:

> The method of control the British adopted was largely determined by the success they had in attracting local collaborators and mediators. The greater their success, the more indirect their control. Therefore it is the Empire and its periphery, rather than the imperial capital of London, that holds the key to understanding both the timing and the nature of [British] imperialism (2007: 30).

The particular local collaborators were tribal families that signed trucial protectorate agreements that, at least through oil exploration, enabled a more distant and preferred British participation, within the regional southern Gulf periphery around the central British interests in India.

In January 1820, the British marked the defeat of the Qawasim with the signing of the General Treaty of Peace with the regional sheikhs of Bahrain and what was then northern Oman (which included the present-day UAE), where all agreed to end "piracy" attacks both among each other and on British trade ships. This truce agreed upon in the Treaty would commit Britain to maintain and enforce this peace, mostly in the interest of their trade pursuits. The "Trucial System" was coined officially in 1835 when the British declared a truce between the Bani Yas tribe from the lower Shakhbut (present-day Abu Dhabi) area and the Qawasim as a means to secure a peaceful pearling season for merchants of the lower Gulf. This truce was again signed by all factions in the Ten Year Maritime Truce of 1843, and then finally ratified into perpetuity (over the next century) through the Perpetual Treaty of Truce in 1853, which stipulated for the British government to "watch over and protect" the southern Gulf region "for evermore" (Heard-Bey 1982: 164). The Treaty also renamed the region as Trucial Oman, or the Trucial States, which was of course, better than the region's previous British title, the "Pirate Coast."

Malcolm Peck points out that the British agreed to back regional sheikhs in power at that particular moment with their military in exchange for a guarantee of peace—most importantly for their trade routes through to India, but also for the pearling sector of the lower Gulf:

> By freezing the power relationships that existed between tribes or tribal confederations, thereby preserving a number of small states that otherwise would probably have been swallowed by larger neighbors. Eventually the British role in the affairs of the Trucial States would carry their evolution toward western-style statehood a step further by defining territorial boundaries (1986: 32).

With a few strokes, a mix of British magnanimousness and clear economic self-interest established a static territorial, political, and social structure for the Trucial States, which was previously characterized by far more fluid inter-tribal power relationships. The British officially installed a Political Resident in Bushire (Persia), which had already served as a diplomatic base since 1778,[2] and in Sharjah in 1823 to "meet the treaty commitments" (Nyrop 1977: 24, Hamza 1968). The treaties established a precedent for an increasingly paternalistic British intervention into the inter-tribal affairs of the lower Gulf as both mediator and military enforcer, wherein British colonial obligations were not as specifically defined as in other areas of the Empire. These treaties brought the region into the sphere of British colonial administration at a point when many in London believed that the region was not worth what it would cost to oversee. The resulting "'cut-price' imperial system of indirect control required local rulers to sign anti-piracy peace treaties and to accept the authority of small British residencies" in exchange for British trucial protection (Davidson 2008: 17). The military backing of local sheikhs in exchange for peace for British maritime routes was a low price for Britain to pay for hegemonic and exclusive control of the lower Gulf, particularly with regard to other competing European powers, along with Russia and the United States.

---

2 See Onley (2007) for more detailed explanation of British political structure within the region.

The Bani Yas and the Qawasim were rival tribes in the late eighteenth and early nineteenth-century. Because the British treaties focused specifically on maritime truce, the Bani Yas (not coincidentally given the British predisposition against the "pirating" Qawasim) were benefited due to their land-based power, in contrast to the Qawasim sea prowess. Though the treaties sought to end the warring factions of the region, the Qawasim and Bani Yas would continue their inter-tribal battling until the end of the nineteenth-century. The Bani Yas were originally from the Najd region, and were comprised of many subsections, both seafaring and Bedouin.[3] During this time, the Bani Yas controlled Shakhbut and areas south, and in addition to fighting the Qawasim, they were also battling against the Wahhabi, which resulted in a strained tribal power structure at its base in Shakhbut. In 1833, 800 members of the Al Bu Falasa subsection of the Bani Yas left to settle in a point between Sharjah and Shakhbut led by Maktoum bin Buti and Ubaid bin Said Al-Falasi. By the late 1820s, the British Political Resident had already reported that the creek of Dubai had approximately 1,200 residents, so the new arrivals nearly doubled the population, and this is generally recognized as the official foundation of Dubai (Davidson 2008: 12–13, Wilson 2006: 29). Al-Falasi died soon after in 1836, thus consolidating dynastic rule of the Maktoum family with the official recognition and security of the 1835 British treaty. The Maktoum dynasty has been the ruling family in Dubai ever since.

Dubai of the Nineteenth Century

The origin of the name "Dubai" is a topic of debate. Some believe it comes from the Arab root word *daba*, signifying a kind of locust that was known to periodically infest the creek, while others claim it the result of fusing the Hindi word *doh*, or two, and the Arabic word *bayt*, house, in reference to a pair of white houses located near the entrance of the creek (Davidson 2008: 10, Wilson 1999: 19, 2006: 23). The Al-Maktoum dynasty was established in 1836, with the associate monarchical intrigues of loyalty, lineage, and succession. Though power was negotiated with the merchant classes of Dubai, the absolutism of the ruler was established in Dubai since its founding. Sheikh Maktoum's rule lasted until his death in 1852 when he was succeeded by his brother, Sheikh Said. Sheikh Said's rule was brief, until 1869, when he died and was succeeded by his nephew Hashar bin Maktoum. After Hashar's death in 1886, there was some dispute for heir status between his brother Rashed and his son Maktoum, which was resolved by the family in favor of Rashed. Maktoum bin Hashar became ruler after Rashed's death

3 Heard-Bey enumerates the many Bani Yas subsections, which along with the Al Bu Falasa includes Al Bu Mahair, the Rumaithat, the Qubaisat, the Mazari, the Hawamil, the Maharibah, the Al Mishaghin, and the Sudan. In addition to the Bani Yas tribe, she also describes the subsections of the Manasir and Dhawahir tribes, who were less numerous than the dominant Bani Yas in the region (1982: Chapter 2).

in 1894, and would lead Dubai with liberal policies that would become part of a larger developmental blueprint for the new century (Hamza 1968).

In spite of the overarching trucial treaties, which focused principally on the sea peace, Dubai's tenuous status between the Qawasim and the Bani Yas required a mix of political cunning and natural luck to keep each group at bay from overtaking the fledging town. Not unsimilar to the larger political intrigues of the previous centuries among the Portuguese, Dutch and British, the three factions frequently shifted allegiances toward their own benefit. By 1840, the Qawasim and Bani Yas resolved some of their larger conflicts and sought to overthrow the Maktoum in Dubai, agreeing to split it along its creek line, with Bur Dubai on the western side to go to the Bani Yas and Deira for the Qawasim (Davidson 2008: 15, Hawley 1970). An outbreak of smallpox in Dubai made this acquisition less appealing, and Sheikh Maktoum bin Buti was also able to counter-strategize against the two to divert their attacks. This kind of plotting was to occur continuously, albeit mostly under the somewhat myopic radar of the trucial agreements, but as the century wore on, Dubai's condition as a buffer zone between the two tribes was generally accepted as beneficial to all in its existence. The division certainly helped the British solidify control of the region, and the 1853 Perpetual Treaty and its ratification sought again to freeze a regional power structure toward British benefit.

The second half of the nineteenth-century proved to be more prosperous for the lower Gulf region, particularly for the pearling sector run by the merchants. The maritime truce offered a calmer environment for pearling, and the increased business demonstrated how the sector benefited from this. Between the 1870s and the late 1890s, pearl exports from Dubai grew ten-fold (Davidson 2008: 22–3, Gabriel 1987: 139, Lorimer 1970), and the harvests drew regional attention that boosted immigration to Dubai, particularly among Persians and *Banians*, British Indian Hindu merchants (Onley 2007: xviii). Dubai merchants were well-integrated into the distribution patterns of the lower Gulf, and operated principally out of the Persian Lingah port, which was a key hub for British trade between India, Persia and Europe. Because banking was considered to be against the Muslim law, it was the Banians, with the support of Bombay banks, who took up the banking sector in Dubai and funded the yearly pearling expeditions. The Persian community was involved mainly in retail and food trade, and Arab bourgeoisie focused mainly on pearling and trading (Al-Sayegh 1998: 88). The 40 shops and 100 traders in the *souq* recognized by Sheikh Maktoum in the 1840s grew steadily (Davidson 2008: 68), and by the end of the century, Dubai claimed the highest number of men employed in the pearling sector in the region (6,936), 335 pearling ships, and was clearly becoming the economic and commercial center of the Trucial States (Al-Sayegh 1998: 89).

The commercial buzz and economic boom of the Gulf at the end of the century escaped neither the British nor other European countries interested in taking advantage of the strategic and commercial benefits of the region. The opening of the Suez Canal in 1869 increased maritime trade routes and connectivity between Europe and Asia, thus increasing the Gulf/Indian Ocean region's strategic importance (Rammin 1999). French, Russian, German, and Ottoman expeditions to court diplomatic relationships, either real or imagined, precipitated greater British commitment to the region, which of course required a similar reciprocal commitment from the Trucial States. In March 1892, exclusive agreements were signed which stated that no territorial sovereignty could be ceded to any other international power without British consent (Peck 1986: 35–6). This changed the Trucial States status from simply a commercial interest for Britain to a strategic one, and this would be particularly important for the future oil explorations concessions of the early twentieth-century. J.P. Bannerman suggests that before oil explorations, the political unit in the Trucial States was understood as "people-centered," based on personal agreements, and not territorially defined with specificity (Bannerman 1986: 76–7). In this sense, with British backing already secured through previous agreements, any pretense of mutual benefit present in previous treaties had now disappeared. The Gulf became known as the "British lake," and the British became the diplomatic arbiter of the Trucial States through signed and internationally-recognized agreements.

While successful pearling expeditions intensified trade for Dubai, during the latter part of the nineteenth-century it was still the Persian port of Lingah on the other side of the Straits of Hormuz that served as the principal distribution center for Indian goods for the region. Lingah's hub status was established since the eighteenth-century and continued throughout the nineteenth-century, which attracted many Indian traders to settle in Lingah and mix in with the Persian trade community. Over time, Dubai traders also mixed with this trading group, and from 1873 through 1902 they controlled distribution trade from Lingah to the Trucial Coast (Al-Saleh 1998: 89). At the turn of the century, however, Lingah's fate would suffer drastically due to the imposition of Tehran's restrictive Imperial Customs tariffs and controls for re-exported goods, which reached up to 400 percent on some goods, particularly for Arab traders (Ibid.). In 1904, in what would prove to be a regional coup, the ruler of Dubai, Maktoum bin Hashar, at the *majlis* (council of the merchant class), declared the Dubai port to be tax-free and control-free by removing the already low 5 percent customs fees, and this quickly attracted re-export activities from Lingah across the Gulf to the Dubai port (Gabriel 1987: 71). All commerce between Great Britain and India would then pass through Dubai, such that by 1905, some 34 steamers were calling regularly, raising the annual volume of cargo to 70,000 tons (Fairservice 2002: 23). The prominent British India Steam Navigation Company essentially shifted its distribution center, firmly establishing Dubai's vocation as a strategic *entrepôt* for British imperial trade routes. As a result, the merchant class greatly benefited from the rapid increase in trade throughput, and large sectors of the Lingah Persian and Indian trading communities migrated to Dubai along with the trade route business.

Maktoum bin Hashar's free port policy announcement at the *majlis* was not coincidental, as it was this council that was chaired by the leaders of the merchant community. Fatmah Al-Sayegh's research explores the relationship between the Dubai merchant class and the ruler throughout the twentieth-century, and underscores the importance of this sometimes delicate relationship in understanding the development projects of the emirate. The free port policy attracted a larger merchant community from Lingah, which meant that this tacit balance of power needed to be cared for all the more prudently. Al-Sayegh describes this understanding between ruler and merchant class at the beginning of the twentieth-century:

> Since the ruler's income was not as high as that of the pearl merchants, and sometimes fluctuated with the market, the ruler often turned to the merchant for financial assistance, a fact which increased his dependency on them. This caused a unique situation where in fact the merchants were often in a position to dictate their wishes. The ruler was fully aware of this fact, and in return for merchants' financial contributions he appointed them to his Majlis, or advisory board (1998: 90).

The *majlis* then served as kind of pre-municipal group, led by the ruler, wherein merchants' financial power gave them significant sway over governing issues. The merchant leaders promoted certain civic initiatives through philanthropic projects for several schools and a hospital, which established a precedent both for specific concern for these kinds of foundational infrastructures, and to a more general degree, a blurring of public and private spheres within the ruling system.

Urban Morphology at the Beginning of the Twentieth Century

While the port was taking on increased international trade functions, at the turn of the century, Dubai was still a town of 10,000 people, of which almost 7,000 were involved in the pearling sector. The urban layout included three areas located around the mouth of the creek: Deira, consisting of 1,600 houses and 350 *souq* shops for the Arab merchant community, Al Shindagha, a residence of the ruling family that included 250 houses, and Bur Dubai, the smallest of the settlement areas with 200 houses and 50 *souq* shops, mostly populated by Persian and Indian merchants (Heard-Bey 1982: 242). Spatially, the town was perhaps more divided than the blurred public and private functions mentioned above, with the ruler's fortress located in Al Shindagha, across the creek from the merchant area of Deira. Oddly, the Bur Dubai area was perhaps the lesser important of three areas in terms of Dubai's political economy, but it housed the cemetery, which holds symbolic importance for many urban cultures (Mumford 1961: 7).

It is important also to underscore the morphological precedent of this outlay in order to better understand subsequent urban development. First, the simultaneous separation and agglomeration of the three settlements around the water element of the creek required a transportation mechanism (*dhow* river transport, later enhanced through bridge and tunnel construction) in order to communicate each

Figure 2.1 Dubai's original settlements, featuring the creek, Deira to left, Al Shindigah below, and Bur Dubai above

Source: Dubai GIS Office

area. While the silt accumulation allowed residents to cross the creek during seasonal low tides, the creek generally required a form of transportation to cross. Furthermore, the creek served as center, because it was the essential entry and exit point for the pearling economy, and because it was the element that joined the three separate settlements. Second, the spatial separation of function, maintaining the Al Shindigah area dedicated to the ruler and his family, and the Deira area for the merchant class, along with Bur Dubai, though to a lesser extent. While this would eventually change with a mixing of spatial functions among the three settlements, the initial urban layout can be understood as a precursor to the later modern and modernization projects that spatially isolated districts for specific functions. Equally important, while always subordinate to the final power of the ruler, different areas of the burgeoning town could be understood as overseen and associated with certain communities in addition to the ruler. Finally, and related to each of the previous points, Dubai was a megalopolitan urban structure. By this I mean that while the creek must be understood as a central urban element and a structuring mechanism for urban articulation and development, these three settlements were also separated by the creek, and each settlement required a transportation armature for functional coherence.[4] Thus, the fluid nature of the creek as center was essentially centrifugal, such that as development moved beyond the walled areas of the city, Dubai's polycentric characteristic, and its ability to have a shifting central hierarchy, were established within Dubai's initial settlement pattern.

In Search of Reform

While World War I had little impact on Dubai, it was the period between the wars that would greatly alter Dubai's economic structure. The world-wide crisis precipitated by financial events in October 1929 would devastate international markets, and Dubai was hit heavily, essentially ending the pearling sector and the associate ancillary activities. As early as July 1929 there were already signs of pearling fleets that could not go out because of lack of financing, and by 1933, the international price for pearls had dropped by 20 percent (Al-Sayegh 1998: 94). Once the crisis hit, sectors of the merchant class felt part of the blame should be directed toward Britain. The British treaties had prevented other countries from investing in the local pearling industry, and merchant leaders felt that this had denied them access to improved technology for more competitive and efficient pearling (Davidson 2008: 30). Indeed, Britain sought to prevent international interlopers into their Gulf "lake," but also consciously wanted to block excessive economic success for the Gulf, particularly in a sector that they did not benefit from directly. The Banians, who were hit particularly hard by the crisis as the principal financiers, requested that Britain intervene to pursue their debtors, but these pleas went unanswered (Ibid.). The introduction of the cultured pearl by the Japanese would also bring international prices down for pearls, and mark the end of this long pearling history in the lower Gulf which had lasted thousands of years.

The end of the pearling industry also interrupted the tacit governing agreement between the ruler and the merchant class in Dubai. This occurred for two reasons. First, while sectors of the merchant class and the *majlis* were involved in port and regional distribution activities, most of the merchant class wealth was based on profits from pearling. Once this ended, they no longer controlled Dubai's purse strings, and thus, there was a shift in the balance of power established during the pearling era to the benefit of the ruler. Second, this shift also occurred because of concessions for oil exploration and air use. In 1939, the British Political Resident for the lower Gulf remarked, "… a key reason for the goodwill between the British and the rulers was that negotiations over air and oil gave the rulers a square deal which carried a money bag rather than a big stick" (Davidson 2008: 24). British oil exploration throughout the Gulf region dated back to the turn of the century, but

4 Gottmann (1961) introduces the concept of "megalopolis," and Pope (2008) discusses contemporary projects in Dubai as "megalopolitan."

similar preventative strategies that inspired the 1892 Gulf treaties to keep Russia and other European countries away from Gulf resources also drove the British to establish oil exploration concession agreements with countries in the region. In 1935, the London-based Anglo-Iraqi Petroleum Company (later renamed Petroleum Development (Trucial States)) formed a subsidiary company called Petroleum Concessions Ltd., which was responsible for signing exclusive oil exploration concession agreements in the lower Gulf (Peck 1986: 37). In 1937, Dubai's ruler Sheikh Said Al-Maktoum signed a 25-year oil concession agreement with Petroleum Concessions Ltd., wherein the ruler received 60,000 rupees at signing, an annual income of 300,000 rupees, with an additional 200,000 rupees if oil were discovered, and an export price of 3 rupees per barrel (Davidson 2008: 27).

The British also sought exclusive air rights in the region for their Imperial Airways line to be able to land and refuel for flights from Basra to Bombay and Cairo to Karachi (Davidson 2008: 25). Again, these concessions were signed directly with the rulers, beginning in the early 1930s with Ras-al Khaimah and Sharjah, and then again in 1937, with Sheikh Said in Dubai (Ibid.). While it was initially believed that there was no appropriate land site for an airstrip, the agreement took advantage of the linear form of the Dubai creek as a landing site for water planes. Sheikh Said received 5,000 rupees in the first year of this agreement, and it is believed that in order to secure this agreement, he would buy up all empty seats on planes that were not full when leaving Dubai to retain Imperial Airways patronage (Ibid.).

With direct passive revenue streams coming from air and oil concessions, Sheikh Said assumed a much stronger position *vis-à-vis* the *majlis* and the merchant class, placing him in a position of greater financial power after having to depend on pearling merchants for an income. Other Gulf countries that also depended on pearling faced similar shifts in the ruler/*majlis* power shares, which precipitated a wave of reform movements in the region, particularly in Kuwait and Bahrain. Clearly these movements were the result of disgruntled merchants that had previously controlled local affairs, who, with the end of the pearling industry, lost much of their wealth, but perhaps even more importantly, much of their power and status. Merchant leaders in Dubai emboldened by the success of the reform movement in Kuwait and Bahrain sought similar reforms.

In October 1938, 400 merchants from various families, including the ruler's, tried to impose a set of political and economic reforms on Sheikh Said (Davidson 2008: 32). The reforms included a new 15-member consultative *majlis*, of which the ruler would be president, whose main functions would be to administer the public coffer, to be drawn from 85 percent of the concession revenues. Importantly, the reforms also included a list of infrastructure investments, such as the dredging and widening of the creek to help boost trade throughput and increase economic activity for the merchants, still reeling from the end of pearl trade, particularly to create advantage over the competing port of Sharjah, which also silted heavily (Davidson 2008: 33). While comprised of disgruntled, status-stripped merchant leaders, the democratic aims of the reforms strove to extend the political and economic decisions of Dubai beyond simply those of the ruler. The reform movement enjoyed some initial success, but Sheikh Said, with the continued support of the British, along with Bedouin tribes on the outskirts of Dubai, was able to regain power. While the power had shifted locally in Dubai because of the end of pearling, the power agreement between the British and the regional rulers, and Sheikh Said in particular, had not changed, and the British, at least at this point, preferred to continue to conduct their business with one person and not a potentially quarrelsome elected *majlis*. A combination of gun-boat diplomacy (several ships from the Royal Navy were stationed within sight of Deira), several low-flying Royal Air Force planes, and the kind of Al-Maktoum cunning that had kept usurpers at bay for over a century, helped Sheikh Said to regain power (Davison 2008: 34).

On March 29, 1939, through what appeared to be a peace offering, Prince Rashid, son of Sheikh Said, was to marry the daughter of a prominent merchant class family involved in the reform movement. Since the October initiative, the Deira side of the creek, controlled by the merchants, had been guarded against any kind of retaliation from the ruler. After some months, this guard seemed unnecessary for the event of the March wedding. On the day of the wedding, however, Bedouin troops crossed the creek and declared that Dubai was once again unified (Ibid.). Instead of the consultative *majlis* that the reform movement demanded, a *Majlis al-tujjar* was established, which would continue to include some selected merchant leaders, but only at the ruler's discretion. From this point forward, Prince Rashid took over the affairs of Dubai in the name of his father, though Sheikh Said would live on until 1958. Rashid was more sympathetic with the merchants' plight, and upon taking power officially, he would proceed to implement many of the infrastructural projects that the reform movement petitioned. Once Sheikh, Rashid would also establish a municipal council that would open some of the technocratic municipal decision-making processes. The important difference, however, is that the merchant class could not force his hand into these projects, and he made sure that the projects were cleared and coordinated with the British political agents. The reform movement marks the beginning of the era of Prince (and subsequently Sheikh) Rashid, as a kind of trial by fire in political intrigue. His marriage into the reformist merchant family, and the intelligence to understand the logic in some of the requests of the reform movement, particular as a means to further Dubai's development, helped to form a more cooperative collaboration with the merchant community. Nevertheless, the outcome of the reform movement, the *counter*-reform if you will, signified that an unclear distinction between overall development objectives and those of individual merchant interests could continue to exist comfortably, with the very clear understanding that each was ultimately subordinate to the Al-Maktoum ruler and his British backing. The outcome also demonstrated that the infrastructural reforms to promote economic concerns for the merchant class were attended to (albeit not until the 1950s), but the political reforms calling for democratization were both repressed and ignored, which again, would serve as a kind of *modus operandi* for what could and could not change within the regime, essentially until today.

Oil Exploration and Increased British Paternalism

The end of World War II marked the beginning of the Cold War, and soon afterward, Indian independence in 1947 ended the British colonial project in the Subcontinent. However the British Raj remained in the Gulf region for 20 more years for various reasons: first, the oil interests pursued since the beginning of the twentieth-century; second, Cold War motives to keep Russian influence in the resource-rich region at bay; and finally, the remaining hubris of Empire, and an inertia which saw no reason to abandon a situation of good relations with the rulers of the region (Peck 1986: 40). Oil exploration continued, and if we consider Bannerman's point about "people-centered" understandings of political sphere and influence before oil (1986: 77), then once concessions were established with the British territorial delineation took on a much greater significance for Gulf rulers. We've already seen how this impacted local ruling dynamics, but at the same time, when oil concessions were signed with both Dubai and Abu Dhabi in the late 1930s, an initial disagreement on territorial boundaries was sparked. Though World War II temporarily halted explorations, they resumed in 1945, as did the border dispute, which flared in 1948 when a Dubai raiding group killed 52 Manasir allies of Abu Dhabi in a border battle (Peck 1986: 41). British political intervention helped to resolve the conflict by drawing up territorial boundaries from the coast to the interior that both Abu Dhabi and Dubai agreed to, but the border would remain a point of contention between Dubai and Abu Dhabi through the UAE formation in 1971. Thus, the British understanding with Trucial rulers could be used both to back those rulers against reformist merchants, and to pit the rulers against one another, with British paternalist intervention as the final word on matters.

As oil exploration resumed after World War II, British institutions moved to Dubai to establish a presence in the growing town. In 1947 a British political resident was set up in Dubai, and in the previous year the British Imperial Bank of Iran (which would change its name to British Bank of the Middle East—BBME—in 1952) signed an agreement with Dubai to set up an office there that would enjoy a banking monopoly until 1963. While profits for BBME were initially more modest in Dubai compared with other Gulf branches in Kuwait and Bahrain, the bank enjoyed good relations with Prince Rashid, and this would eventually pay off well for them (Jones 1987: 150). Beginning in the early 1950s, gold became the new resource to replace pearls in Dubai. While Kuwait had previously been the principal exporter of gold to India, their discovery and subsequent concentration on oil in 1950, along with Dubai's economic growth and geographic proximity to India, attracted gold trade flows southward (Green 1973). After India's independence was declared, the sale of gold was officially outlawed for Indian merchants. For Dubai merchants, who were forced to find other sectors for business opportunities (both legal and illicit) after the pearling decline, a market for the covert sale of gold to Indian merchants began. Thus, all international gold trade with India (including Britain's and Switzerland's) would pass first through Dubai, where its dhow traders would then transship the gold for the final trek to meet with Indian traders off their coasts (Ibid.). The BBME in Dubai would offer "free dollars" for gold trade, even though Dubai still was part of the sterling region, and in this way, a curious three-way exchange for currency and bullion traders emerged that generated profits of 300 percent or more (Gabriel 1987: 142, Green 1973). The BBME, of course, also profited handsomely. With the same vision and flexibility demonstrated in competition with Persia, Dubai, again, utilized a lax regulatory system and a willingness to encourage business to solidify its economic and geographic position.

Politically, events in the 1950s throughout the Middle East began to stir, with nationalist movements in Egypt with Jamal Abdul Nasser and in Iran with Mohammad Mosaddeq. Christopher Davidson explores how this influenced civic movements in Dubai and the lower Gulf, particularly among teachers and students. A group known as the Front for the Liberation of Occupied Eastern Arabia (FLOEA) was a teacher-led group in Dubai that was sympathetic to similar Arab nationalist movements in the region, and advocated independence from British protectorate rule, as well as from the local ruling oligarchy (2008: 42). By 1953, a group was formed known as the Dubai National Front, which sought to promote nationalist activities, and along with an increasingly strong presence in the Dubai schools and among students, the National Front also promoted public demonstrations. There were only a handful of schools in Dubai during this time, and the nascent education system had to import foreign teachers to teach students. With these foreign teachers coming from Iraq and Egypt, also came the nationalist discourses felt throughout the region. While similar kinds of nationalist discourse informed the reform movement in the 1930s, much of the literature that inspired reform of that era had previously come through merchant contacts with India (Al-Sayegh 1998). Nevertheless, many of the same families that had supported the reform movement also joined the National Front for similar reasons.

The resulting response to the rising nationalist and anti-regime sentiment marks an interesting turn of events for Dubai and the British. In 1951, the Trucial Oman Levies (TOL) were established as a policing group representing the British to keep peace throughout the Trucial sheikhdoms and protect British political agents (Peck 1986). The Levies were augmented in the mid-1950s to approximately 1,000 men, and their name was changed to the Trucial Oman Scouts. A further demonstration of strength occurred when Sheikh Rashid officially took over as ruler in 1958. The HMS *Loch Insh* British warship brought the letter of official recognition, as yet another demonstration of British force backing both their interests and those of the ruler (Davidson 2008: 51). In addition, in 1960, Sheikh Rashid appointed Banaga Al-Amin, a Sudanese friend of the British resident, as Director of Education to help purge the education system of the subversive nationalist element. Education had been funded through merchant largess in the early part of the 1900s, and the British were hesitant to invest in education during the 1940s and 1950s, as they had in health care, for fear that a more educated Dubai population may rebel against British paternalistic rule. Whether this was simply on principle, or inspired by the political activity in Dubai schools at the time, it was not until the early 1960s that the British understood that investment in education could also counter nationalist propaganda and formation (Davidson 2008: 52). In protest to Sheikh Rashid's decisions, Egypt sent various delegations to meet with him personally and register formal complaints. These delegations, along with all flights on Egypt Air, would notably be refused landing at the new Dubai airport throughout the 1960s (Ibid.).

Dubai Urban Infrastructure

The historic relationship between Dubai and the British government—and their associate interests in promoting British institutions—cannot not be overemphasized as part and parcel of the emirate's modernization project. Geoffrey Jones's history of the BBME underscores the kind of unorthodox relationship established between the Bank and Sheikh Rashid:

> As in Kuwait, BBME had a monopoly of banking in Dubai after opening in 1946. In Dubai, as elsewhere, the responsibilities of monopoly encouraged BBME to undertake functions beyond the scope of a normal commercial bank … Moreover, from the late 1950s BBME played an important part in the Ruler's plans to modernize Dubai (1987: 150).

Since proposed in the *majlis* reform movement of the late 1930s, the dredging and widening of the creek was understood as Dubai's most imperative infrastructural project to help increase throughput of traffic, as well as accommodate the landing of heavier equipment necessary for oil exploration. In 1954, through contacts of both the British Raj political agencies the BBME, Prince Rashid called upon Neville Allen—an engineer for the British Sir William Halcrow firm who was working on hydrographic surveys for the development of the Shuwaikh Port in Kuwait—to carry out similar surveys for the creek and its eventual dredging scheme (Jones 1987: 154). Allen's survey determined that the cost for dredging would be £388,000, and in 1955 Prince Rashid and the British political agent approached the BBME to try to secure a loan for the project (Ibid.). The bank would not agree to the loan without the guarantee of the British government that it would pay in case of default, which was not immediately forthcoming. An alternative route through this same network helped to secure a £400,000 loan from the Ruler of Kuwait, under the auspices of the Kuwait Development Fund that offered regional help to developing neighbors since Kuwait's oil discovery in 1938. The BBME helped to negotiate favorable lending conditions and also agreed to guarantee payments in case Dubai defaulted (Ibid.). The initial dredging and widening of the creek was completed by the end of the decade, and increased throughput capacity to allow local vessels and coastal steamers of up to 800 tons to enter. Grey Mackenzie & Sons, also a British firm working in the Gulf since the late nineteenth-century, operated barges that unloaded cargo in the creek for offshore ships over the 800-ton limit (Gabriel 1987: 141, Jones 1986). The Sharjah creek had silted to a point beyond use long enough for Dubai to secure the infrastructural advantage.

In addition to creek dredging, through the same regional networks, Dubai also contracted the British architect/planner John R. Harris to draft the first 1960 master plan to direct booming expansion and infrastructure projects. Harris had also been involved in architecture and planning work in Kuwait (Humaid Al Tayer 1999). As creek activity and development increased, Sheikh Rashid either foresaw, or was persuaded, that this kind of urban development and expansion needed proper planning to guide it. Whether Sheikh Rashid saw what was happening in Kuwait and Bahrain and wanted to follow their example with the advice of British institutions and consultants who would benefit, or these infrastructure projects were part of his larger vision for Dubai is conjectural. Clearly Sheikh Rashid's political cunning, along with a family history of business-friendly policy to facilitate trade, demonstrated the ruler to have the intelligence to both identify and create opportunities for Dubai. But it was with the financing and technical expertise of both British and Gulf networks that these projects were ultimately realized.

Harris's 1960 master plan was principally a road map outlining the transportation armature to help structure the city's growth. The plan included general land use indications for industrial, residential, commercial, and public (future schools, hospitals) uses, but these were broad-brushed, and could later be changed circumstantially according to new project and investment requirements (Harris 1994). A 1968 promotional booklet on Dubai announces as much in its "Town Planning" section: "The whole plan has an inbuilt flexibility enabling it to be adapted to new conditions and major development projects" (Hamza 1968).[5] While initially a part of the reform movement's petitions, the Dubai Municipality was officially established in 1957 as the institution in charge of carrying out the indications of the Harris plan. By the end of the decade, the small fishing town began to grow southward along the creek's natural urban axis with the help of muscular, ambitious engineering projects to guide expansion. Dredging and land reclamation, and Harris's first master plan occurred at the same time as Sheikh Rashid promulgated the Land Law of 1960, which was essentially a homestead declaration giving land ownership to those Dubaians who could prove having lived on their property for a certain period of time. All other land belonged to the ruler, land could not be owned by those who were not Dubaians, and if the municipality needed privately-owned land it was committed to paying the appropriate price (Gabriel 1987). Prince Maktoum bin Rashid Al-Maktoum headed the land regulation committee, and the Land Law

5 The Engineering Department of the Dubai Municipality was responsible for the plan's implementation.

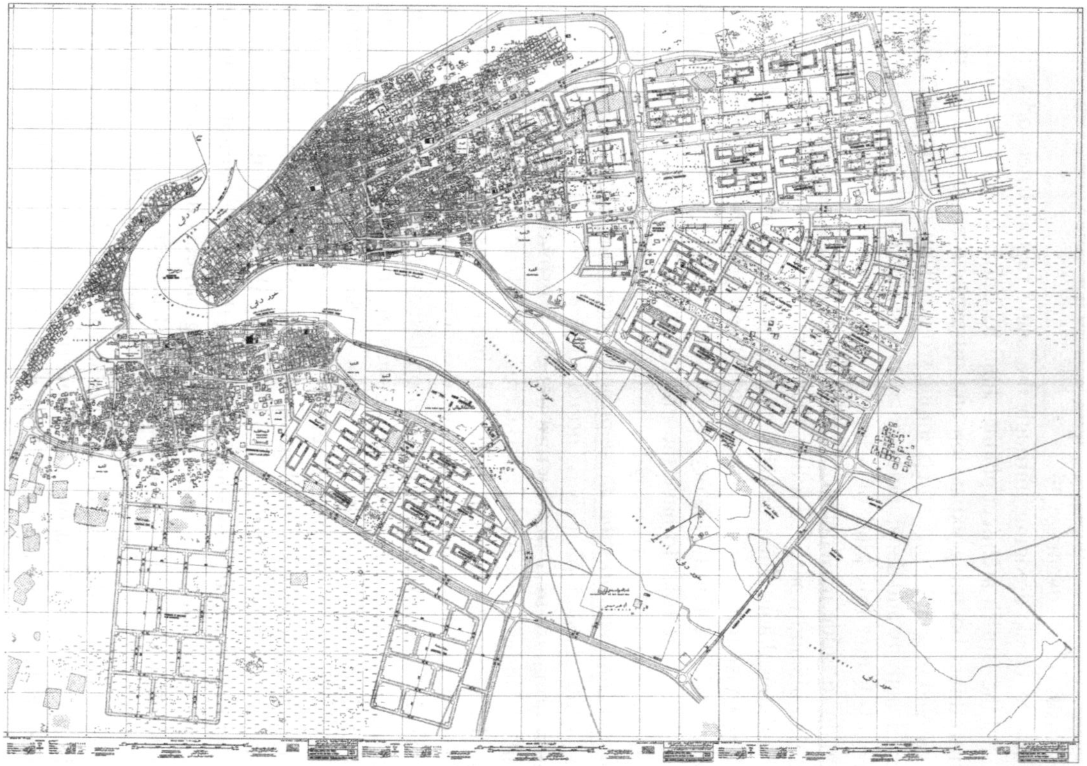

Figure 2.2 John Harris 1960 Master Plan

Source: John R. Harris and Partners

was structured specifically on the Sudanese land law, which had recently been completed after Sudanese independence in 1956 (Balfour-Paul 1991). Sudanese consultants were contracted to help formulate the law based on their recent experience (Hamza 1968). Though within a different sector, the Land Law is another example of consulting expertise contracted through regional networks based on British spheres of influence (though recently independent, Sudan had also been a part of the British Raj). The law was also an essential to step legislate land capitalization for wealth accumulation. It was directly linked to the first master plan as parts of the larger strategy to invest in Dubai as a territory through large infrastructure projects, take advantage of the resulting land value increase from these projects, and also help to guarantee the loans needed for these projects by capitalizing land for wealth accumulation.

Other infrastructural projects were also initiated during this period with financial help from the above-mentioned networks, including the Qatari ruling family, which like Kuwait had also recently discovered oil within its territory (Jones 1987). Projects included drilling for additional fresh water resources for the growing population (the site of Al-Awir would become an important water resource, along with the enhanced Bedouin well systems) (Davidson 2008: 92, Wilson 2006: 177), the Dubai State Telephone Co., along with the founding of the Dubai Electric Company, which the BBME also helped form based on the foundational structure and articles of the Baghdad Electric Company (Jones 1987: 155). The Halcrow firm, which by this point was firmly established as the chief engineering group for Sheikh Rashid's plans, was also contracted to build the first bridge the across the creek. The Al-Maktoum Bridge finally connected Bur Dubai with Deira, facilitating alternative passage for vehicles in addition to the creek water passage by *dhow* and *abra*.

Sheikh Rashid initiated many infrastructural projects during this boom period between his assuming the title of ruler in 1958 and 1966, when oil was struck. It is important to underscore that along with the more traditional infrastructural and municipal services projects mentioned, there was also a conscious effort to establish banking and hotel infrastructure to further attract trade and diversify financial possibilities. The financial arrangements through local and British contacts to finance the engineering projects often resulted in Dubai using borrowed money to pay international (mostly British) consultants to carry out ambitious projects, such as creek dredging and road construction, but Sheikh Rashid also understood that at some point, these institutions would need to be created locally. Recalling Gerschenkron's work, while Dubai could borrow these strategies from regional neighbors, it was also important to establish the institutions to accompany this form of technological and developmental import.

The BBME had enjoyed a monopoly in the Dubai banking sector since the late 1940s, and though officially their profits where less than in other parts of the region, gold trade throughout the 1950s earned the bank an important income. In 1959, during a trip that Sheikh Rashid made to London, he is said to have made an agreement with the BBME to extend their monopoly banking privileges,

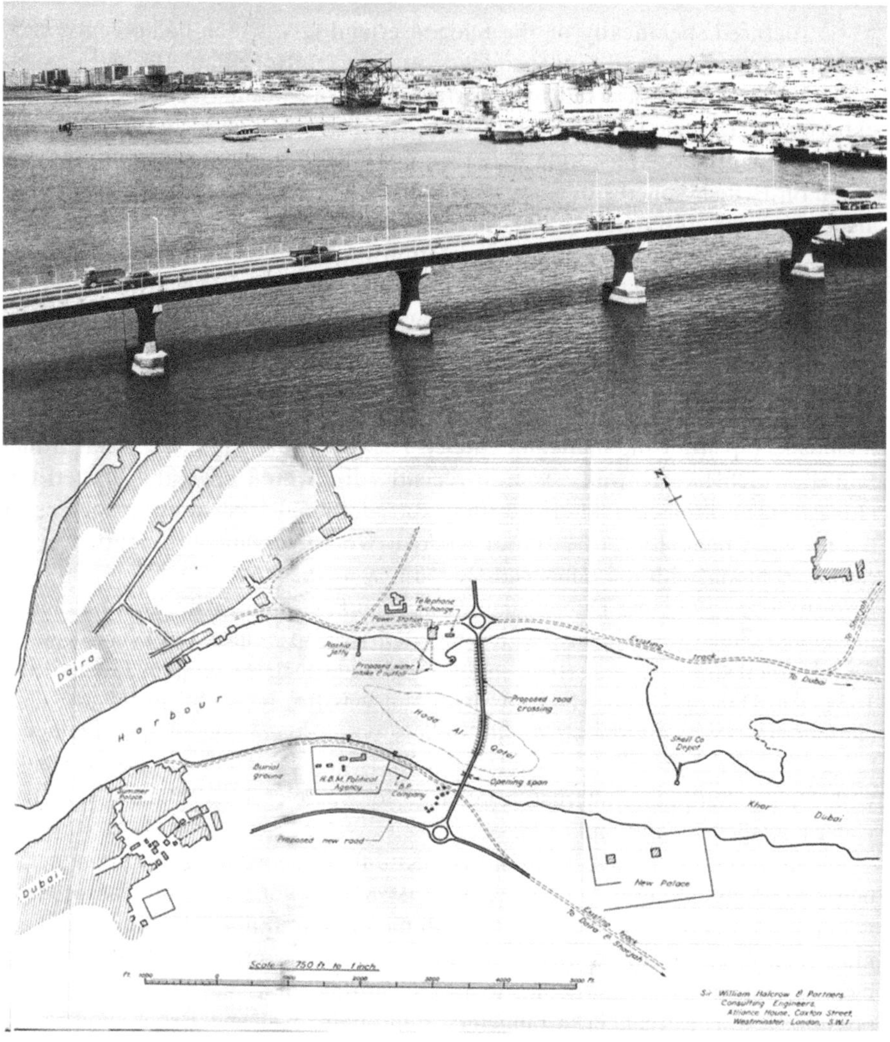

Figure 2.3 Halcrow drawing for Al-Maktoum Bridge 1961 and an image of the bridge

Source: Halcrow Archive

which were previously scheduled to end in 1967, for an additional seven years, or through 1974 (Al-Gurg 1998, Jones 1987). Nevertheless, beginning in 1962, Dubai representatives went to Kuwait to study the National Bank of Kuwait, and to offer them a 30 percent share in helping to establish a National Bank of Dubai in 1963 (Jones 1987: 156). The National Bank of Dubai, to the BBME's surprise, opened in May 1963. In Geoffrey Jones's history of the BBME, with an obvious bias, he states, "BBME's decision not to oppose the formation of the National Bank was the only practical choice ... There was great disappointment, however, when further breaches of BBME's monopoly followed" (Ibid.). These "further breaches" included the opening of the First National City Bank of New York (Citibank) in January 1964 as a part of the oil concession agreement of 1963 with the United States firm the Continental Oil Company. By 1968, along with these three banks, six other banks had opened offices, from neighboring Gulf countries, the UK and the US, and this number, of course, would continue to grow apace with Dubai's economic prosperity (Hamza 1968). Sheikh Rashid's decision to first establish a National Bank, and then to subsequently diversify the international bank presence in Dubai may have origins in the fact the BBME had initially refused his petition for a loan to widen and deepen the creek, and that his desire to use their presence as a quasi-public coffer had clear limits. The merchant community, which had a history of anti-British sentiment, may also have influenced Sheikh Rashid's decision. But it seems just as likely that he observed the moves of neighboring Gulf countries and believed that Dubai's financial autonomy would require the founding of a national bank as well.

Dubai also saw the beginnings of its hotel sector in the early 1960s, with an increasing number of visits from international businessmen attracted by the prospect of oil exploration, along with many visiting Dubai in relation to gold trade activities. The three first-class hotels, the Carlton (112 rooms) on the Deira side of the creek, the Bustan (32 rooms) by the airport, and the Airlines Hotel (26 rooms) in Bur Dubai, were advertised with swimming pools and tennis courts (Wilson 2006: 186, Gabriel 1987: 143, Hamza 1968). Additional hotels included the Ambassador (46 rooms) and the Oasis (36 rooms), and those along the creek were still ground+nine buildings (Harris 1994: Section 4.2.8). Foreshadowing future supply-side infrastructural decisions, hotel construction preceded the demand capacity, and many rooms were initially vacant. As the decade would progress, and investments increase, these kinds of vacancies would not last.

Air and Sea Ports

The municipal services, financial institutions, and nascent tourist infrastructure projects sought to complement those core elements of Dubai's trade and *entrepôt* functions, but Sheikh Rashid's projects still centered on large-scale trade infrastructure. Though the creek had been widened and dredged in the late 1950s, the air concessions agreement with the British Royal Air Force from the 1930s to use the creek as a landing strip for water planes was signed mainly with the interest of warding off other international courters. The actual use of the creek as an airstrip is recorded only from 1942–1947 (Al-Gurg 1998). The principal airport for the lower Gulf was the Sharjah International Airport established in 1939, but just as Dubai wanted to compete for maritime trade with Sharjah by dredging the creek, Sheikh Rashid realized quickly that an airport would be necessary to attract international business directly to the city. When presenting the idea to the merchant community, however, he made sure to underscore his firm belief in an "open skies" policy (Davidson 2008: 94), and not repeat the exclusive agreement signed in the late 1930s by Sheikh Said. Sheikh Rashid also emphasized the different circumstances to downplay any bad memories of the power change that the air concessions deal of the 1930s had caused the *majlis*. Easa Saleh Al-Gurg, who served as an advisor to Sheikh Rashid and an early employee of the BBME, recounts in his autobiography of how he and Sheikh Rashid, during their 1959 trip to London, met with International Airadio Limited, the British air-traffic control firm, where they committed to running a new Dubai International Airport. Nevertheless, upon returning from the trip, Sheik Rashid still had the British Political Agent in Sharjah to contend with, who, along with the Sharjah ruler, were set on defending Sharjah's airport advantage by blocking Dubai's petition (1998).

During the London visit, Sheikh Rashid also had the chance to meet with the renowned British R.A.F. pilot Freddy Bosworth, who flew flights for, and directly benefitted from, the London-Dubai-India gold trade with Imperial Airways (which would later become British Overseas Aviation Company, and later still, with the help of Bosworth, splinter off and become Gulf Aviation) (Davidson 2008: 95). Bosworth agreed to deliver the Dubai petition for a new airport in person to the principal British Political Agent in Bahrain on behalf of Sheikh Rashid, in which Sheikh Rashid emphasized that he would not ask for any money from the British to build the airport, so he did not see why the British had the right to prevent him from doing so. Sir William Luce, a senior British diplomat, served as Political Resident in Bahrain, and it is said that once he heard that Sheikh Rashid would finance the airport, his response was, "In that case you may certainly have your damn airstrip. In fact you may have ten airstrips if you want them" (Al-Gurg 1998: 106). A plot of land was indentified between the Al-Ghusais and Al-Rashidya areas in early 1960, and by the end of the year the terminal and air tower were completed. The airport was managed by International Airadio Limited, and flights from Gulf Aviation and Kuwait Airways immediately began routing through Dubai. British Overseas Aviation Company, though initially reluctant, also eventually began flying through Dubai, as the result of Sheikh Rashid incorporating his father's policy of buying up any vacant seats on flights so that the BOAC could meet its minimum of 60 percent occupancy (Davidson 2008: 95).

In addition, by 1965 increased trade along the creek continued to serve the construction and oil exploration boom of the 1960s, and it was clear that a deep-water port was needed to alleviate month-long queues of ships waiting to unload cargo for the city. While 40 Grey and Mackenzie barges worked to unload offshore ships, it simply could not keep apace, and in several cases, helicopters were contracted to help throughput. In 1965, Halcrow was summoned once again to begin surveys for a deep-water port just south of the creek's entrance in Al Shindigah. The initial plans for the new Port Rashid were complete in 1967, but only included four berths based on conservative British growth projections for trade. As we will see, even

Figure 2.4 Port Rashid general aerial view of the first four berths from the southwest, June, 1971

Source: Halcrow Archive

Sheikh Rashid's insistence on 16 berths proved below the mark. All berths were oversubscribed when Port Rashid opened in 1971, which would then have to be expanded 37 berths by the end of the 1970s (Walker 1984).

Oil Discovery

By the early 1960s, the 25-year oil concessions contract that Sheikh Said had signed in the late 1930s with Petroleum Concessions Limited (PCL) was ending. The first round of concessions contracts throughout the Gulf, roughly from 1910 through World War II, were generally forced on rulers through the British political agencies. The oil companies were not required to train nor include local labor, offer participation of the host country, foster any commitments toward industrial development, and were generally established on unjust financial arrangements (Al-Otaiba 1977: 39–40). In the case of Dubai, the end of the pearl trade and the financial advantage of direct payments to Sheikh Said offered a politically attractive way to strike a new power contract with the local *majlis*, but this is not to say that the concession contract were just. After PCL acquired the concession rights, World War II interrupted oil exploration in Dubai, but once it resumed after the war three separate sites for onshore drilling (notably, Jebel Ali was

Table 2.1 Dubai's crude oil exports, 1969-1975

Year	No. of Tankers	Export in barrels	Revenue in US$
1969	12	3,561,094	376,114
1970	79	30,949,134	11,556,000
1971	98	45,323,357	37,587,000
1972	110	55,595,650	54,128,000
1973	153	81,151,245	108,536,000
1974	146	88,317,655	558,042,000
1975	123	91,635,272	600,000,000*

Note: * Estimate
Source: Al-Otaiba 1977

one) were explored during the 1950s. By the time the contract was up, oil had been discovered in commercial quantities in other regions of the Gulf, and the frustration of unsuccessful drilling meant that the British were not as eager to renew. In 1963, Dubai signed an oil exploration contract with the US Continental Oil Company (CONOCO), and set up the Dubai Petroleum Company (DPC) to run the onshore concession; the Dubai Marine Areas Limited was also set up as a joint venture with British Petroleum and Compagnie Française de Pétroles for offshore exploration (Ibid.).

This arrangement would change several times through quick sales of percentages within these joint ventures from one international oil company to another, but on June 6, 1966, the DPC discovered crude oil in the offshore "Fateh" field (meaning "good fortune" in Arabic) at 7,600 feet below sea level. Subsequent fields known as "Fateh South" and "Rashid" were also successful, and oil production began three years later in 1969. On September 22, 1969, the first shipment of 180,000 barrels arrived at the UK CONOCO refineries, and on October 15, 1970, Dubai became an official member of the club of oil exporting countries (Ibid.). By the end of the first year, the Dubai oil fields yielded 3,561,094 barrels of crude oil, with revenues of $376,114. By the end of the following year, 1970, revenue jumped to $11,556,000, and by the end of 1975, estimated revenue reached $600,000,000 (Al-Otaiba 1977: 67).

The Blueprint

While oil discovery would bring revenue to Dubai that would change the city's physiognomy and move it beyond the initial three creek settlements, it is clear that Dubai's status as a dynamic *entrepôt* for international trade and transshipment, its foundational infrastructure projects, its free-port policies to attract merchant communities from throughout the Gulf and the Indian Ocean, and licit and illicit trade for re-export to Persia/Iran and India were solidly established before "black gold" was struck in Fateh field. Dubai's trade vocation existed before the arrival of the British, but their indirect protection (with clear costs and benefits to Dubai), along with the fact that British merchants were not attracted to local Gulf trade because profits were considered too low for their efforts, allowed for a community of Banian, Persian, and Arab merchants to settle in Dubai and assume their own positions of power and influence (Owen 2008). Though initially because of the ruler's dependence on the merchant community trade wealth, and subsequently because of Sheikh Rashid's focus on trade, as Enseng Ho states, before oil Dubai was a "'trading state' in which the ruling family, the Maktoums, combined the role of both ruler and chief merchant" (2008, Owen 2008: 7, Ho 2008). Indeed, through both marriage and family, Sheikh Rashid is perhaps the best example of this, such that his ruling style would become imbued in both the responsibilities and political understandings expected of the sheikhdom title itself.

Sheikh Rashid was able to carry out the infrastructure projects solicited by the *majlis* in their reform movement, and though the merchant community was hit strongly by the end of pearling, by the end of the 1940s gold trade profits for the Dubai merchant community helped to quell reform rumblings. Once the creek was dredged and widened, with Harris's master plan and the 1960 Land Law in place, the Dubai municipality saw the strategic opportunity to reclaim land on the Deira side of the creek by using what was removed from the dredging project. Creek dredging and land reclamation in the late 1950s and early 1960s provided a new surface on which to guide southern creek development. This reclaimed land then became the corridor for office, hotel, and municipal development, which the municipality was in turn able to either lease or sell without having to buy out any existing landowner plots within Deira—one of the densest parts of the city. Thus Baniyas Road would become the city's central business district, mixing heavier industry with commercial and office uses. This strategic use of ambitious infrastructural projects, and those institutions which would help establish future economic sectors for Dubai (i.e., numerous banks as a financial infrastructure, hotels as a tourism infrastructure) for multiple developmental objectives, would also mark future infrastructural projects and overarching developmental strategies.

Thus Dubai's development blueprint was being forged while the city was still a Gulf outpost and British protectorate up through oil discovery: large-scale engineering projects to facilitate trade movement (which, in turn, attracted more trade); urban expansion along the new trade route (initially, the creek); spatial planning reduced essentially to providing transportation infrastructure to facilitate and loosely structure growth; and, as I'll discuss more in Chapter 5, a replication and amplification of building typologies to accommodate the swift speed of this new development.

Chapter 3
Boom

The period following oil discovery in Dubai markedly changed the emirate in many regards. The developmental blueprint forged by Sheikh Rashid prior to 1966, with oil profits, was amplified through more grandiose plans and projects that pushed the city into its hinterland and eventually moved it southwest-ward along the Gulf coast toward its border with Abu Dhabi. The development boom attracted low-wage laborers, mainly from the Asian Subcontinent, in such great numbers that between the years of 1968 and 1975, the Dubai population more than tripled from 59,000 to 183,000 (Dubai Statistics Center 2010). In parallel to this rapid development, the British announced in 1967 that it would abandon all of its commitments east of the Suez Canal by the end of 1971, which meant that Dubai, somewhat reluctantly given its ambivalent relationship, would no longer be under trucial agreement with Britain. These events would presage the tumultuous decade of the 1970s, both for Dubai and the larger Gulf region, but the same factors on which Dubai had built its success up to oil discovery would remain its key strategic components.

Before the British withdrew they encouraged sheikhdoms of the Trucial States to come together as one new federated nation, which sought to maintain British influence in the region, check Arab nationalist expansion, and, under pressure from the United States, prevent larger Soviet advancement into the Gulf. The result was an odd kind of nation-building mosaic called the United Arab Emirates, which federated seven of the sheikhdoms in an arrangement that was clearly hierarchical: those who had discovered oil (Abu Dhabi and Dubai) and those who had not (Sharjah, Ras al-Khaima, Fujairah, Umm al-Qaiwain, and Ajman). Though Sharjah would discover oil soon after federation, the relationship between Abu Dhabi and Dubai, and the size and wealth the two largest emirates, would essentially determine the new nation's leadership agenda; which in many ways is still true today.

British withdrawal also signified the end of Aden's primary port and refinery capacity in the region, which meant that regional states would compete throughout

Table 3.1 Dubai population, 1900–2005

1900	1939	1968	1975	1980	1985	1990	1995	2000	2005
11,000	21,000	59,000	183,000	276,000	371,000	490,000	689,000	862,000	1,321,000

Source: Dubai Statistics Center 2010

the 1970s to attract the commercial and industrial activity abandoned in South West Arabia. This competition was escalated with the two oil price booms during the decade's international oil crises, which radically increased regional wealth. The need for expanded trade capacity to keep up with increased imports, the fiscal attempt to temper the inflationary pressure of this new wealth, and the full attraction and force of modern, grandiose nation-building sparked an intensified regional race for commercial and industrial trade infrastructure and its ancillary facilities and services. The recession of the early 1980s, and the subsequent fall in oil prices, eventually stepped in to end the race, but during the 1970s, while the British withdrew its interests east of the Suez, its consulting engineering design organizations won many lucrative large-scale infrastructure contracts as a part of regional trade capacity competition. Though a "latecomer," Dubai was very much a part of this regional competition, and during this period urban development increased exponentially in the emirate. The only limit to Dubai's construction pace was the reduced offloading capacity at its overcrowded creek and the new Port Rashid. In its extramural push outside its original three settlements, Dubai literally arrived at its port facilities as primary imported construction material to be converted into a metropolis.

The decade of the 1970s began in Dubai with John Harris's second master plan in an attempt to order the ebullient construction activity into a modern, ring-radial metropolitan form centered around the creek. But as the decade progressed, the plan's influence receded and large-scale infrastructural projects determined territorial organization and development in parallel to the coast toward the southwest. Sheikh Rashid's development strategy clustered infrastructural elements and systems to enhance Dubai's international trade profile. The chapter will look at this dynamic decade between oil discovery and the commissioning of the Jebel Ali Port and Industrial Area, both in Dubai and the larger region. The chapter ends with a review of Dubai's infrastructural projects, and how they collectively determined the emirate's economic and territorial development throughout the decade.

The British Empire is Dead—Long Live the Empire

By the end of the 1950s, the British colonial free port of Aden in South West Arabia was one of the busiest ports in the world. Strategically located where the Red Sea and the Indian Ocean meet, Aden served as a principal British military base since becoming a crown colony in 1937, though it had loosely been under British jurisdiction in a manner not unsimilar to the Gulf protectorates since the 1830s. As a crown colony, it was Britain's only official, direct colonial relationship in the Gulf region, in contrast to the system of regional protectorates described in Chapter 2. Aden's location, with British protection, helped turn it into a thriving *entrepôt* that attracted a prosperous merchant class from the region, particularly after the British declared it a free port in 1850 (Balfour-Paul 1991: 54, Stanford

Research Institute 1971: 26). Trade throughput in Aden increased dramatically after the opening of the Suez Canal in 1869. With the objective of both capitalizing on Aden's strategic location and keeping the French interests in check, the British purchased eight square miles of land on the western end of the crescent-shaped peninsula and named it "Little Aden," as a trade center removed from the larger town (Balfour-Paul 1991: 56–7).

In 1951, as a result of the British-Iranian crisis in Abadan, British Petroleum decided to build a large oil refinery and port facility in Little Aden, which was a massive project that involved the dredging of a deep water channel, building a massive breakwater, reclaiming 200 acres of land, and importing 15,000 laborers from South Asia and Somalia to carry out the work (Longhurst 1959: 250). Residential camps were built to house both the contractors and the laborers. The camps were described by one account as "temporary townlets, each complete with its own living quarters, mess, recreation centres and other facilities" (Longhurst 1959: 253). The British concentrated on the western side of the Aden peninsula and the laborers to the rocky east, in an area known as the "Crater" because it was located on an extinct volcano (Stanford Research Institute 1971: 68).

Upon completion, Aden had two ports. The inner port to the east of the crescent was equipped with 20 "first class" berths for vessels of up to 37-foot draughts, seven "second class" berths for vessels with up to 18-foot draughts, and a 600-foot cargo wharf also for vessels with 18-foot draughts. The oil port was on the western end, which could simultaneously receive four tankers of up to 42,000 tons and a maximum of 39-foot drafts (Stanford Research Institute 1971: 92). On April 27, 1954, Queen Elizabeth II inaugurated the oil refinery and port, and until 1967, Aden was one of the world's largest oil bunkering ports, after Rotterdam, Liverpool, London and New York (Ledger, 1983: 32, Stanford Research Institute 1971: 30). During this period, of the 30,000 British troops located east of the Suez Canal in the Sudan, South West Arabia, and the Gulf trucial sheikhdoms, 20,000 were stationed in Aden (Peterson 2006: 78). Thus Aden served as both the principal military base for British interests in the region, as well as a key commercial point for trade, including the increasingly important regional oil trade from the Indian Ocean and the Gulf to the West.

This period was a politically active time for the Middle East, headed by Jamal Abdul Nasser's Arab nationalist movement in Egypt and growing independence actions in Iran led by Mohammad Mosaddeq (Kinzer 2003, Yergin 1991). Egypt was the preeminent local power of the region, and Nasser's charisma had cultivated a post-war sentiment throughout the Middle East that opposed colonial subjugation and pushed for a United Arab Republic. The British had emerged from World War II as the uncontested power of the Gulf region, and the United States used British military forces to keep Soviet advancement into the region checked (Peterson 2006). While this policy was not new, the Cold War scenario of the 1950s and 1960s intensified the geopolitical situation. Because of this (and Egypt's own history with British) the British were a central target in much of Nasser's anti-colonial rhetoric, even though the British Labour Party made great efforts not to

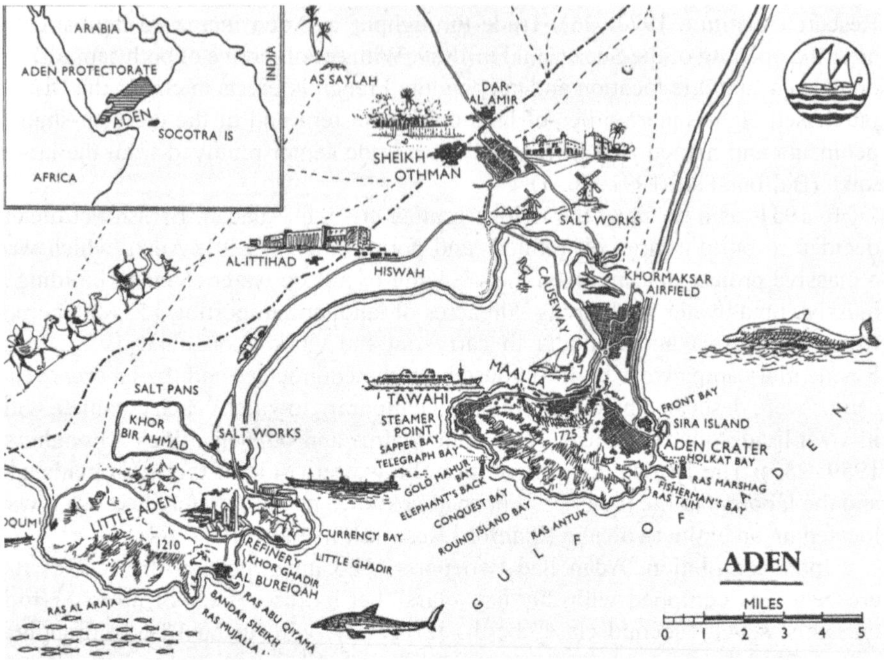

Figure 3.1 Plan of Aden from October 1962
Source: J.M. Bel 1998

see itself as a colonial power and tried to appease Nasser. Thus, from the post-war period through 1967, Nasser and the British played a kind of "cat and mouse" with one another, usually by proxy, where each suffered from their own particular kind of hubris and neither could claim to have achieved their ultimate goals.

The first Suez Canal crisis of 1956, the Civil War in Yemen after Imam Ahmad's death in 1962, federation struggles in Aden in the early 1960s, the 1967 Egyptian-Israeli Six Day war where, rightly or not, Nasser was able to paint the British as pro-Israel, and the 1967 closing of the Suez Canal were all events that accelerated, if not precipitated the final official withdrawal of the British colonial presence east of the Suez. These events, coupled with a significant devaluation of the British pound and, headed by Harold Wilson, the Labour Party's "increasing distaste for empire" (Peterson 2006: 116), all made it difficult to justify international expenditures to maintain the regional political, commercial and military infrastructure while Britain experienced economic hardship at home. Saudi estimates at the time gauged British annual profits from oil and related industries to be in the realm of £1,300 million, while its costs to maintain its infrastructure were approximately £1,250 million (Peterson 2006: 115). Clearly companies from other countries, including the US, France and Spain, were able to reap profits from oil extraction in the region, so within these circumstance, it became harder to justify a British presence simply in the name of oil, much less as a kind of "civilizing influence." The full intrigue surrounding the British withdrawal from east of Suez is beyond the scope of this book (see Peterson 2006, Smith 2004, Balfour-Paul 1991), nevertheless, the power vacuum left by the British would be one of the key reasons that the US allied with Saudi Arabia and Iran (until 1979) to ensure peaceful oil extraction and to keep the Soviets at bay. The British left their Aden headquarters in 1967, and the region all together by the end of 1971, and the Suez Canal remained closed until 1975. The economic impact of these events would prevent Aden from returning to its pre-1967 regional *entrepôt* eminence.

The rulers of the Trucial States, unsurprisingly, were reluctant to change their relationship with the British. While not free from problems, the British had truly protected the ruling families, and the fact that the British dictated the foreign policies and international intrigues of the day allowed the rulers to focus on their own domestic development. When Nasser's project began receiving international attention, the British formed the Trucial State Council in 1952 as a way to exert more political influence on the region. The British political agent initially presided over the Council, and it was subsequently headed by the rotating sheikhs (Peck 1986: 44). The Council was little more than a symbolic union, but taking into account the border wars of the region in the late 1940s, it was a way to create a kind of common project among the region's neighbors, if for nothing else, to at least calm tensions. The Trucial State Council also marked the beginning of what would eventually be the formation of the United Arab Emirates in 1971, as we will see.

It should be noted that British "withdrawal" was the official process to describe the events previously mentioned leading up to 1971, but British firms and interests, through private relationships established during the protectorate period of modernization, would continue to figure importantly throughout the future UAE and the entire Gulf region.

United Arab Emirates Formation

On February 18, 1968, shortly after the British government informed the sheikhs of its plan to withdraw in January, Sheikh Rashid met with Sheikh Zayed at Al-Sameeh of Abu Dhabi near their mutual border (Wilson 2006: 264, Al Abed 2001: 128). Sheikh Zayed had recently become ruler of Abu Dhabi in 1966, and it is debated as to how seriously he and Sheikh Rashid were committed to a federation, which at this point included the future seven emirates, along with Bahrain and Qatar. Each probably still had hopes that the British would ultimately change their mind and stay, at least with the Trucial States. Sheikh Rashid had the additional suspicion that entering into any kind of formal alliance with Abu Dhabi would certainly place Dubai in a secondary position given their respective size, population, and oil reserves.[1] Nevertheless, the British likely asked the two sheikhs to publicly commit to a federation project as a way to engage the other Trucial States. Their meeting, in this sense, was successful, and only a week later, leaders from all nine sheikhdoms met in Dubai on February 25 and agreed to jointly form the "Federation of the Arab Emirates" (Al Abed 2001: 128). The project, however, was by no means finished.

The nine sheikhdoms brought together to form a federal alliance all had very different development trajectories, not unsimilar to other unifications movements in the region (i.e. Nasser's United Arab Republic). Indeed, throughout history, those same countries who try to come together after significant competition, and sometimes outright warfare, make for very difficult bedfellows, particularly when such an alliance can threaten the autonomy of any individual members (i.e. European Union, NAFTA, etc.). Of the nine sheikhdoms, this was particularly true for Dubai. Dubai had just discovered oil, but it was still a merchants' city at heart, and the possibility of interrupting commercial relations with its trading partners, particularly Iran, India and Pakistan, in favor of political allegiance to any kind of sheikhdom grouping would be a very hard sell, to say the least. As John Duke Anthony states:

> Left to their own devises, Dubai's leaders believed they could maximize the prospects for maintaining good relations with the emirate's customers, companies, and investors, and thereby assure continuity for Dubai's well-being. By contrast, if they were made to bend to the policy dictates of others whose interests and priorities would not always be similar, the prospects for being able to maintain good ties with its vital partners would be constrained (2002: 91).

In spite of this, Sheikh Rashid was well aware that he could orchestrate the situation to his advantage. He was not obligated to enter into any federation with the other eight emirates, and he knew that a federal structure would favor Abu Dhabi, so he regarded these negotiations as an opportunity. To achieve the kind of federation that the British had in mind, the responsibility and bargaining would fall on Sheikh Zayed, as the leader of Abu Dhabi and the sheikhdom most likely to benefit from any agreement. The onus would be on Sheikh Zayed to piece together a federation by wooing the other emirates.

These dynamics played out at their initial meeting, when Sheikh Rashid and Sheikh Zayed, before discussing their possible political partnership, first resolved those onshore and offshore territorial conflicts that remained between Dubai and

---

1 While crude oil and natural gas reserve estimates for the UAE have changed over time, the proportion is generally constant, with Abu Dhabi possessing 90 percent of each, and the remaining 10 percent divided among the remaining emirates, particularly Dubai and Sharjah. In 1986 Peck estimated UAE oil reserves at 32 billion barrels, and in 2009, the UAE web page estimates 98.2 billion barrels. See: http://www.uae.gov.ae/Government/oil_gas.htm.

Abu Dhabi. Sheikh Zayed agreed to cede the contested areas to Dubai, including the site of the future Jebel Ali Port, Industrial Area, and Free Zone, along with an offshore Gulf area that included "Fateh South," which would produce generous oil supplies for the future (Al Abed 2001: 128). As negotiations continued from 1968 through 1971, Sheikh Rashid was also designated as the Vice President of the Federation, and it was agreed that while Abu Dhabi would temporarily be the capital, a new capital city was to be built on the Dubai-Abu Dhabi border (Al Abed 2001: 131).

On December 2, 1971, seven emirates formed the United Arab Emirates, which finally included Abu Dhabi, Dubai, Sharjah, Ras al-Khaima, Fujairah, Umm al-Qaiwain and Ajman, but did not include Bahrain or Qatar. Issues of unified defense, fiscal policy, and joint governing structures proved to be insurmountable for the two sheikhdoms. In hindsight, however, since the founding of the Emirates, Dubai has been able to retain a good deal of political autonomy, while also receiving significant funding from the UAE Central Bank for many of its projects. The federation relationship has been particularly important recently during Dubai's debt crisis, as Abu Dhabi has loaned it over $25 billion to address these debts (*Economist* Briefing 2009). Dubai, for its part, also contributes to a UAE development fund, similar to the Kuwait fund that it benefited from, to help the poorer emirates that have not discovered oil within their territories. Though not free of its own kinds of conflict and intrigue, it is clear that Sheikh Rashid's decision to negotiate and form the UAE with Abu Dhabi and other five emirates proved beneficial for Dubai.

Bi-furcated Expatriate Communities

During British withdrawal and the formation of the UAE, the development boom proceeded at a rapid pace in Dubai. Construction along the creek included mixed-use buildings and hotels, with an increased demand for office space due to expanded business activity resulting from oil discovery. Construction of Port Rashid began in 1967, just south of the creek's entrance in the Al-Shindigah district, and a large portion of the imports to Dubai at this point was comprised of building materials to keep pace with the numerous projects of the city. By 1969, construction workers made up seventeen percent of the estimated 24,014 total active labor force in Dubai (Pacione 2005: 259), and this number would continue to rise exponentially. If the first great wave of immigration to Dubai occurred after the free port declaration at the beginning of the twentieth-century, the late 1960s marked the second immigration wave, largely as the result of British contractors and consultant firms working in Dubai recruiting low-wage laborers from throughout the region, but particularly from India, Pakistan, and Iran (Pacione 2005: 258).

While most of the second wave of immigration came from the region and the Asian Subcontinent, a portion of immigrants were also the contract workers from Britain, Europe, and the United States. Low-wage laborers, as today, were provided with informal housing barracks on construction sites, but the rising number of the consultant class was beginning to overfill the city's hotel infrastructure capacity. Fast-track hotel projects would continue in the 1970s to respond to this growing population, but in the meanwhile, Dubai entrepreneurs saw an opportunity:

> I realized that after the Dubai Petroleum Company had been established to manage the state's oil affairs, the increasing number of expatriate personnel would require accommodation of a quality higher than available in Dubai at the time. In partnership with the oil company I built 48 American-style villas on the site [opposite the cement factory], the actual building costs being financed by the oil company … The villas are still standing today and have certainly more that earned their keep (Al-Gurg 1998: 179).

As pointed out, at least half of the housing stock in Dubai by the end of the 1960s was comprised of "barasti" houses, with palm frond roofing and wall structures built of clay and corral fragments, which was not surprising given that the first house to use concrete blocks was not recorded until 1956 (Pacione 2005, Harris 1994, Gabriel 1987: 80, Heard-Bey 1982: 260). The ground+one (G+1) "American-style villas" (in fact, international in style) were to become a housing typology that would proliferate throughout Dubai, particularly in the Jumeirah residential neighborhoods. As the passage states, these houses were first intended specifically for those expatriate personnel, implying British, European, or US, from whom rents could be generated. In this case, the housing was provided for Dubai Petroleum Company (DPC) contractors and consultants, but this practice of building G+1 villa housing for expatriate personnel was also carried out by the Halcrow Company, responsible at this time for the management of the Port Rashid construction.

The antecedents for this kind of housing division can be traced back to company town urban structures in nineteenth-century United States and England, where "skilled" and "non-skilled" labor housing were separated. The urban design established facilities for workers and management as a means to maximize efficiency and production. Within the "paternalistic order" of the company town (Crawford 1995: 15), housing becomes another kind of infrastructure, within the larger town armature, to serve the production process. The company town layout essentially takes Fordist production and extends its spatial rationale beyond the factory to the town scale. The housing model proliferated throughout the first part of the twentieth-century in projects around the world, particularly within *de novo* circumstances, often based on the need to house a relocated labor force for resource extraction projects. Both the American Arab Oil Company in Saudi Arabia and the British Persian and Iranian Oil Companies incorporated this same housing logic for oil extraction towns such as Abadan, Dhahran, and the aforementioned Aden (Sutherland 1989, Seccombe and Lawless 1987, King 1984, Nawwab et al. 1980, Planhol 1964, Longhurst 1959). The machinistic qualities of this kind of urban structure were manifest in Dubai through the predominance of large-

Figure 3.2 Images of Al-Gurg's 48 villas development, July 10, 1968
Source: Halcrow Archive

scale infrastructural projects, which in turn, contained their own smaller sets of infrastructure to help facilitate production or oil extraction. Much of the terminology for later development in Dubai called these large-scale projects "cities within the city," which is a reflection of the infrastructure within infrastructure strategy that these original expatriate villa housing projects represented, and would become a replicated pattern in many subsequent developments.

If we think back to Joan Busquets's point about the territorial hierarchy of infrastructure in Barcelona expansion, this infrastructure model develops ancillary, secondary, and tertiary infrastructure systems within one another. The hierarchy is developed from the primary infrastructure, which in this case, were the offshore oil rigs and Port Rashid. The housing example demonstrates how these infrastructures can be spun out of a primary facility or system, and then subsequently clustered as a component of a larger developmental package. This diachronic, incremental process of expanding concentric, hierarchical infrastructure systems within one another would increase in programmatic complexity and scalar intensity as Dubai's development moved toward the southward. As I will discuss in Chapter 4, this also would be become the pattern for Dubai World Holding Company and its clustered components.

The Second Harris Master Plan

Urban growth and initial oil revenue gave Dubai both cause and resources for John R. Harris to produce a second master plan in May 1971, just before the official formation of the Emirates. Harris had produced a report in 1965 to reflect upon his first 1960 master plan, recognizing that it had been completed just before the construction boom of the 1960s occurred. The recommendations proceeded in the same fashion, outlining road structure, zoning, the concurrent need for both outlying residential areas and a new town center (Harris 1994: Section 3.4.5), and building regulations that stipulated a ground+nine height maximum, which was made official in 1969 (Ibid.). Harris's second plan was comprised of sections, with the first four dedicated to listing an inventory of Dubai's urban elements, infrastructure, services and facilities, and the last two sections recommending urban growth patterns and suggestions for their implementation. Jumeirah is identified as an area where "high-class" residential accommodations were built, which have "become the standards for others" (Harris 1994: Section 4.6.5). The plan suggests that the irregularity of plot sizes could prove to be an obstacle for growth, and recommends that future development should correct this irregularity. If we think back to Cerdà's *example* plan as a prescribed, geometric rationality for urbanization, Harris's recommendation for orthogonal plot symmetry stems from the same modern conception. Jumeirah, to a large degree would develop in this modular fashion, but as we will see, Harris's modern dictates would not contain Sheikh Rashid's competitive urban ambitions.

Harris's plan prescribes a ring-radial urban form centered on the creek and fanning outward on each side, to underscore the continued function of this water element as the structuring growth axis for the city. As he suggests:

> The Creek, with sheltered waters, offered a natural site for development. Dubai thus shares with many great cities of the world the advantages and disadvantages of lying on both sides of a stretch of water; water which is a focal point, a centre

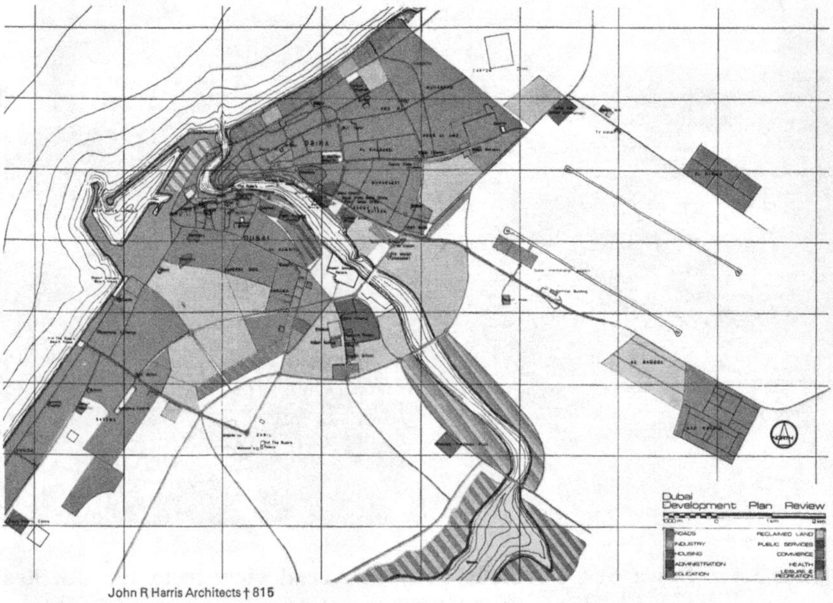

Figure 3.3 John R. Harris 1971 Second Master Plan for Dubai
Source: John R. Harris and Partners

> of activity, and also a major barrier between the development of either bank … Both from a functional and an aesthetic viewpoint, therefore, developing Dubai should still be centered on the Creek, where marine activity continues to flourish. The clear implication of this is that there shall be future development inland on both banks of the Creek (1994: Sections 5.1.1 and 5.1.5).

Harris's emphasis on creek development came with the additional recommendation that with increasing car use, Dubai would also have to increase the number of creek crossings, either by bridge, tunnel, or both. It also implied that future development inland along the creek would require further engineering, dredging, and widening, to continue its central structuring function. This presaged the ambitious creek dredging that moved it inland during the 1970s, along with both the Garhoud Bridge below the Maktoum Bridge and the Deira-Al Shindidah Tunnel above it. Harris correctly recommends that a connection would be necessary to facilitate traffic between Deira and the new Port Rashid, once completed. He cautions that because a bridge would require a 120-foot height clearance and long approach ways that would cut deeply into the urban fabric on each side, a tunnel was the best solution. Both the tunnel and the bridge would be completed by 1976; each, again, by the Sir William Halcrow engineering firm.

Figure 3.4 Deira Sea Corniche Project. Aerial view from the northeast. Land reclamation in the central foreground. Port Rashid and creek entrance in the top left, January 14, 1973

Source: Halcrow Archive

Thus from the large-scale creek dredging that preceded Harris's first plan, he understood and then recommended the implementation of such ambitious engineering as an important part of Dubai's urbanization process, and these projects would quickly follow the publication of the second plan. Harris's ring-radial structure relied on a bilateral symmetry of both the construction of Port Rashid in the Al-Shindigah district, and the large land reclamation project on the Deira side named the "Deira Corniche." A semi-circular ring road is prescribed to move around the creek and connect the urban structure, and radial roads to move outward from the Deira-Al-Shindigah center. This same ring-radial structure was common in many developments throughout the Gulf at this time (Kuwait, Bahrain), mainly because it was often the same small group of planning contractors working throughout the region ("Everything According to Plan" 1983). British firms in particular likely referenced Abercrombie's 1944 London Plan as a kind of template for ring-radial form in varying contextual scales.

Finally, the language used in the second Harris plan shows clear signs of the change in the regime's orientation. The outlying residential areas that Harris recommends were to be enclaves both for "low-income" housing, as well as for Dubaian communities that would specifically separate them from the international expatriate community in Jumeirah. Increased health care, schooling and land for housing for the citizens of Dubai, free of charge, are all underscored in the plan. Roger

Owen suggests that this kind of move away from the more cosmopolitan sensibilities of the pre-oil period toward more of a welfare state orientation had occurred previously in those sheikhdoms north of Dubai who had discovered oil first:

> In the event the model chosen, first by Kuwait in the 1950s, and then adopted up and down the Gulf, was a type of development based on a local version of the welfare state, with free health, education and largely free housing for those of its residents deemed to be local nationals. This in turn required the import of high numbers of temporary workers from wherever labour was the most cheap, while providing them with only limited access to local services and no possibility of owning property or their own businesses or of obtaining proper social security or other benefits (2008: 5).

Clearly Dubai is a mild example of this kind of inward turn, in contrast to other Gulf examples. But the initiation of state magnificence for those considered to be of Dubai—including the first wave immigrants from the turn of the twentieth-century, but not most of the imported labor of the late 1960s and 1970s—with oil to fund this state-oriented project, was certainly present in the discourse of the second plan; likely at the request and design of Dubai's leadership. Import-substitution-industrial policies of the 1970s would also reflect this attitude in Dubai. The dual tendency of outward-looking economic liberalism and trade orientation mixed with a more socially restrictive welfare policy each still have their political advocates in Dubai today. It was as if once oil was struck in Dubai, the regional precedents of the Saudi Arabian welfare state and the contrasting, more open Bahrain merchant state were synthesized. Though these political, social, and cultural voices do not play out within an electoral environment, their associate interests are manifest in the plans and projects throughout Dubai's developmental history. While commercial and retail spaces may provide for more permissive public interaction than some its Gulf neighbors, many of the neighborhood projects still tend to cluster nationals and international residents in discrete, separate areas. I explore this cellular spatial model further in Chapter 4.

1973 Oil Boom and Regional Infrastructure Development

At a Baghdad Conference held from September 10 to the 14, 1960, 13 oil exporting countries, including Kuwait, Saudi Arabia and Venezuela, together formed the Organization of Petroleum Exporting Countries (OPEC) as a way to consolidate bargaining power against oil companies, mainly from the US, Britain and Holland, who were pressuring oil-exporting countries individually to push prices down. Abu Dhabi joined OPEC in 1967, and this membership transferred to the entire United Arab Emirates, including Dubai, in 1972. In 1968, the Organization of Arab Petroleum Export Countries (OAPEC) formed as a subgroup of 12 Arab exporting countries, for the same general reasons, but with the further motivation of regional solidarity. In the early 1970s, international inflation both within the US and abroad saw western export prices increase dramatically to keep up, and in October 1973, fighting broke out again between Egypt and Syria and Israel in the Yom Kippur War. These two events, along with the ongoing pricing disagreements between OPEC and oil-import companies, saw oil prices jump from $3 per barrel to $5.12 per barrel, and by December 1973, oil prices reached $11.65 per barrel (*The Middle East* 2005: 144). This continued throughout the 1970s, and by 1979, with the Iranian Revolution, the second price shock brought oil prices up to $18 per barrel in the Gulf, and $20 per barrel in other oil-exporting countries. It is within this international context that Dubai's revenue from oil goes from $376,114 in 1969 to $600,000,000 by the end of 1975.

For Dubai—along with Abu Dhabi, who also shared the same common dirham UAE currency (Wilson 1987: 113)—this vertiginous influx of capital brought with it two main challenges: how to invest this money and avoid the strong inflationary effects on UAE currency, and how to develop the trade infrastructure capacity to receive the dramatic increase in imports. The first challenge for monetary stability was correlated to its low monetary absorption rate, meaning essentially the danger that the local economy was not developed enough to absorb that quantity of money in such a short period of time (Morgan 1979). The second challenge, shared also by Gulf oil-exporting countries, was the concern for trade capacity and infrastructure to respond to the dramatic spike in the already-booming import sector. As A.R. Walker wrote:

> In the era of (post '73) rapid change, both the adequacy of the Gulf's seaports and the efficiency of the sea transport systems serving the region are of crucial importance if the development process occurring in the wake of accumulating oil revenues is not to be undermined by congested ports and absent cargoes (1984: 182).

Throughout the region, Gulf States did not have the proper port infrastructure to meet the high import demand. They quickly responded by launching a series of fast-track port construction projects to meet the high demand, resulting in massive regional investment in infrastructure development. Between 1973 and 1980, Gulf States invested an estimated $4.7 billion developing their commercial ports and $3.0 billion on industrial port construction (Walker 1984: 187). In Dubai, Port Rashid opened in 1972, and by 1973 it had 13 fully operational berths (Owen 1978). With the increase in imports, however, the offshore queue of ships waiting to dock at the new port reached up to 150, reminiscent of times five years earlier when creek infrastructure could not keep up with import demands. From 1972 to 1976, deadweight tonnage offloaded at Port Rashid jumped from 600,000 to 3.4 million, and the number of days required for a ship to offload cargo went from six in 1974 to 60 in 1976 (Walker 1984: 180,186). It was clear that Dubai would have to invest further to enhance its trade infrastructure capacity.

For Dubai, investment in trade infrastructure, and the accompanying ancillary and industrial activities to support the trade sector, was understood strategically. Large-scale infrastructure investment was a way to alleviate port congestion, to make large capital investments of oil revenue profits that would help dampen inflationary pressures on its currency, and direct investment in sectors beyond oil (though still arguably related), so as to diversify the economy and avoid the so called "rentier" status that heavily oil-dependent economies worried about (Hayami 1997: 100). This diversification did occur in certain new industrial areas in Dubai. Trade, however, was nothing new to the emirate, so more than diversify, the investment in large-scale trade infrastructure amplified existing facilities to accommodate the staggering growth of the 1970s.

The Queen's Visit

In 1972, Sheikh Rashid held the first major trade exhibition of the lower Gulf in Dubai in the newly-constructed airport terminal. The new terminal is mentioned in Harris's second plan, and its quick completion by 1972 was carried out under the management of the Halcrow firm. Queen Elizabeth II was on a state visit to Australia in September of that same year when she was suddenly called back to the UK due to the collapse of Prime Minister Edward Heath's government. After completing her duties, the Queen would return to Australia to resume her visit, but instead of her usual stop-over point in Bahrain she decided to stop in Dubai, at the invitation of Sheikh Rashid, to visit the new airport terminal and exhibition (Humaid Al Tayer 1999). The two had developed a friendship during Sheikh Rashid's various visits to London since 1958 (Al-Gurg 1998). Surely Sheikh Rashid had seen pictures of the Queen inaugurating Aden's oil refinery port, and in a competitive spirit to follow Aden's example, wished to have the same honor. Queen Elizabeth landed at the Dubai airport at 3am, where she was greeted by Sheikh Rashid and his team and they proceeded to tour the new terminal and exhibition. After the tour, the Queen and her party departed for Australia, and Sheikh Rashid's team returned to bed. It is said, however, that Sheikh Rashid did not go back to sleep, but stayed up all night thinking of the kind of trade facilities necessary to host traders and international firms for international trade meetings (Humaid Al Tayer 1999).

It is these kinds of events that make up Dubai's history, which, in the absence of elections or other kinds of temporal bookmarks, were staged precisely as markers of progress. The events also ring of the same kind of infrastructural "ribbon cutting" performance that flatters all leaders. But in Dubai, the event, and the historical anecdotal recounting of the event, is an intentional and repeated occurrence that stage and construct history. Over time, these events included both the announcement of a project and its inauguration, as we saw with the Dubai Metro project, and the media has become an important way to promote these events. In contrast to political grandstanding in Western contexts to garner local political support/capital, Sheikh Rashid's invitation of the Queen to the trade show and the opening of the airport terminal projected more international aspirations. The Queen transmitted a confidence in Sheikh Rashid, Dubai, and the larger UAE project, in the immediate wake after its federation, that he knew would announce their arrival to the international community. Furthermore, it was under the auspices of a trade event, with clear overtures to an international business community that projected a willingness to "do business," in contrast to countries of what was understood as an otherwise tumultuous region. Finally, perhaps the invitation also sought to potentially lure the Queen's stop-over point from Bahrain to Dubai, with the associate prestige that this would signify. The invitation, the event, and the airport terminal were was strategically interwoven.

To further explore Sheikh Rashid's infrastructural strategy, and Dubai's subsequent investment throughout the 1970s, it is useful to bring in Michael E. Porter's work on the concept of "clusters," and how strategic infrastructural investments mutually enhance one another:

> Clusters are geographic concentrations of interconnected companies, specialized suppliers, service providers, firms in related industries, and associated institutions (e.g., universities, standards agencies, trade associations) in a particular field … Clusters, or critical masses of unusual competitive success in particular business areas, are a striking feature of virtually every national, regional, state, and even metropolitan economy, especially in more advanced nations (2000).

One can see how the trade sector infrastructure was a physical extension of Dubai's vocation and competitive advantage as a regional trade hub. This integral and overarching cluster strategy that focused on trade, with associate forward and backward linkages, would continue on throughout the development of the city and diversify into different areas (De Langen 2004). Sheikh Rashid could both cluster various strategic objectives within a single infrastructure project, as demonstrated in the airport terminal, and cluster larger infrastructure projects into a unified strategy that fused both business and territorial considerations and aspirations. Sheikh Rashid invested strategically throughout the decade, in reaction to regional infrastructure competition and to augment Dubai's trade capacity and international profile. This strategic clustering found its maximum territorial expression in the Jebel Ali Port, Industrial Area, and Free Zone, and later, as an international business strategy, for the Dubai World Holding Company. Just as he joined the urbanization, land capitalization, finance, and master planning in 1960, with increased oil revenue Sheikh Rashid's continued to strategically cluster infrastructure investments toward larger developmental and political objectives throughout 1970s. In this way, infrastructure assumed functions and meanings beyond those of its primary trade capacity expansion.

But this is only part of the story. Sheikh Rashid's "great man's vision" (as it is often recounted) that the above portrays cannot be denied as part of these investment decisions for the 1970s, but international consultants (again, mostly

British) were also a part of carrying out these visions with technical expertise. The story must also acknowledge the fact that those consultants that had Sheikh Rashid's ear were also recommending projects in which the newly wealthy emirate may want to think about spending its money. A.B. Zahalan's work on the Arab construction industry during this boom period notes the importance of British consulting engineering design organizations (CEDOs) and underscores their prominence in the region:

> The hostility of the British government to Egypt during the Suez adventure of 1956 undermined business opportunities in the region temporarily. After 1963, UK CEDO business began to pick up, but it is clear that there was a major shift away from Iraq, Egypt and Sudan, those Arab states which were the traditional clients, and towards the emerging markets of the oil-producing countries of Libya, UAE, Qatar, and Saudi Arabia. During the early 1970s, the share of the Arab world in UK foreign activity began to increase fairly rapidly, and oscillating around the 50 percent level … The Arab market is of vital importance to UK CEDOs partly because of their large share in it, and partly because it is one of the few major construction markets which does not impose many restrictive practices (1984: 84–5).

Clearly UK CEDOs were working in Dubai previous to the early 1970s, the Sir William Halcrow firm being the prime example, but the capital investment in large-scale infrastructure throughout the region, particularly in the UAE, Qatar, and Saudi Arabia, were "in the air." Large infrastructural projects were also suggested by international lending institutions as the recommended investment strategy for developing nations. Projects taken on by UK CEDOs included airport construction, harbor, docks and sea defense work, land planning and development, roads, bridges and tunnels, desalination plants, and industrial sites, among others (Zahalan 1984: 58). UK CEDOs far outnumbered those from other countries in the region, so while the British had officially withdrawn, the relationships before 1971 gave them a clear advantage for acquiring, and even inventing, infrastructure project commissions for oil-exporting Gulf countries throughout the 1970s ("Everything According to Plan" 1983).

Industrial Flooding

Given the above-mentioned factors and international players vying for how to best leverage exponentially-increasing oil wealth, it is not surprising that similar development projects were shared and replicated within the region; among other reasons, as quick, large-scale investment development strategies to swiftly channel the enormous wealth. A.R. Walker, in writing about this period, suggests, "The determination to transform oil-based, weakly developed economies of the Gulf states has overridden the inevitable regional competition

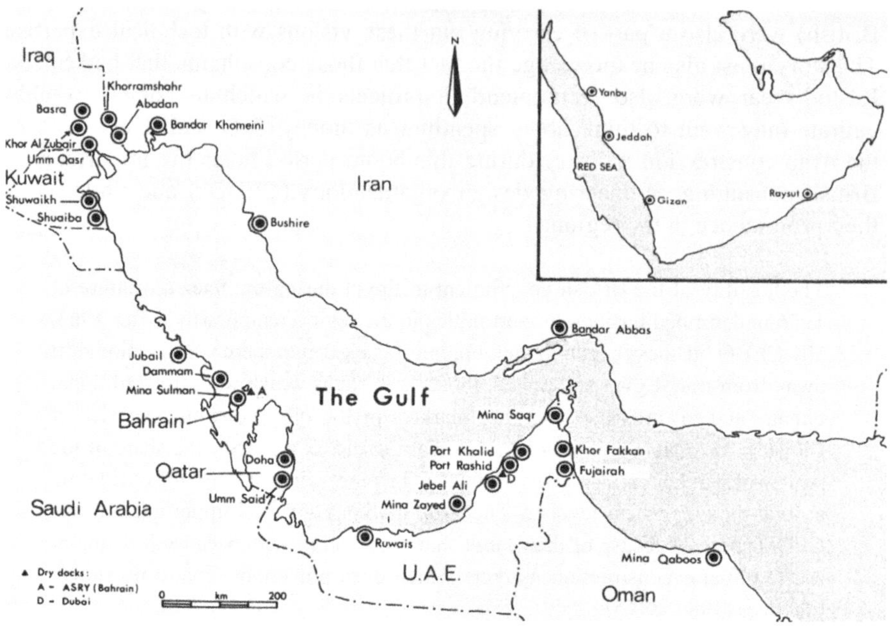

Figure 3.5 Major seaports of the Gulf in the early 1980s
Source: A.R. Walker

in industrial development and is represented by a plethora of new industrial projects and industrial berths, most of which have been constructed in the post-1970 period" (1984: 190). He goes on to list the regional industrial projects of the region: Khor Al Zubair (steel), Basra (petrochemicals), Bandar Khomeini (petrochemicals), Shuaiba (petrochemicals, fertilizers), Dammam (fertilizers), Jubail (petrochemicals, fertilizers, aluminum, steel, hydrocarbon-based industries), Yanbu (petrochemicals, hydrocarbon-based industries), Bahrain's Arab Shipbuilding and Repair Yard Company (ASRY), Bahrain's Aluminum Bahrain smelter (ALBA), Umm Said (steel, petrochemicals, fertilizers), Ruwais (petrochemicals, fertilizers, hydrocarbon-based industries), Jebel Ali (aluminum, cables, steel, cement, hydrocarbon-based industries, Dubai's ship repair and dry dock facility, and Mina Saqr (cement) (Ibid.). Within the region, the overarching strategy of utilizing oil export as the core for industrialization by combining oil and oil-derivative processing within industrial port complexes and facilities was clearly popular.

Fatima S. Al-Shamsi, in her work on UAE policy of the late 1970s, writes that one of the explicit points of the UAE's 1979 industrial strategy was "enhancing government participation in large-scale, capital intensive projects and encouraging private investment in productive joint venture activity" (1999: 84). This practice clearly occurred in those industrial projects throughout the 1970s, as most sought a joint-venture strategy as a means to train local workers and facilitate technology transfer (Ghanem 1992). Nevertheless, Al-Shamsi goes on to warn that "given the characteristics of Gulf state economies, the drive for industrial development will remain restricted unless it acquires a real [Gulf] regional dimension … Adherence to a regional strategy may lead to a more efficient resource allocation through reducing the cost of duplication and excess capacity of industrial projects" (1999: 102). The outsiders' analysis and subsequent warning against this kind of project replication occurred in parallel to international CEDOs encouragement of these projects. This is not to deny the region's agency in making these decisions, but the number of cries against regional project duplication, both during and then after the construction boom, take on an almost comic light. The warnings, of course, were correct, and when oil prices fell in the 1980s, price-cutting completion and other events would benefit some projects over others. Nevertheless, as Mary Ann Tétreault suggests, when looking at the UAE's overall investments at this time, project duplication had a specific logic:

> UAE investments, particularly those made by Dubai, have been criticized as egregious examples of differential accumulation at the expense of regional partners. This is disputed by analysts who cite disparities in exchange rates, pricing policies and taxation across the GCC [Gulf Cooperation Council formed in 1981], which though they are diminishing, are the chief culprits blocking the growth of regional trade. Indeed, such impediments make duplicate investment economically rational (2000: 138).

As she points out, this was particularly true for Dubai. Dubai's success throughout the twentieth-century was based precisely on this combination of infrastructure and policy as a means to excel in competition. Dubai duplicated the functions of Lingah at the turn of the century, and within an environment of a particular kind of regional industrial development strategy based on oil and oil wealth, Dubai threw its hat in again with similar infrastructural investment, combined with important differential elements that would have lasting consequence for the emirate. In addition, the British withdrawal from Aden in 1967 removed key port and refinery infrastructure capacity from the region, and this had to be redistributed to other ports. Dubai's history as an *entrepôt* made it the obvious heir, but it was not the only port vying for the position. The race for infrastructure capacity and political will to fill the role of Aden was yet another factor to fuel the regional construction boom of the 1970s.

Dubai Industrialization

In Dubai, infrastructure investments followed the regional trend, but with an intensified ambition and scale in projects that sought to outdo its competitors. Throughout the 1970s, Dubai construction of large-scale trade infrastructure proceeded with a kind of hubris that initially focused on building beyond the scale of its regional competitors, and ended the decade building the largest industrial port in the world. Within this incremental and intensified construction race, Dubai appeared not only to be competing against its oil-producing neighbors, but also against time itself, with the belief that the quantities of its oil reserves were low compared to other OPEC countries, and therefore it needed to invest in "brick and mortar" projects before the oil reserves ran out. Thus the pace, scale, and intensity were strongly influenced by the time factor. Dubai was a "latecomer" to industrialization and oil discovery, and as a result, a kind of insecurity *vis-à-vis* neighboring Gulf States inspired increased grandiosity in projects, and a kind of "go for broke" attitude. If the scalar ambitions of Dubai's infrastructural projects seemed wildly out of proportion with production and trade flow demands, the belief seemed to be that to successfully out-build competing infrastructure projects would reap subsequent rewards. An infrastructural supply-side approach, launched with a kind abandon of a new nation with more new oil wealth than it could even fathom. Perhaps in light of the great wealth that befell Dubai on that day of oil discovery in June 1966, the same kind of fortune would smile on its 1970s infrastructure projects if it had the ambition and will to carry out the largest and greatest projects. Again, this is not to say that Sheikh Rashid's strategic investments in infrastructure during the 1970s were mere folly, for clearly they were built on a strong tradition of the emirate's trade history. But the projects were inspired by competition for the future rather than hard facts of the day, and this continually bedeviled consultants of the time who warned against project replication. Sheikh Rashid was a close follower of those regional precedents set in the region by Aden, Bahrain, and Kuwait, and his supply-side driven strategy sought to compete with these same regional neighbors to attract trade activity and leverage Dubai's strategic geographic location on the lower Gulf.

Mary Ann Tétreault, in her work on the economics of national autonomy in the UAE, refers to the concept of a "competitive state," citing the work of Ronen Palan and Jason Abbot (Tétreault 2000, Palan et al. 1996). The two authors point out, first, that the competitive state implements policies that will promote national competitiveness as the driving force for economic development and increased standards of living, and second, in pursuit of this objective, the government switches its focus from traditional demand-side measure to the supply-side measures. Viewed in these terms, Dubai is a clear example of a competitive state. The supply-side "policies" to promote its competitiveness were channeled into the scalar and capacity differential of its infrastructure projects, and here again, we see how its strategy for economic competitiveness fused with the specific large-scale trade projects and their territorial impacts. A closer review of Dubai's infrastructure projects of the 1970s helps to better illuminate this point.

Port Rashid

Plans for the deep-water Port Rashid were commissioned in 1965, before oil was discovered. Halcrow's preliminary plans for the port were completed in 1967, calling for four berths, but Sheikh Rashid immediately insisted that the port should have 15 berths. Port Rashid opened in 1972 with 12 completed general cargo berths, and because of the increased imports since 1967 and the closure of Aden, it was already oversubscribed upon initial completion. By May 1976, the wait to unload cargo reached 60 days, and Sheikh Rashid commissioned another expansion of Port Rashid, which was to increase its capacity to 37 berths by 1980 (though it was inaugurated in 1979) to become the largest modern Gulf port (Owen 1978: 166).

The expansion also made the important decision to equip the port with new trade technology, including two container crane berths, roll-on/roll-off facilities (ro-ro), and lighter aboard-ship systems (LASH), which other port construction projects in the northern Gulf had decided against, favoring the traditional bulk general cargo facilities (Walker 1984: 185). The decision to risk investment on the new container technology and equipment would prove decisive in Port Rashid's competitiveness over other regional ports (Sucharov 1977: v). When the Suez Canal reopened in 1975, Aden was also not equipped to handle container movement, which put it an important disadvantage. Halcrow completed the Port Rashid project in a joint venture with the British firm Costain Taylor Woodward under contract for $214 million (Sucharov 1977: vi). From 1967 through 1979, Port Rashid went from four berths, to 15, and finally to 37, demonstrating both an incremental and exponential amplification logic, which in the case of Port Rashid, was self-referential, as I will explore further in Chapter 5.

Figure 3.6 Erection of the "Tango 80" container crane on Berth 10 at Port Rashid, April 7, 1977

Source: Halcrow Archive

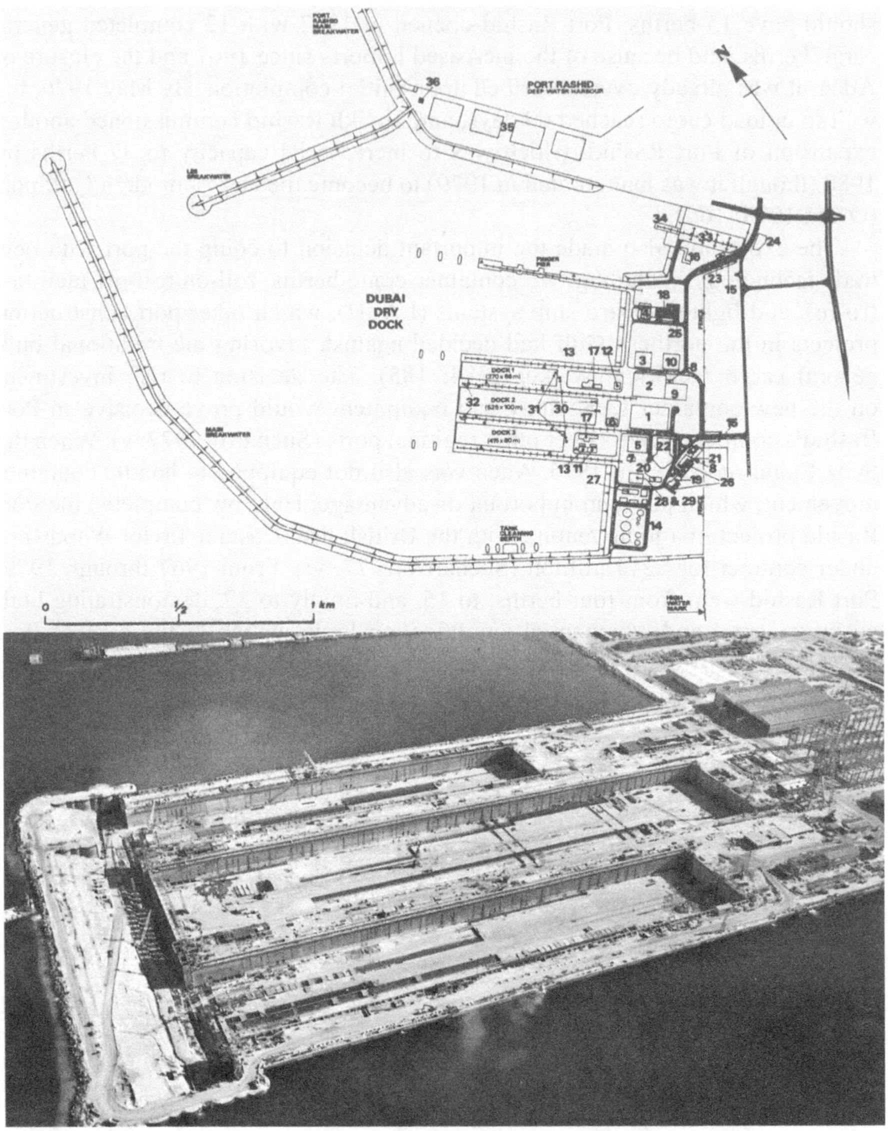

Figure 3.7 Dry dock and ship repair facility diagram and image
Source: Cordery 1979b. Halcrow Archive

Dry Dock and Ship Repair Facility

Shortly after Port Rashid opened in 1972, a contract was signed, again with the Halcrow, Costain, Taylor Woodward joint venture, in December 1973 for $275 million for the construction for the Dubai Dry Dock and Ship Repair facility, as an ancillary activity to be located just south of Port Rashid (Ibid.). Though industrial port construction was largely replicated throughout the region, after forming the *Organization of Arab Petroleum Exporting Countries* (OAPEC) in 1968, member countries Bahrain, Iraq, Kuwait, Saudi Arabia, the UAE, Qatar and Libya all agreed to mutually invest in a dry dock and ship repair facility. After internal debate over where the facility would be located, it was eventually agreed that Bahrain would host the facility, and construction began on the Arab Shipbuilding and Repair Yard (ASRY) at the beginning of the 1970s. Opened in 1977 (Walker 1984: 193), the ASRY was operated by Estaleiros Navais de Lisboa SARL of Portugal, and it had four repair berths with the capacity to repair tankers of up to 500,000 deadweight tons (dwt).

Though the UAE was part of the joint venture to build the ASRY, leaders in Dubai decided that even though they weren't selected for the OAPEC facility, that they would proceed to build their own dry dock and ship repair yard. While the Dubai dry dock only had three repair berths, one of these berths had the projected capacity to repair tankers of up to 1,000,000 dwt, which gave it the kind of differential edge in duplication mentioned above (Ibid., El-Mallakh 1981). The facility would also make Port Rashid more attractive for maritime trade as an additional clustered service. Thus, the move demonstrates both scalar amplification and programmatic intensification, which we will see as characteristic throughout Dubai's development. The Dubai Dry Dock and Ship Repair Facility opened on February 26, 1979, with the largest dry dock berth in the world, measuring 525 meters long by 100 meters wide (Cordery 1979b: 65), though the projected capacity for 1,000,000 dwt vessels would take longer to achieve. As with future projects, within this competitive environment, strategies to promote and exaggerate scale and capacity could both help to create a promotional "buzz" around a given project and aspire to attract future business based on the marketing techniques.

World Trade Center

Though the second Port Rashid expansion and the dry dock facility were both completed after Harris's second master plan in 1971, they essentially did not break with his ring-radial urban structure that centered on the creek. The break with this morphology began in 1974 with the location choice for the new World Trade Centre facility. When Queen Elizabeth made her late-night visit to the Dubai trade exhibition at the new airport terminal in 1972, Sheikh Rashid knew that a proper facility was needed to host future trade events. Trade centers were springing up in cities around the world, and the World Trade Center was under construction in New York. Upon completion, New York's trade center would be the tallest building in the world, and this surely inspired Sheik Rashid as well. Clearly Sheikh Rashid understood the important function of a trade center and was intrigued by the possibility of it being housed in an iconic building.

Shortly after the Queen's visit, Sheikh Rashid commissioned John R. Harris, who had already designed the Rashid Hospital and authored both master plans, to design a world trade center facility. Harris's original plan was for a low-rise office complex with several display halls and an auditorium, but Sheikh Rashid complained that it was not tall enough. Harris then revised the project, including a 39-storey tower, which was to be the tallest building in the Middle East at that time, and the first building in Dubai to have an elevator (Davidson 2008: 107, Humaid Al Tayer 1999). Though the trade center was originally planned for a location at the mouth of the creek in Deira, aviation patterns for the airport would have limited Sheikh Rashid's ambitious height requirements for the project. As a result, the project was relocated for a site on the Abu Dhabi Road, which at the time was far removed from the urban limits. The new location did not have height restriction problems, and it also offered more space for car parking (Humaid Al Tayer 1999: 31), which was an issue that was becoming more important with the emirate's increased automobile use. The World Trade Center opened a new southwestern growth axis perpendicular to the creek.

Figure 3.8 Construction of the World Trade Center
Source: John R. Harris and Partners

Figure 3.9 Diagram of the National Cement Company, including: 1. Crusher 2. Raw material storage 3. Weightfeeders 4. Slurry and cement mills 5. Slurry basins 6. Rotary kiln 7. Fuel oil tanks 8. Fuel heating station 9. Kiln planetary coolers 10. Clinker silos 11. Cement silos 12. Packing plant 13. Workshop and stores 14. Garage 15. Main 33 kv substation 16. Workers' amenity 17. Administration building 18. Laboratories 19. Weighbridges 20. Electrostatic precipitator

Source: R.D. Mackenzie

National Cement Company

Along with the World Trade Center, development moved southwest beyond Al-Shindigah and Bur Dubai with the construction of the Dubai National Cement Company. A large portion of imports throughout the 1960s was comprised of construction materials for the building boom, including large quantities of cement that came from Kenya, Japan, West Germany, and Belgium (El Mallakh 1981: 54). The use of cement blocks for housing did not begin until 1956, but subsequent construction relied heavily on the material, though extensive experimentation by contractors was necessary to find the adequate mixes to accommodate the local climate (Crowder 1983, Fleming 2008). While the leadership was investing to expand trade facilities to reduce the delay of construction projects due to the slowed supply-chain cycle for construction materials, in parallel, Sheikh Rashid decided in April 1968 to contract the British Halcrow, Costain, and F.L. Smidth and Co. groups, and the Swiss Holderbank Group (Mackenzie, date unspecified), for the construction of a national cement company as part of a larger strategy for import-substitution-industrial investment.

The Holderbank Group conducted a land survey for the cement factory in 1970, and because of sand, fuel, and water requirements, they recommended that the factory locate near the coast beyond Al-Shidigah in the Al-Qouz industrial district. Though aluminum oxide and iron oxide had to be imported, cement was produced with local lime-rich coastal and silica-rich inland sands to feed the process, along with gypsum that was mined at the inland quarry in Jebel Ali. The process also required treated water pumped from the municipal sewage plant located seventeen kilometers away, along with fuel pipelined in from Dubai's new offshore oil supply. Measures were taken to reduce dust output from the cement production, and exhaust gases were reduced to 0.2g/Nm3 (Ibid.). The cement company's significance, beyond its production value and the continued move southwestward through infrastructural facilities, lies more in its machinistic qualities that strategically clustered production processes around various local and international inputs. The use of treated sewage water to feed the production process, along with local oil, gypsum, and sand, mixed with some imported materials, was not unsimilar to other more complex industrial processes. However the company's isolated and agglomerated functions that included disparate and coordinated inputs with strategic linkages would also become a model for the future Jebel Ali Port and Industrial Area, and yet another example of the kind of machine-like, infrastructure-within-infrastructure development promoted in Dubai throughout the 1970s.

The Queen's Return

On February 26, 1979, Queen Elizabeth II returned to Dubai at the invitation of Sheikh Rashid. She had a busy schedule. This time the visit was not a stopover, but an official state visit and a momentous occasion on which she was to inaugurate some of the most ambitious engineering projects the world had ever seen. First, John Harris's World Trade Center complex, which included a 39-storey tower—the tallest in the Middle East at that point—was appropriate for her to open because her first visit had inspired its construction. Second, she was to inaugurate the extension of Port Rashid, along with its neighboring Dry Dock and Ship Yard

Figure 3.10 Photos of Queen Elizabeth II and Sheikh Rashid for the promotion material announcing her visit in February 26, 1979

Source: Halcrow Archive

facility, which were each constructed by the Halcrow firm. The Dry Dock had three large facilities which could repair the world's biggest tanker ships, and Port Rashid was extended in its second phase by an additional 22 berths to become the largest in the Middle East. Finally, the Queen would inaugurate a new port and industrial complex 35 kilometers southwest from the creek, which was the largest port construction and excavation project ever completed. Mina Jebel Ali (*mina* meaning "port" in Arabic) was also a Halcrow project, and it was touted to be one of the three projects, along with the Great Wall of China and the Hoover Dam, that were visible from space. Beyond the fanfare and hyperbole, Mina Jebel Ali would change the course of Dubai.

While the World Trade Centre can be understood historically as a large-scale trade infrastructure which began to move Dubai beyond the dictates of the second master plan, and the National Cement Company also pushed development southwest toward Abu Dhabi, it was the scale and force of impact of the Jebel Ali Port and Industrial Area (and subsequently, its Free Zone) that truly changed Dubai's metropolitan form.

Boom

The period in Dubai between oil discovery in 1966 and the commissioning of Jebel Ali ten years after was one of intense construction, population growth, and urban expansion, along with dramatic political change as the era of the

British protectorate came to a close. The combination of economic prosperity as a result of oil discovery, amplified by the 1973 international oil crisis, and the political reorganization of the seven sheikhdoms in the formation of the United Arab Emirates changed both the region and Dubai decisively. Though initially unwilling to see the British leave, Sheikh Rashid soon realized that the onus of UAE formation fell on Sheikh Zayed of Abu Dhabi, allowing him to negotiate the terms of Dubai's inclusion in the new federation to his favor. Abu Dhabi retained capital status, and Dubai essentially benefited from UAE funding that helped it realize ambitious infrastructural development of the 1970s without the need to surrender political autonomy to Abu Dhabi. In addition, the decline of Aden's port protagonism as a result of Britain's withdrawal and the closing of the Suez Canal represented an opportunity that Sheikh Rashid also surely identified.

The 1973 international oil crisis flooded the Gulf region with profit liquidity, causing a sharp increase in import demands, which caught the region's port facilities by surprise. The combination of demand-side requirements to increase trade infrastructure capacity, along with the decision of many of the region's oil-producing countries to launch ambitious investments in industrialization that were generally either aimed at internal import-substitution-industrialization (I-S-I) or regional trade, produced a decade of furiously-paced growth. The two kinds of investments also represented two seemingly divergent national aspirations of merchant trade cosmopolitanism (which was traditionally Dubai's hallmark) and a kind of inward-looking welfare state insularity of these I-S-I policies. The interplay of these two tendencies would express themselves differently throughout the region (including Dubai); a tension which certainly continues through today. While the British had officially left by 1971, British consulting firms took advantage of the contacts and relationships established during the British protectorate period, such that they were involved in the planning, engineering, and construction of many of these regional projects.

Dubai's investment in trade infrastructure and industrialization followed regional trends, and also involved British CEDO firms, guided by a clustered investment strategy that built on the emirate's historic trade profile. Dubai's projects focused on increasing trade infrastructure capacity, and replicated regional oil-derived industries, competing with other regional facilities through either price or efficiency differentiation, thus continuing patterns of infrastructural replication and amplification. Harris's second master plan launched Dubai's most intensive growth decade in 1971, building upon his first plan, but also including some regulatory measures (height maximums, uniform plot sizes, etc.) that would not hold against Sheikh Rashid's increasingly ambitious growth aspirations. Infrastructural investments were the motors for larger urban development aspirations: municipal services including water, electricity, and roads; ancillary infrastructure such as the banking system for the finance sector; hotels for tourism; the Jumeirah ground+one villas for the growing ex-patriot community; and, the World Trade Center complex to host trade shows and facilitate international trade negotiation. All components built upon the infrastructural urban development patterns that had been established in Dubai from the period before oil was discovered. As I will explore in Chapter 4, the culmination of these clustered projects would be the Jebel Ali Port, Industrial Area, and Free Zone.

Chapter 4
Jebel Ali

> The decision to develop a modern port facility in Dubai proved to be one of the most enlightened taken during Sheikh Rashid's reign, for Dubai's exceptional port facilities and the subsequent foundation of the Free Zone at Jebel Ali have contributed more, perhaps, than any other innovation to the present success which Dubai enjoys (Al-Gurg 1998: 80).

In nineteenth-century journal entries of the British navy, the area of Jebel Ali is mentioned variously as "Gebil Ali," "Jebel 'Alí," "Jabal-al 'Ali," and "Jabail," and in 1864 was described as, "the only hill on this coast is in Dibai [sic] territory: it is 220 feet high, flat-topped, and lies 19 miles southwest of Dibai town and four miles inland, being separated from the sea by a strip of low desert" (Trench 1994: 304). Located approximately 20 miles (35 kilometers) southwest from the Dubai creek toward Abu Dhabi, Jebel Ali is located close to the border with its neighboring capital emirate. *Jebel* means "hill" or "mount" in Arabic, as referred to in the passage, and the Jebel Ali mount is one of the few examples of exposed rock made of sediment salt deposits near the UAE coast, not including the rugged interior mountains (Gabriel 1987: 23). In the early 1950s, Jebel Ali was one of the first onshore oil drilling test sites, known as "Bab One" (Davidson 2008: 100), but after proving fruitless, exploration moved offshore. In late 1966, a radio station was constructed at the Jebel Ali location for communication, although the location was still a contested territory with Abu Dhabi. However, when Sheikhs Zayed and Rashid met at Al-Sameeh in February 1968, it was agreed that the territory would be ceded to Dubai.

With imports increasing dramatically after oil discovery, in 1972, the same year of the Queen's first visit, Sheikh Rashid was already thinking of a larger port complex for Dubai. As the story goes, Sheikh Rashid was surveying the Dubai coast for the exact location of the new port. The consultants from Sir William Halcrow and Partners group accompanied Sheikh Rashid on his walks, and observed as the ruler gazed over the landscape to find the pre-destined spot. The consultants' conventional wisdom suggested that the port should be located at what was then known as Chicago Beach, named after the industrial company from Chicago that built the floating oil storage structures known as "khazzans" (and home today of the Jumeirah Beach). This location offered closer proximity to the city center, and coastal currents were less burdensome so as to require a shorter approach channel for the new port (Davidson 2008, Fleming 2005). Sheikh Rashid had other plans.

Figure 4.1 Aerial photo of Mina Jebel Ali and the stretch of land northeast toward Dubai

Source: Halcrow Archive

What seemed to be defiance of conventional consulting wisdom—the mysticism of lore, along with a dash of monarchical megalomania—may all have been part of the scenario, but Sheikh Rashid's decision to locate the ambitious new port that he had in mind at Jebel Ali was neither irrational nor difficult to comprehend. While the territory agreement was struck at Al-Sameeh four years earlier, the border definition had previously been disputed over and had caused bloodshed for both Dubai and Abu Dhabi, so it is not difficult to understand Sheikh Rashid's desire to punctuate the 1968 territory agreement with the world's largest port construction project to "seal the deal." In addition, such an ambitious port project so close to their shared border could help to give Dubai a competitive edge over any future Abu Dhabi port facility, and could potentially offer regional port services to both emirates. Knowing that Dubai itself had already chosen to duplicate the Bahraini Arab Shipbuilding and Repair Yard with its own dry dock facilities, Sheikh Rashid certainly knew that the same duplication could and would be employed by Dubai's neighbors, even after the 1971 federation of the UAE; particularly so since the same consulting groups were operating throughout the region. Finally, it is also likely that Aden's duel port structure that sited its industrial port on the western edge and its commercial inner port on its eastern side may have influenced Sheikh Rashid's dual port strategy.

In neighboring Saudi Arabia, as a part of the government's first infrastructural development plans, the newly-formed Royal Commission for Jubail and Yanbu contracted Sir William Halcrow and Partners in 1976 to help build two major industrial cities on both the Gulf and the Red Sea, respectively. Until this project, Jubail had been only a small Gulf coast port town with a history of pearling. Its new industrial city would include four distinct areas for leisure, residence, industry, and transportation. Transportation infrastructure included the King Fahd Industrial Port along with an airport area that covered 250 kilometers, a commercial port, and the industrial area, which all spanned over 8,000 hectares (Pampanini 1997, Korea Development Institute 1980). The close proximity of Jubail to Dubai along the Gulf coast, a very similar time line, and the same engineering consulting company make it more than coincidence that the Jebel Ali Port project, though planned for since 1972, was officially announced by Sheikh Rashid in the same year, with ambitions to specifically outdo the parallel Saudi industrial and commercial port projects.

On August 2, 1976, Sheikh Rashid contracted the Halcrow International Partnership as chief consultant for construction management, the Gulf Colba group for land dredging, and the newly-formed Mina Jebel Ali Construction, as a part of the larger joint venture for the construction of the Jebel Ali Port and Industrial Complex (Cordery 1979a). Construction began soon afterward, and by 1978, five berths (of the future total of 67) were fully operational, with a 20 kilometer approach channel that augmented the need for construction materials for the ambitious project. Port construction was complete by 1983, with extensive industrial, logistics, and residential facilities. The Jebel Ali Port and Industrial complex replicated other regional prototypes and models, but its machinistic qualities, ambitious scale, and morphological repercussions transformed the development into a new kind of urban and industrial product that would consequently be replicated in Dubai, the greater region, and beyond. Reviewing some of the elements of the port, industrial complex, and their ancillary components, I will explore how this new model emerged.

Mina Jebel Ali Port

The announcement to build Jebel Ali in August 1976 came only months after the announcement to expand Port Rashid in May. The Port Rashid expansion was to make it the largest in the Gulf region with 37 berths. Shortly afterward, Jebel Ali was announced to become the largest man-made port in the world, with 15 kilometers of waterfront and 67 berths (Broeze 1999: 178). Internally, the *majlis* questioned Sheikh Rashid's decision (Wilson 2006), but his vision for increased trade capacity and economic industrialization and diversification would eventually prove to be shrewd and successful foresight.

Part of the *entrepôt* trade success that Dubai enjoyed after the fall of Aden in 1967 was an extension of its free port policy by offering free sea-air cargo transfer, which, in light of Harris's second plan, made the Deira tunnel, Al-Garhood bridge, and the ring-road around the creek all the more urgent to facilitate this cargo transfer (Ho 2008, Wilson 2006: 489). This was one of the key reasons that the Jebel Ali port and industrial development originally also included an international airport to reduce the commute time for sea-air freight transfer. When Sheikh Rashid lobbied for an airport with the British political agent back in the 1950s, one possibility that Sharjah promoted was for the auxiliary airstrip to be built near the Jebel Ali location, though clearly history turned out otherwise (Davidson 2008: 94). The elusive Jebel Ali airstrip(s) would not be completed until 2010.[1]

Figure 4.2 Jebel Ali construction in 1978
Source: Halcrow Archive

1 The Al-Maktoum International Airport of the Dubai World Central project is presently scheduled to open in 2010. See: http://www.dwc.ae/.

As noted by A.R. Walker, along with economic growth and political ferment, another main issue for port expansion throughout the Gulf, and in Dubai in particular, was technological innovation (Walker 1984). The plans for Port Rashid's extension project included two berths that would be equipped with cranes to handle container movement, which would be part of a larger internal breakwater that Halcrow built on top of a large swath of reclaimed land (Cordery 1979b). Mina Jebel Ali was to amplify the emirate's gamble on new port technology with many more ambitious container berths, and equipment, and technology imported from Japan and South Korea, who by this time were the premiere trading partners for Dubai, and the larger UAE oil (Broeze 1999: 181–5, Walker 1984). In addition to the imported equipment, Sheikh Rashid signed an agreement with the US Sea-Land company to manage the new port (Owen 1978).

Sea-Land was founded by a trucking impresario named Malcolm McLean, who became involved with shipping after concluding that the movement of cargo on land and sea could be understood as a streamlined process that could mutually benefit one another through improved technology for higher efficiency. Historically, on April 26, 1956, a large crane lifted 58 of McLean's recently-invented aluminum container boxes on an old oil tanker ship known as the *Ideal-X* at the Port of Newark, New Jersey, where it then took five days to move its cargo down to Houston, Texas (Levinson 2006: 8). This is understood as the birth of containerization, which revolutionized the industrial freight and logistics industry by establishing specific standard dimensions for the aluminum containers (20, 30, and 40 feet in length by 8.5 feet in height). The containers could then be loaded and offloaded from ships at ports far quicker through mechanization, and at far less cost than maintaining itinerant armies of port longshoremen and stevedores, particularly those who were unionized. McLean began his contracting of container transport and services mainly within the US during the early 1960s, but the Vietnam War offered him the opportunity to work with the US Army to help ship military cargo more efficiently in this new form. Simultaneously, McLean signed partnerships with Europe, and then Japan, to establish triangulated trade routes, where specific ports had invested in container technology. The Japanese had a strong shipbuilding tradition since the nineteenth-century, when the Mitsubishi family first invested in the sector (Wray 1984). By the early 1970s, the containerization phenomenon was spreading throughout the world, and McLean's Sea-Land company, logically as its inventor, was the premiere company for container transport and port management looking to expand its trade routes. After signing the agreement to manage the new Jebel Ali Port, which was to open its initial container berths and services in 1979, Sea-Land initiated its first container routes to India in 1980 (Henning 2010). Sea-Land viewed the management of the Jebel Ali port as an important stronghold for the region, and a strategic point for throughput for the new container route to India.

The port design for Mina Jebel Ali was based on research conducted on a 1:120 hydraulic model constructed at the Hydraulic Research Station at Wallingford in the

United Kingdom. The model generated data on channel alignment and breakwater positioning so as to minimize wave activity for both the approach channel and the areas below and above the port's entrance ("Mina Jebel Ali" Date unspecified: 2). The predominant wave direction came from the northwest, and after running tests using both hydraulic and mathematical models, it was determined that a bend was required in the entrance channel, preferably as close to the entrance as possible, to maximize the energy of wave generation off the channel entrance. Construction of the inland berth areas involved massive dredging and excavation, and the sand and earth brought up was mainly compacted on the adjacent site to elevate it appropriately for industrial use. As Maraqa et al. describe:

> The harbor at Jebel Ali is the largest manmade port in the world ... The approach channel has a depth of 14-15 meters and a width of 280 meters reducing to 235 meters. It bends after 10 km and becomes the entrance channel. It widens to 300 meters at the bend and to 340 meters at the entrance channel. There are two basins within the port. The outer 14 meter deep basin is 2.3 km long and 600 meters wide, while inner basin is 3.7 km long and 425 meters wide, with a depth of 11.5 meters ... The area of Jebel Ali Harbor is about 5 by 5 km^2 (2008: 105).

It is important to underscore, with this, that the engineering for the ambitious project required elaborate modeling to design and construct the port, which involved closely studying the wave direction and how to best harness its energy. As future projects are planned around Jebel Ali (Palm Jebel Ali, Jebel Ali Port extension ... ?), this will clearly alter those wave patterns that the original Jebel Ali port was designed for, and this may generate new challenges for such additions. The same difficulties have arisen with various plans for coastal preservation, wherein those flushing stations set up to preserve the Dubai coast are now disturbed by new reclamation projects off the coast (Fleming 2005). This process of engineering on top of other engineering projects has been a consistent difficulty for Dubai, and reflects a wider cellular construction model where project coordination is a perennial challenge.

Along with its central trade activity, the industrial area included other facilities and functions in its clustered agglomeration, as I explore below.

Marine Industrial Development Area

When oil was discovered in Dubai in 1966, it was clear from the beginning that this would be a limited source of capital for the emirate and that complementary and diversified strategies would have to be developed in order to secure future wealth accumulation. In the 1970s, Dubai's economic diversification strategy emphasized large-scale industrial infrastructure investment to help absorb liquidity from oil revenues and stave off inflation concerns that often accompanied oil profits and have historically demonstrated oil to be a mixed blessing for many countries in the

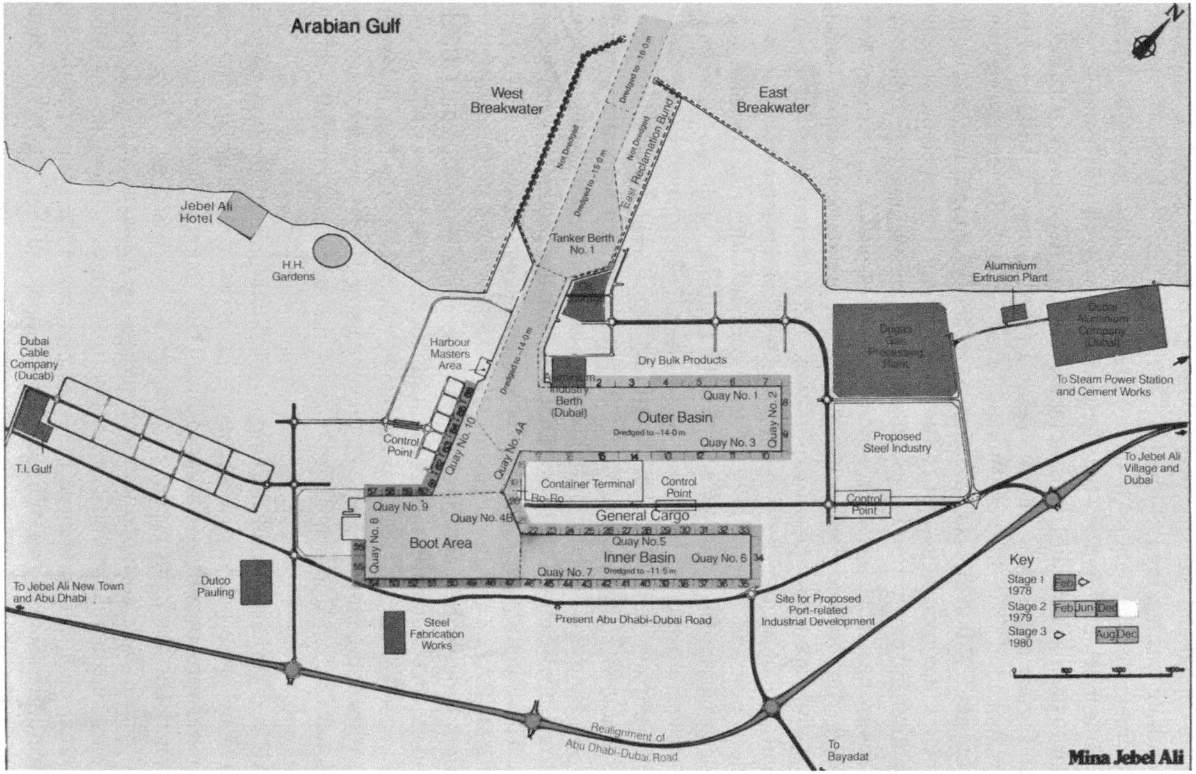

Figure 4.3 Diagram of the Jebel Ali Port and Industrial Area

Source: Halcrow Archive

developing world (Morgan 1979).[2] Going back to Al-Shamsi point, these large-scale, capital-intensive projects that sought joint venture activity were a quick path toward industrialization that took advantage of oil profits and could bring in trained human capital and industrial technology for potential knowledge transfer, which the emirate was lacking (Al-Shamsi 1999: 84).

Some elements of the Jebel Ali model drew on regional examples of oil-derivative industrial development, but the ambitious overall port complex was more similar to the marine industrial development area (MIDA) projects launched in post-war Europe and Japan. André Vigarié's (1981) work on MIDAs in the early 1980s looked at four different models based on their different scales and locational impacts. Within this classification, Mina Jebel Ali closest resembles the Japanese model, incorporating what is known as the *horikomi* method of heavy land reclamation and excavation in previously "sandy or swampy zones" that was central in achieving the Japanese economic miracle of post-War recovery from 1960 to 1975 (Rimmer and Taniuchi 1989). Dubai maintained a close trading relationship with Japan through oil exportation, and in return, received Japan's expertise and technology transfer in port management and machinery.

The interaction and functionality of the port and industrial complex took on strategic, machinistic qualities that would continue with the subsequent ancillary services mentioned below. It was originally comprised of the Dubai Aluminum Company (DUBAL), an aluminum smelter and extrusion plant; Dubai Gas Company (DUGAS), a liquefied petroleum and natural gas works to process gas from the offshore oilfields that also produced the energy to run DUBAL; the Dubai Cable Company (DUCAB) for the production of electric cables; and a desalination and steam power station run by the heat energy output produced by DUBAL. The natural gas for DUGAS was generated from offshore oil extraction, though the capturing process was initially inefficient. Oilfield services and other related activities; particularly those of the Shell Oil Company, previously located along the creek would also be relocated to the new industrial site. In this regard, the industrial area can be understood as an expanded version of the National Cement Company, with various interactive and mutually-reliant components and inputs.

Jebel Ali is a curious mix of the import-substitute-industrialization policies demonstrated by these industrial components, as most of their production was internally aimed for Dubai use—similar to Jubail and Yanbu in Saudi Arabia, and echoing Robert Owen's point earlier in Chapter 3—but based on a large trade facility and with a more cosmopolitan free port policy that was truer to Dubai's pre-oil origins and merchant vocation. While the industrial elements of Jebel Ali were perhaps not as important as the trade platform, the resources at the site would be useful for some degree of import substitution, and these elements would help pave the path for the future light manufacturing activity in the Free Zone.

2 Hayami (1997: 100) refers to this mixed blessing as the "Dutch disease," describing potential developmental challenges because of a country's oil assets.

In addition, while other industrial areas had been established along the creek—near Port Rashid, and the close to the airport—the scale of Jebel Ali's industrial component attracted much of the emirate's industrial activity, thus freeing up land closer to the creek and what was still considered "downtown" Dubai.

Regional Growth Pole/Growth Corridor

In the literature on regional planning and development of this time (Hoyle and Pinter 1981, Friedmann and Weaver 1979), the increased spatial demands of port and cargo technology often required port expansion and relocation in cities throughout the world, particularly in France, England and the Netherlands. "Growth-pole" theory was often applied in the regional planning of new port facilities as a way to both understand and plan for the infill development projected along the corridors connecting new or expanded port facilities to the city center (Dawson 1996, Hoyle 1996, Richardson 1978). Mina Jebel Ali is a clear example of this.

John Harris's second master plan responded to the accelerated urban growth of the 1960s, but when it was published in 1971, Mina Jebel Ali had not yet been commissioned. In the first part of the 1970s, the large-scale projects of Port Rashid and the Dry Docks in Al-Shindigah were counterbalanced with the Deira Corniche land reclamation project on the northeast side of the creek. This maintained the creek as the central element and urban growth axis for Harris's ring-radial structure, even if these projects pushed urban growth outward a bit further from the creek than the 1971 plan had prescribed or predicted. The tipping of this symmetric balance around the creek began with the World Trade Center, followed by the National Cement Company located further to the southwest in the first Al-Quoz Industrial Area. These moves can be understood as incremental changes from the 1971 Plan, but it was the ambitious scale of the Mina Jebel Ali Port and Industrial Zone that truly broke with Harris's ring-radial structure. Jebel Ali established a new growth pole and growth corridor perpendicular to the Gulf coast along the Abu Dhabi-Dubai Road, which would become Sheikh Zayed Road. During its planning and initial construction, Jebel Ali was to be a new town project, as we will see below, which enhanced its perceived impact further in terms of the force of a dual urban system—the original walled settlement and the new industrial/capital city of Jebel Ali—changing Dubai's regional morphology. New city aspirations were scaled back when oil prices fell in the early 1980s, but the morphological impact of Jebel Ali as a growth pole, and the establishment of a new growth corridor along the Abu Dhabi-Dubai Road, were already in place.

Infill development occurred in a predominantly modular form, in which large swaths of land in Jumeirah were divided into superblocks, and then subdivided symmetrically to form various geometric sub-block patterns with subtle, angular variation. The high-rise construction along Skeikh Zayed Road, in a replicated pattern, built southwestward along the corridor with buildings of similar height, in curtain fashion not unlike those that line the creek, with the difference being that

Figure 4.4 Aerial image of Jumeirah modular infill patterns
Source: Peter G. Rowe

they no longer needed to obey a ground+nine height regulation. The area between Jumeirah and Jebel Ali, as well as inland from this corridor, would eventually be subdivided into a larger mosaic of superblocks for residential, commercial and limited industrial use. Contrary to Harris's wishes, however, superblock infill was less geometrically consistent and increasingly large as development approached Jebel Ali.

In 1988, the office of the Greek architect and planner Constantinos A. Doxiadis published the Dubai Urban Area Plan in a series of reports that detailed an exhaustive inventory of the land usage and resources of the metropolitan area. The Urban Area Plan made this insightful observation:

> Development of spatial growth in the urban area will essentially conform with past practices. That is, the majority of the growth will occur on an East-West axis extending from the Central Business District (CBD) to the airport, with the majority of infill development occurring in a North-South axis extending from the CBD to Jebel Ali (Dubai Municipality 1988: xiii).

Doxiadis's team understood that Dubai's urbanism historically followed the growth corridors established by large-scale infrastructure projects, and projected

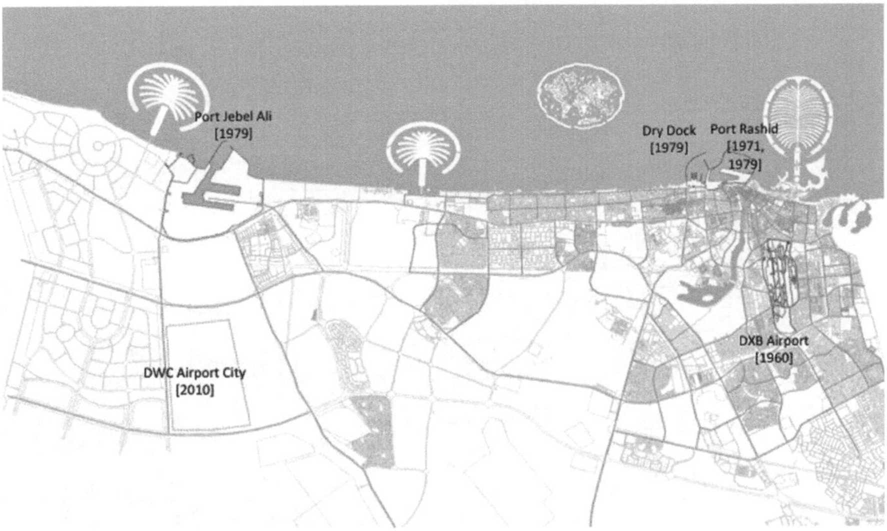

Figure 4.5 Ports and airports map with inaugural dates
Source: A map created by author

that future circumstances would follow the same pattern. The process of creating instant real estate value for land between city centers and ex-urban projects was clearly an important strategic element of Dubai's large-scale trade infrastructural investment; particularly with the Jebel Ali agglomeration.

From a traditional urban design perspective, the punctuation of transportation corridors with large-scale trade infrastructure facilities assumes the same function that monuments serve within a smaller contextual scale. In Dubai, trade infrastructure was built to monumental scale and imbued with this monumental significance to truly transmit the ethos of an international trade *entrepôt* at the metropolitan scale. Here again lies the seeming contradiction of constructing the largest port and industrial facility in the world, to compete with and exceed all competition, yet keeping that same facility generally out of site and off limits to the majority of the local population. This same kind of contradiction would eventually also characterize the Palm/World projects, which are visible for air travelers and magazine photography, but impossible to perceive as whole projects at the ground level. While the reasoning for this exclusivity can be as common as real estate marketing, trade security issues, and even the protection of illicit activity within these trade spaces, the larger effect of removing the very monuments Dubai builds for the international community from local spaces of *civitas* is indicative of the importance of this perceived, invisible, powerful "global" community expressed locally in the scale and significance of these projects.

Figure 4.6 Sketch of Jebel Ali New Town
Source: Peddle, Thorp, Chapman, and Taylor

Industrial/Capital New Town

> By the end of the century Jebel Ali could well have mushroomed into a city of 300,000 with its own international airport—possibly to become in time, the natural capital of the Emirate (Brown 1978).

This quote from a 1978 report on the Mina Jebel Ali construction highlights another function of the project as a new town for Dubai. Although the Dubai population at this time was little over 250,000 (Dubai Statistics Center 2010), ambitious growth aspirations mixed with a "build it and they will come" (i.e. supply-side driven) attitude sought to include an entire new town appendage as a part of the new industrial port complex, demonstrating a progressive programmatic intensification around the central trade infrastructure. This attitude was also present in neighboring Saudi Arabia, where the planning and construction of the new industrial cities of Jubail and Yanbu were launched in 1976.

During negotiations for the formation of the UAE, it was agreed that Abu Dhabi would assume temporary capital status for the seven emirates until a new capital could be built near the border between Abu Dhabi and Dubai. While the quote suggests that the Jebel Ali new city could become the "natural capital" of Dubai, it was originally planned as the capital of the entire UAE. Costs, inter-emirate politics, and international circumstances would slowly scale back both capital ambitions, but the planning for the new city (though much of it would not be built then) also helped to forge the larger development blueprint that the overall Jebel Ali project signified for Dubai.

The Jebel Ali New Town master plan commission was awarded to the British consultants Peddle, Thorp, Chapman, and Taylor (PTCT) on September 9, 1976, soon after the port and industrial project were announced in August. Port and airport facilities were to be designed and overseen by Halcrow as separate from the PTCT Plan. The loose guidelines Sheikh Rashid provided PTCT for the commission offer an interesting priority list for how the ruler interpreted urbanization:

1. Provide the conceptual framework for future development and examine and suggest the layout of the infrastructure of the area.
2. Examine the provision of basic services, i.e. water, drainage and power supplies, and suggest how they might be accommodated and provide information on the basic road and transportation network, with particular reference to the possible realignment of the main Dubai/Abu Dhabi road.
3. Suggest the location of the various components of the town, in conjunction with the proposed industrial element, and make recommendations on the siting and layout of the related residential areas, together with ancillary functions such as educational and medical facilities and shopping areas.

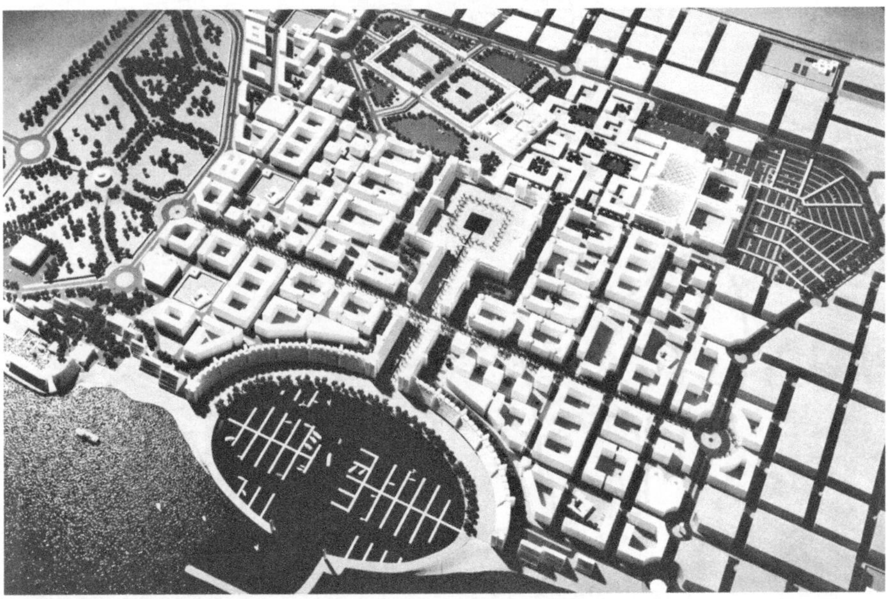

Figure 4.7 Model for Jebel Ali New Town Center
Source: Peddle, Thorp, Chapman, and Taylor

4. To give particular attention to landscaping and the creation of an attractive environment for those who will live and work in the area, and make recommendations as to how such needs might be met.
5. Liaise closely throughout with the Municipal Authority and Halcrow Middle East Limited the consultants retained for the new port and airport project.
6. Prepare the report in six months, with an interim report after three months. Restricted timetable dictated by the fact that construction work on the harbor and some of the basic industries had commenced and it was essential to establish an overall framework for the town and the basic infrastructure provision at the earliest date possible (Peddle et al. 1977: 1).

With the Jebel Ali New Town, the dual urban structure proposed with the original Dubai settlement would split complementarily functions: "Jebel Ali becoming the main industrial location with its port and airport providing for full international

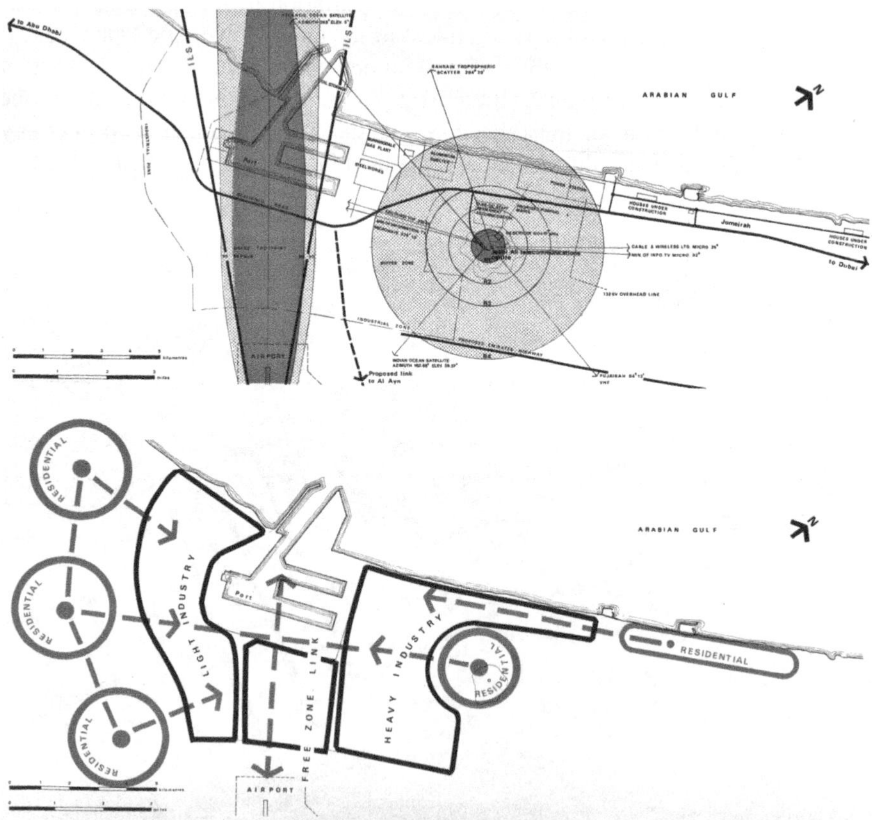

Figure 4.8 Jebel Ali New Town diagram
Source: Peddle, Thorp, Chapman, and Taylor

needs, and Dubai continuing to develop as the social, commerce and administrative centre" (Peddle et al. 1977: 4). The modern programmatic isolation of industrial and administrative functions between the proposed new town and the original creek settlement echoed Aden's bi-polar metropolitan structure, and its development agglomeration around its two ports.

PCTC's Plan suggested four phases, scheduled for completion in 2007, with high, medium, and low population and employment projections for the new town. Programmatic square-meter projections were also given for economic development projects, and the corollary number of schools, health clinics and hospitals required for growth projections. Heavy industry is located just north of the port, and there is a band of heavy industry that connects the port to the airport through a free zone. Another band of light industry is located to the southwest of the port. The new town center is located further to the southwest, divided from the light industrial area by a thin strip of parkland. Circular residential areas are located both to the southwest of the town center and just north of the heavy industrial area, where they meet with the existing residential areas of Jumeirah. The town center includes a waterfront corniche around a small recreational port, with a monumental axis moving inland toward a main square. There are varying-sized parcels to accommodate different housing densities and types, but the diversity of urban forms (interrupted grids with varying block sizes, an angled mall that does not quite arrive to the central square, etc.) make it difficult to see how the city would function. To be fair, the time constraints were very tight, but one senses that the larger programmatic layout took priority over the specific urban design of the "downtown." Finally, the PTCT Plan also included an elevated mini tram for public transportation throughout the new town, and northward to the new residential areas projected just south of the Jumeirah district. As mentioned in the Introduction, though also put on hold when the Jebel Ali New Town was scaled back, the present Dubai Metro project picks up on the limited scope of the proposed monorail for the Jebel Ali region and expands it for the entire emirate. In addition to the amplification of the project, the Metro also demonstrates how southwestern development, and the cumulative lessons learned in the process, are now moving northeasterly back toward the creek.

In his book *An Urban Profile of the Middle East*, Hugh Roberts says the following about Jebel Ali New Town's potential capital aspirations for the UAE:

> The UAE as a federal system is still developing a stable political form in which co-operation between the various states is becoming a matter of course. It has not yet reached this stage as the duplication of investment plans for international airports, high-rise buildings and industrial diversification proposals between the Emirates tends to illustrate … If the role of capital city (for the UAE) is ever considered for Jebel Ali, a new exercise in planning will be needed to cater for the significant change of role which will be the result … although the recent decision not to construct a major new airport at Jebel Ali may weaken the town's claim to capital status for the Emirates as a whole (1979: 146).

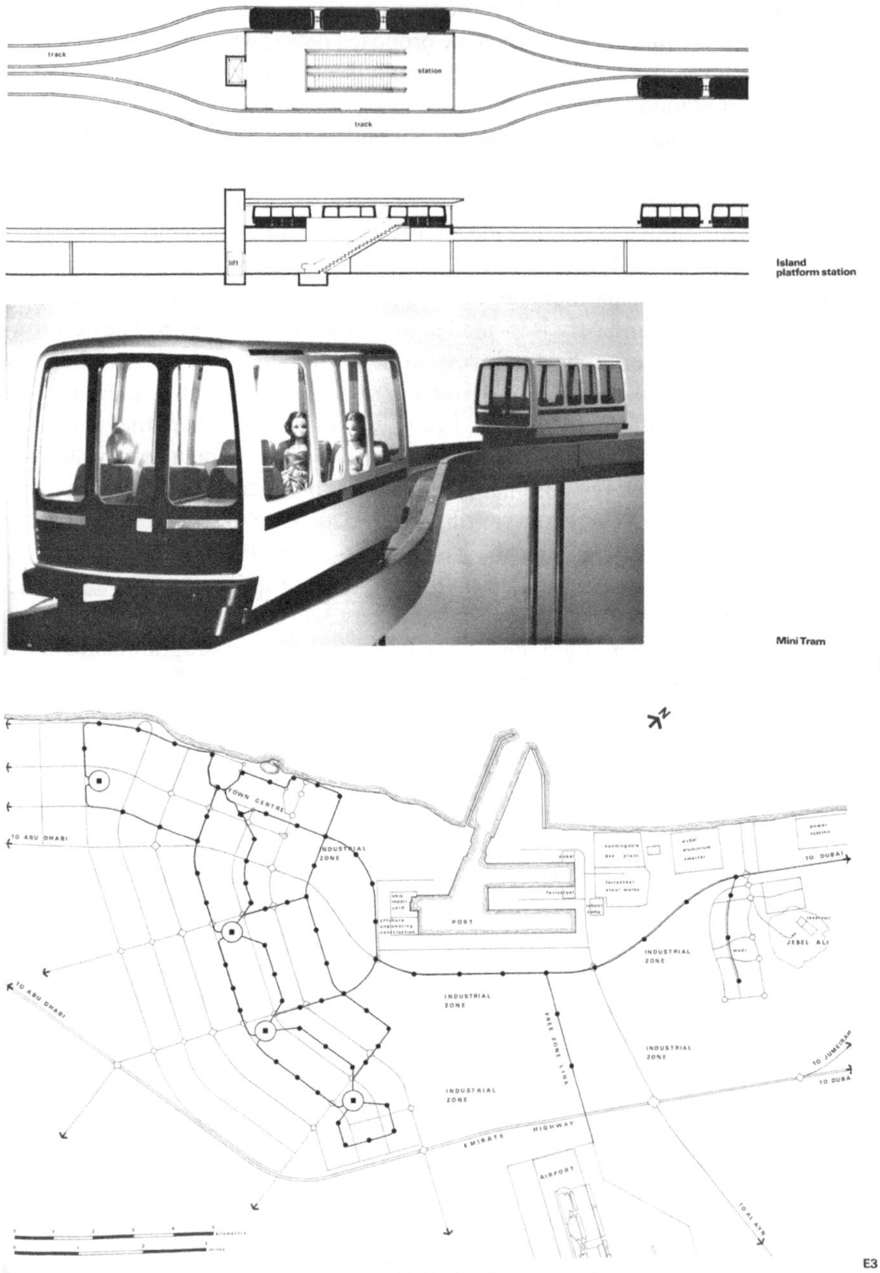

Figure 4.9 Jebel Ali New Town monorail diagram, image, and map
Source: Peddle, Thorp, Chapman, and Taylor.

As Roberts points out, by 1977, plans for the airport at the Jebel Ali New Town had already been dropped, and Dubai and Abu Dhabi had agreed to allow the latter to retain capital status for the UAE. Whether because of inside political agreements, or the belief that the UAE, and Dubai in particular, had overextended their large-scale investments, or a combination, with political economic sobriety the Jebel Ali New Town project was scaled back significantly, and very little of the PTCT Plan was built. The port and industrial area were completed, as was the free zone by 1985, but the new town and most of its residential surroundings would remain on the shelf in the PTCT document, and would not be revisited until 2005 when the Office for Metropolitan Architecture would be commissioned to design a new "Waterfront City" in its place. The sea-air connection for cargo planned for Jebel Ali with the airport–port combination would also have to wait until the construction of the Al-Maktoum International Airport, which is planned for inauguration in 2010. In the years since Jebel Ali's completion, cargo first traveled along the realigned Dubai/Abu Dhabi road (later named Sheikh Zayed road) from Jebel Ali to the original Dubai International Airport. More recently, as non-cargo traffic increased on Sheikh Zayed Road, this freight travel moved inland to the interior Emirate Road.

Along with the guidelines mentioned above for the PTCT Plan, also indicative of Dubai's overall urbanization priorities are the projects that were constructed for Jebel Ali. Along with the port and industrial projects, the only remnants of the new town plan were a residential enclave described in the first phase of the PTCT plan, and a luxurious hotel with a small recreation port. Each project was structured as a joint venture to be managed, again, by Halcrow, and Halcrow would also serve as architects for each project. The hotel was originally envisioned as a three-star facility to accompany the rest of the new town, but once the new town aspirations were scaled back, the hotel project took on more importance as a "luxury class" facility to properly receive and accommodate international industrialists at the Jebel Ali location, saving them the long trip to the original settlement. The Jebel Ali Hotel and its marina were completed in 1981.

Halcrow also designed the residential Jebel Ali Village, which was a project of 300 two- and four-bedroom detached units. The village project included a community center, a primary school, a small clinic and supermarket, and was modeled essentially on both the US company town and the British Garden City, with 30-meter by 30-meter residential plots ("Jebel Ali Village" Date not specified). In this regard, the village was similar in spirit to the villas that were built in the late 1960s for the DPC expatriate consultants in Jumeirah, only with a larger number of villas and expanded school and clinic facilities for the village families. The village was initially built to house the professional team working on the Jebel Ali project, but was projected to eventually be passed over to those who would work at the functioning port complex. The isolated and autonomous residential area of Jebel Ali Village would serve as a model typology for future semi-autonomous residential areas throughout Dubai (i.e. The Gardens, Emirates Hills, Jumeirah Lakes etc.), along with the shopping malls in the southwestern end of the emirate

Figure 4.10 Aerial images of Jebel Ali Village
Source: Halcrow Archive

Figure 4.11 Villa types for Jebel Ali Village
Source: Halcrow Archive

that were aimed at serving these residential community districts. In the case of both the hotel and the village, each again served as infrastructural elements within the larger international industrial strategy for Jebel Ali; infrastructure within infrastructure described as a "city within a city" even after the new town plans had been abandoned. The strategy demonstrates an instrumentalization of space and territory toward clear economic objectives of enhanced trade and manufacturing capacity for competitive regional advantage, industrial diversification, and investment opportunities to defend currency from inflationary pressures.

Free Zone

Finally, continuing Dubai's tradition of free port policy to help attract regional trade routes, Jebel Ali was to be an economic free zone. Though the Jebel Ali Free Zone adjacent to the port did not open officially until 1985, this element was included in the project plans from the late 1970s. The closing of Aden after 1967 gave Dubai the opportunity to aspire to Aden's previous role as a leading free trade *entrepôt* for the region, and of course Dubai already had a strong history of preferential merchant policies to fill this role. Free ports, free trade zones and export processing areas have received ample attention in planning and economic literature (Ho 1996: 9, Butler 1991, Hall 1991, Pollock 1981, Pounds 1981), and it is particularly this strategy, as a part of the larger *entrepôt* trade cluster, which inspires the many parallels between Dubai and the Asian ports of Singapore and Hong Kong.

The Jebel Ali Free Zone began as a 10,000-hectare facility (with 42,000 square meters dedicated for cold storage) for transshipment and re-export, particularly for goods passing along the East Asia-Europe corridor (Broeze 1999: 178). As the percentage of import/export for Dubai and the Gulf region hinterland grew, there was an increasing need for processing and assembly functions in the Free Zone. Restrictive land laws prevented foreign companies from owning land.[3] In 1984, Abu Dhabi passed the Commercial Companies Law, based on the *kafil* system, which stipulated the only way for international firms to set up offices or factories throughout the UAE was through complex sponsorship agreements with local entities, wherein the local firms would assume 51 percent ownership (Davidson 2008: 114). With the establishment of the Free Zone in 1985, Sheikh Rashid was able to sidestep the federal law by allowing international firms to rent warehouse and small processing facilities in Dubai without having to find sponsorship. As Michael Pacione describes:

> Jebel Ali free zone [opened] in 1985 as an enclave where businesses could operate outside Dubai's customs and legislative barriers and benefit from a ready

3 The 1960 Land Law of established that non-nationals could not own land in Dubai, similar to the Kuwaiti land law which had already been passed. The 2002 Land Law in Dubai established freehold areas where non-Emiratis could own land, but this was primarily for residential development.

> supply of low wage non-unionized labor. By 1992, Jebel Ali accommodated 480 firms from 56 countries, and by 1995, this figure had increased to 800 firms from 72 countries, and included many major multinational corporations such as Nokia, Daewoo and Reebok seeking to penetrate the markets of the Arabian Gulf-Arab World. The number of firms in the Jebel Ali free zone has continued to increase, reaching 1633 in 1999 and 2051 by 2002 ... The shift to higher value added manufacturing is evident in the Jebel Ali free zone where, as the economy has matured, attempts have been made to attract more high technology industries, (such as assembly of computers and electronic equipment), and to phase out labor intensive industries, (such as textile processing), dependent on expatriate labor (2005: 257).

Thus the character of logistics and manufacturing activities have changed over time, just as the profile of the port and Dubai's economic aspirations have changed.

The free port tradition and policy began in 1904, and continued with Port Rashid, but it took on greater spatial significance with the Jebel Ali Port, Industrial Area, and Free Zone. The British free zone policy, exemplified in the region by the port of Aden under British direction, was certainly also a factor that influenced Dubai's free port and free zone policies at Port Rashid and Jebel Ali. The free zone also recalls Dubai's original morphological structure, where the areas of Deira and Bur Dubai still fell under ultimate control of the ruler, but these small settlements within the greater town were under the local leadership and jurisdiction of their merchants. I will explore the evolution of those leaders into the present holding company leadership of Dubai below, but the free zone is an important example of how spatial organization and political and economic policy mutually informed one another throughout Dubai's development.

Competing Infrastructure in the 1980s

The ambition of Sheikh Rashid's cluster of trade and industrial projects grew throughout the 1970s, superseding first the scale of regional projects, and then, with Jebel Ali, outdoing the scale of any comparable global project. At the time, however, industry experts worried that these projects were overambitious and would become "white elephants." While Jebel Ali Port signed an agreement with Sea-Land Services to manage the port, Dubai initially had difficulty finding a company to manage the Dry Dock (Walker 1984: 192). Concerns over local operating capacity were matched with the potential of Gulf port oversupply as a result of the construction boom precipitated by 1973, due to a general lack of regional project coordination and "an atmosphere of uncertainty, not least because the similar resource base of many of the Gulf States has led each government to invest in broadly similar, often replicated enterprises" (Walker 1984: 190).

Indeed, the Dry Dock project could be seen as simply an expanded version of the Bahraini Arab Shipbuilding and Repair Yard (ASRY), which had opened years earlier; the Dubai Aluminum Company (DUBAL) at Jebel Ali was modeled on Aluminum Bahrain (ALBA), which also predated it; and the Jebel Ali Port itself was very similar to the ambitious Saudi port projects of Jubail and Yanbu. Concerns regarding oversupply were well-founded, and this resulted in rate-cutting competition throughout the region in the early 1980s when oil prices fell (Walker 1984: 195). "By the early 1980s laid up tonnage, especially tanker and dry-bulk, reached record levels (internationally) and was reflected in low levels of activity at many ports which only a few years earlier had been frantic in their efforts to expand facilities to accommodate rapidly increasing trade" (Hoyle and Hilling 1984: 6). Economists refer to these cyclical ebbs and flows as longer-term Kondratieff cycles, to which international trade is equally susceptible (Hanappe and Savy 1981). What could not have been predicted, however, was the Iranian revolution in February 1979, and the subsequent conflict between Iran and Iraq throughout the 1980s that solidified Dubai's geographic position in the lower Gulf as a transshipment center for the entire Gulf Cooperation Council (GCC)—the larger regional council formed in 1981 specifically to confront the regional economic downturn of the period.

Attacks on commercial ships in the Gulf during the Iran-Iraq War opened an opportunity for Dubai to receive international cargo flows and re-route them for local and regional distribution (Pacione 2005: 257, Walker 1984: 183). So while fluctuating oil prices would still greatly affect Dubai's growth rate (particularly compared with its vertiginous numbers of the 1970s), regional conflict, in its own way, provided a degree of economic stability for Dubai by bringing increased regional trade through its ports. Dubai was able to take advantage of events within the region, identify them as opportunities for their own benefit, and provide both facilities and policies to capitalize on these trade-related opportunities, similar to the previous experiences with Lingah and Aden. With the Iran-Iraq conflict, increased transshipment throughput was redirected to Dubai's two ports away from Iran and Iraq, and Kuwait, by offering safer port conditions. The United States Navy began to use Jebel Ali as a regional port for its ships during the 1980s (today it is the most frequented non-US port in the world),[4] thus offering the military protection to the port. A port's security has always been essential to its success, and the United States protection helped to assure Jebel Ali's success during this otherwise tumultuous regional moment.

Metropolitan Trade Apotheosis

Jebel Ali was successful in spite of recessionary downturns and the fall in regional oil prices during the 1980s. The various components that make up the Jebel Ali

4 See Global Security. Available at: http://www.globalsecurity.org/military/facility/jebel-ali.htm. A laundry and swimming pool facility is located at the Jebel Ali for the US Navy called the Kasbah Liberty Center, run by the United Services Organization (USO).

megaproject mark a definitive "before and after" moment for Dubai. As I have explained over the past two chapters, Sheikh Rashid forged a development blueprint even before oil was discovered through large-scale, muscular engineering projects that sought to lead and guide urbanization. Creek dredging, bunding, and reclamation allowed larger ships, and thus greater trade flows, to access the creek, which brought the construction materials to extend the city on the reclaimed surfaces along the creek. Trade increased, and the creek airstrip moved from water on to land with a new airport in the early 1960s. Heavier port activity moved from the creek to Port Rashid at the end of the 1960s. Ancillary trade services were also packaged (or "clustered," in Porter's terms) with these new facilities to include a dry dock, a trade center, and isolated residential areas (beginning in Jumeirah and then moving outward) for ex-patriot, Dubaian, and low-income communities. Oil revenue allowed Sheikh Rashid to realize his grandiose projects. Harris's second plan attempted to contain and channel new projects and investment within a similar transportation armature as he had done in his first plan, albeit expanding out wider from the creek. The World Trade Center was the first project to move beyond the dictates of the second plan, along with the National Cement Company, and each, in their own way, influenced the Jebel Ali project.

The scalar ambition of the World Trade Center, to be the tallest building in the Middle East, matched Port Rashid's parallel status after its extension as the biggest port in the Middle East. The Cement Company, located at the Al-Quoz industrial area designated in the second plan, crept toward the southwest, and its different components worked together strategically, demonstrating programmatic intensification by using fuel from offshore oil to produce cement. These machinistic qualities were then further manifest in the Jebel Ali Port and Industrial Zone, with the various industrial components fueling one another, and the port receiving many of the international material inputs for production. Jebel Ali's scalar ambitions—the largest man-made port in the world—clearly followed a kind of marketing hyperbole rather than demand-side numbers.

In this regard, Jebel Ali was all the more indicative of Sheikh Rashid's understanding of urbanism and urbanization as a series of clustered, strategic, infrastructures-within-infrastructure. The scaling back of the fuller development ambitions of the Jebel Ali New Town demonstrated his development priorities: Urbanism reduced to clear, modern, discrete interworking parts, instrumentalized toward the objective of trade, production, and economic gain. The scale of the Jebel Ali project gives one the impression that all of Sheikh Rashid's previous infrastructural endeavors—land dredging and reclamation, industrial areas, trade facilities (including logistics sheds at Port Rashid), residential development, hotel infrastructure for tourism, free port policies, and the airport—were all smaller sketches for the master work that was to be Jebel Ali Port, Industrial Area, and Free Zone. If infrastructure is traditionally understood in urbanism as a blanket element to guide development through systems located underground (water), at ground (roads), or above ground (electricity), within a modernization process, Jebel Ali is a clear example of infrastructure as epic; infrastructure as monument;

infrastructure as growth corridor (including the systems of roads, water, electricity), and growth axes (the creek and then Sheikh Zayed highway); and infrastructure as growth pole, as Doxiadis's plan wisely observed.

Furthermore, returning to Mary Ann Tétreault's point in Chapter 3, Jebel Ali, in her terms, reflects the "sometimes reinforcing sometimes antagonistic processes of industry and business" (2000: 111). Tétreault believes business is defined by the kind of individual gain derived from "differential accumulation," and industry as "the planning and construction of a complex of material processes and subprocesses" (Ibid.) for wider societal gain and development. The ambitious scale and strategic rate-cutting policies, along with the acumen to replicate services of Aden, marked a clear business inspiration for the Jebel Ali mega-project, while the industrial advantages of the project, the complexity of infrastructural components, and eventually, the human capital required to run the port, industrial area, and free zone demonstrated wider industriousness. Joint management of the Dubai ports was taken over from Sea-Land at Jebel Ali and Grey Mackenzie at Port Rashid in 1991, when it formed its own Dubai Port Authority. If these processes were mutually reinforcing, when they were at odds, at least in the short term, the business motivation seems to have influenced decisions for Jebel Ali with greater weight.

Contemporary Planning Challenges

In spatial terms, this division of business and industry could also be divided into the cellular "city-within-city" models exemplified in Jebel Ali and subsequent megaprojects of the emirate, in contrast to more industrious (as Tétreault describes the term) overall development represented by Harris's master plans. If Harris's plans did not seek to overprescribe land-use or spatial regulation or limitation, Jebel Ali marks the end of any serious pretentions toward even loosely coordinating an emirate-wide master plan, although many such plans were commissioned after Jebel Ali was completed. This must be qualified to emphasize that project and megaproject planning has certainly occurred after Jebel Ali, but administrative and territorial repercussions of these megaprojects have generally had to be addressed emirate-wide by following afterward rather than projecting infrastructure planning beforehand. Jebel Ali demonstrated a pattern of a trade infrastructure megaproject that served as structuring agent and monument, extending the emirate's morphology to immediately include the entire coast between the two "dual cities," and allowing infill, with increased real estate value, to be completed afterward.

The challenges of this model codified at Jebel Ali—from a traditional planning perspective—are clear. By incorporating a free port and free zone regulatory measure that frees the port and free zone from regulatory or tax jurisdiction, the entire Jebel Ali project took on a parallel administrative independence. The origins of this, for the Jebel Ali example, must also consider that in contrast to subsequent marketing monikers that described what were essentially mixed-use construction projects, ("Planned Urban Developments" in the US), such as "Falcon City," "Internet City," "Academic City," "Health Care City" (Sarkis and Abulhasan 2005), Jebel Ali was in fact projected as a new city, in parallel to other new city projects of the region during the 1970s (Roberts 1979). Again, this underscores Sheikh Rashid's repeated tendency to closely follow regional trends. Over time, the Jebel Ali Free Zone, in conjunction with some of the original new town aspirations mentioned earlier, increasingly took on the regulatory role for planning, permitting, and construction within the Free Zone, along with all areas owned or controlled by the Ports, Customs and Free Zone Corporation.[5] The free zone model established at Jebel Ali has since proliferated into diversified information and service sectors over the past decade (an example being the Dubai Internet City, which is run under the jurisdiction of Dubai Technology, Electronic Commerce and Media Free Zone). The result of this has been the splintering of Dubai's municipal planning capacity, as many of these autonomous developments are also responsible for their own regulatory and permitting structures.

This kind of Balkanization of project planning, development, and administration has also influenced the real estate sector in Dubai. This pattern connects what Christopher Davidson calls the "old rentiers," whose wealth came from oil and oil-related industries, to the "new rentiers," focused more on the kinds of global F.I.R.E. services (Finance, Insurance, Real Estate) associated with the global city (Davidson 2008: 159, Sassen 1991). Muhammad al-Abbar was director-general of Dubai's Department of Economic Development in the 1990s, and as a confidant of Dubai's present leader Sheikh Mohammad bin Rashid Al Maktoum, was able to start his own property development company, Emaar Properties. In 1997, al-Abbar and Emaar announced the development of a 700-million dirham residential project and golf course to be called "Emirate Hills." With al-Abbar's favored status with Shiekh Mohammad, he was able to do two important things that previous residential developments had not beforehand: first, because property developers had complained at the time that the planning permitting process was too slow in the Dubai Municipality, and technocrats within the planning and permitting departments were holding back developments for higher up technocrats such as al-Abbas, Shiekh Mohammad personally oversaw the project and fast-tracked all administrative and/or regulatory structures in the Municipality. This essentially opened the path for "Emirate Hills," and future preferred fast-track, residential projects to do the same. Second, "Emirate Hills" publically flirted with the possibility of allowing non-GCC citizens to purchase property within the development, which openly countered the UAE land law which prohibited this, and "thus for the first time in the UAE's history, residential plots were being marketed not only for Emirati and GCC citizens, but also to 'those others who can either buy fully built-up villas or plots'" (Davidson 2005: 230). After "Emirate Hills," al-Abbas

5 The Civil Engineering Department (CED) regulates project planning and construction licensing.

and Shiekh Mohammad launched the "Westside Marina," which also opened up the possibility of liberalizing Dubai's land market to include non-GCC citizens to purchase plots, apartments, or villas. It would be two more years until the 2002 Land Law of Dubai officially stipulated that specific residential projects would allow foreign ownership, but the importance of the "Emirate Hills" precedent in helping to precipitate the 2002 law by challenging the non-GCC ownership precedent (though importantly, with the blessing and backing of Shiekh Mohammad) is clear. Dubai's more cosmopolitan history makes it all the more surprising that it took until 2002 to allow foreign land ownership, and in truth, it marked more of a snub toward Abu Dhabi's central land policy than Dubai's own. Both "Emirate Hills" and the "Westside Marina" projects openly encouraged the clear courting of an international, professional ex-patriot community, in the same way that Al-Gurg's first Jumeirah villas did, followed by the Jebel Ali Village project, with the additional caveat that these residential projects would be available for foreign ownership rather than extended leasing. Essentially, the new property law added a legal free zone framework to the previous residential project models to generate a new spatial commodity that would sidetrack municipal planning and regulatory processes and liberalize selected areas of the land market, in the same way that Jebel Ali's free zone policy removed it from legal and regulatory infringement from the Municipality. Similar to proliferation of the free zone model, developers would also eventually develop their own, in-house permitting and regulatory structures that were to be responsible for overseeing their own projects.

Thus as the free zone model was replicated into new sectors, including the real estate and service markets, similar kinds of autonomous, uncoordinated regulatory structures were essentially outsourced from the Dubai Municipality to the governing structures of these free zones and mixed-use residential developments. In this way, the proliferation of the free zone policy opened up new possibilities of jurisdictional administration, wherein the challenge is now to coordinate these different bodies, particularly around shared infrastructure such as electricity, water, and transportation. Dubai's current increased traffic, strained electricity grid and concerns over water supply are all testament to the dangers of this cellular model. By drawing on Palan and Abbott's work on the "competitive state," I demonstrate throughout the book that Dubai's competitive model has repeatedly served as motivation for programmatic and scalar intensification in new projects to outdo the capacity of their neighboring competitors. The cellular model of planning would seem to stem from a similar competition within Dubai, among its various public and quasi-public agencies, which is turned inward and against one another, generating challenges for agency and development coordination (Salem and Jarrar 2009). It is within this unregulated context that the Dubai real estate market, in parallel to the unchecked, accumulated debt Dubai borrowed to pay for these cellular developments, and even the larger international financial community, overleveraged investments and hit crises. In Dubai, territorial development served as the guide for domestic and international business interests, and each strategy—

territory and business—have always been intimately linked. It not surprising then that the contemporary condition has affected all of Dubai's economic sectors.

Beyond Jebel Ali

In 1991 management of Mina Jebel Ali and Port Rashid were joined when the Dubai Port Authority (DPA) was formed, which marked the end of Sea-Land's management of Jebel Ali and Grey Mackinzie's management of Port Rashid. Large-scale infrastructure projects, up to this point, had been structured around joint-venture models seeking international construction and management companies in the hopes that, over time, technology transfer and human capital training would occur and these functions would eventually be filled by Dubai and GCC citizens to replace the international (mainly European, Asian, or US) consultants and companies. There would continue to be human capital challenges for training Dubai citizens at the DPA, which were often filled by international workers, but the management company and structure passed on to Dubai, marking an important move toward capturing management funds within the emirate, and completing a final component of the port investment projects, over 25 years after the first surveys were commissioned for Port Rashid construction. Recalling Gerschenkron's point regarding the need to establish local institutions to accompany technological borrowing, the DPA signified a move toward institutional trade management development as a kind of structural "software," after the port "hardware" was complete. In 2001, DPA merged with Jebel Ali Free Zone Authority (JAFZA), Dubai Customs Department, and Dubai Ports World to form the Ports, Customs and Free Zone Corporation (PCFC), to further streamline port access and management with the logistics and light manufacturing of the free zone. This strategy offered a "one-stop shopping" service provision for import, export, and transshipment of goods in and out of Dubai, and made the ports more efficient and attractive for international trade (Jacobs and Hall 2007). In 2006, all of these components were folded into an overarching holding company called "Dubai World," which essentially added other transportation, logistics, light industrial activities and real estate components to PCFC, and is run by Sultan Ahmed bin Sulayem, who, like Muhammad al-Abbar, is part of the Sheikh Mohamed's inner circle of Director-Generals. While many half-jokingly refer to Dubai's ruling structure as "Dubai Inc.," Dubai World essentially is Dubai Inc., representing the majority of its local and international holdings and investment interests.

Dubai is often referred to as a kind of misplaced Asian tiger in the Gulf, and as discussed, Dubai has an important trade history with many South East Asian countries. The same kind of Dubai World Holding Company structure can be dated back to Singapore's Tamasek conglomerate, the Korean *chaebols*, and further to the Japanse *zaibatsu.* Each began as trade sector firms that slowly diversified over time into a multitude of sectors and acquired many assets. The Korean and Singapore

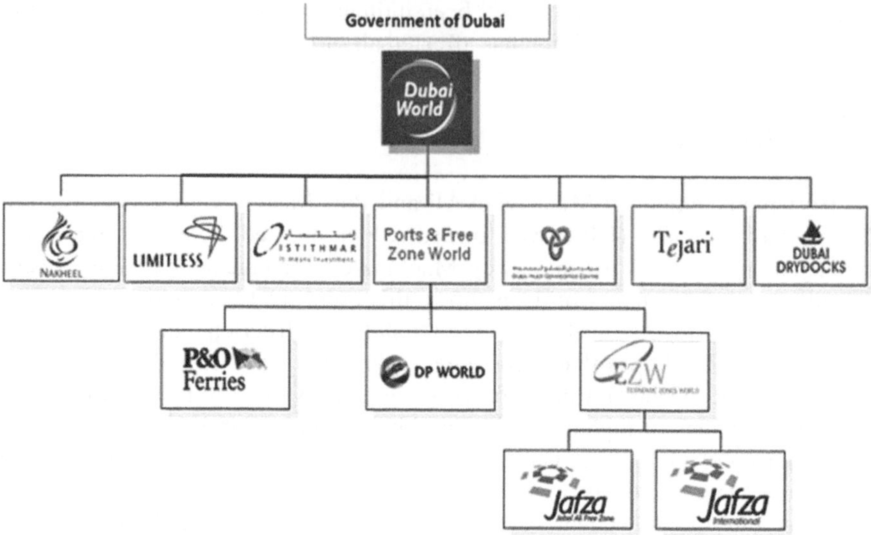

Figure 4.12 This organizational diagram outlines the principal operating subsidiaries held by Dubai World and is a simplified representation of the current legal structure of the Dubai World Group

Source: www.dubaiworld.ae

examples, of course, were central in precipitating the Asian financial crisis of the late 1990s, and were, in theory, restructured to avoid repeating the cross-subsidies and off-book wealth transfers among the various companies of the conglomerates (Nugée and Subacchi 2008, Ahmadjian 2006, Chang 2006, Tsui-Auch 2006). This kind of opaque bookkeeping to spread speculative investment and risk across many companies would also characterize Dubai World's practices, and was also a factor in the recent Gulf crisis. While there are clear contextual differences, each are characterized as conglomerates that began within developmentalist origins, enjoyed preferential state treatment and promotion in their own countries, and over time, became more interested in international private-market investment.

While it is beyond the scope of this book to go into details about the Dubai World business structure, it is important to note that since beginning as DPA back in 1991, incremental additions of different components, in many ways, can be understood in parallel to the same clustering strategy in Dubai that found its spatial expression in the Jebel Ali Port, Industrial Area, and Free Zone. The bundling of trade (port), residential (beginning with Jebel Ali Village), tourism (beginning with Jebel Ali Hotel), logistics and light manufacturing (within the free zone) infrastructures at Jebel Ali served as a template, which was then followed in the clustering of companies within the larger Dubai World Holding Company, both domestically and internationally. JAFZA has its international counterpart in JAZFA

International, DP World, which originally took over port management of Jebel Ali and Port Rashid, is now the world's fourth largest port, and Limitless served as one of the international property development companies of Dubai World. In general, these companies all encounter international development opportunities, and once they have found an investment they can then strategically look for investment opportunities for one of the other arms of the holding company. If DP World is managing the port of Djibouti, it can also investigate logistics opportunities for JAFZA International, with ancillary residential opportunities for Limitless, as has actually been the case. Located just across the Gulf of Aden from what was once the British key *entrepôt*, Dubai has indentified Djibouti as an important location for its multi-faceted portfolio trade investments, and this kind of strategy can be replicated wherever one of Dubai World's companies finds a new opportunity.

In addition to the clustering of components within the Dubai World business strategy inspired by the Jebel Ali precedent, the spatial reproduction of the Jebel Ali project is also occurring in Emaar projects internationally. The King Abdullah Economic City (KAEC) in eastern Saudi Arabia is a new city project that is currently being built on the Red Sea coast, 100 kilometers north of Jeddah and 200 kilometers south of Yanbu. A round of Gulf new cities flourished during the recent boom decade, in parallel to the oil-boom new cities of the 1970s. Contemporary new cities sprang out of the similar circumstances: increased oil revenue due to the steady increase in crude prices (peaking this time in the Summer 2008); the need to manage this wealth and curb inflationary currency pressures; the objective of diversifying investment into n with infrastructural investment, which combines the highly speculative risk/return of real estate with infrastructure's more sound, risk-averse investment. Phasing for the KAEC begins with the seaport and industrial zone, along with two small residential areas, much in the same way the PTCT planned the first phase of the Jebel Ali New Town, and more obviously, the seaport for the KAEC uses the same form and scale as the Jebel Ali port. In a conversation with the designer, he mentioned that he simply transplanted the Jebel Ali port design. Taking into account that Dubai's Emaar is designing the city, it is not surprising that they are merely reproducing what they know from experience at Jebel Ali (Beehler 2008). A contract has already been signed agreeing that DP World will manage the port. Subsequent phases add new residential quarters and a kind of downtown center on the waterfront, similar again to the PTCT's Jebel Ali plan. The parallel circumstances are also comparable given the fact that a severe decrease in the oil prices, along with a depression in the international financial system, could significantly scale back the ambitions and timeline for KAEC, as occurred in the early 1980s throughout the Gulf, and particularly with the Jebel Ali New Town. It is important to underscore, however, that the Jebel Ali model, along with its components, can now be bundled into an urban package that can be delivered by one company.

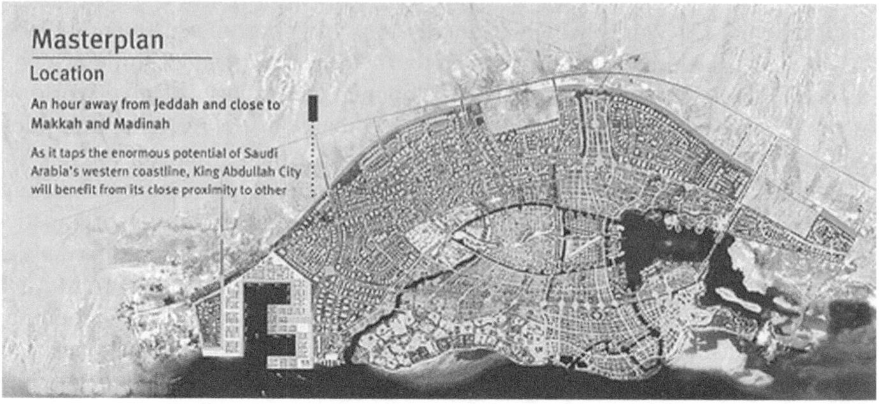

Figure 4.13 Emaar's King Abdullah Economic City Master Plan. Port facilities on the left, with industrial facilities around the perimeter of the development and residential areas along the central waterfront

Source: Emaar King Abdullah Economic City

If the KAEC project is scaled back, the first phase assures the same kind of urbanization priority of trade infrastructure, logistics, and light industry as exemplified by Jebel Ali's first phase, with the associate army of consultants, similar to PTCT, already at work imagining and designing the future city on ready-made models that are now easily transferable. The difference, of course, is that now Dubai no longer imports the idea and model from Yanbu of Jubail in Saudi Arabia, as in the 1970s, but exports the model and design back to Saudi Arabia, in the form—literally—of Jebel Ali and its components, through the Dubai Emaar developer.

Finally, back to Dubai, in the area just south of the Jebel Ali Port and Free Zone, Dubai World Center announced that it would develop an enormous airport city, whose scale is 140 square kilometers (10km by 14km)—twice the size of another international *entrepôt*, the city of Hong Kong—and will be joined to the port by an extension to the Jebel Ali Free Zone, which will be called Jebel Ali South. Again, echoing the press and circumstances of the 1970s port construction, in response, the *Middle East Airport Exchange* trade journal announced that the Gulf Cooperation Council (GCC) has 59 active airport construction projects worth a total of $17 billion, stating that it is one of the few regions of the world with plans in place to meet the demands of continued growth in air travel, which will help it to avoid what the International Air Transport Association has described as a "looming infrastructure crisis." The article continued by identifying the DWC Al-Maktoum International Airport as "far and away the biggest, with a 12 million ton annual cargo capacity, three times the capacity of Memphis International Airport [today's largest cargo hub], and 120 million passengers per year, almost 50 percent more than Atlanta's Hartsfield-Jackson International Airport [the world's busiest passenger airport]" (*Middle Eastern Airport Exchange* 2007: 31). The DWC project becomes the scalar amplification of the Jebel Ali Port, Industrial Area, and Free Zone, with associate programmatic intensification, informed by supply-side motivation to loosely outdo any other similar project in the world, and then plan backward from those objectives. The DWC web site promises that the new agglomeration construction at Jebel Ali will "eventually be home to 900,000 people, with infrastructure costs estimated at $33 billion, and will be comprised of six specialized clustered zones: Al-MaInternational Airport, Dubai Logistics City, DWC Commercial City, DWC Residential City, DWC Aviation City and DWC Golf City," and thus, a "true 'city-within-a-city.'"

In this way, the airport that was to accompany Jebel Ali Port and Industrial Area when it was conceived in 1976 will finally be constructed, with ancillary services and components that can now carry the requisite "city" suffix to accompany it, and all permitting and regulatory mechanisms to be handled by DWC, not the Dubai Municipality. The scalar ambitions of the Al-Maktoum Airport continue the "largest in the world!" strategy, and with extensive real estate options, the development, again, is a diversified investment portfolio with risk spread through speculative and conservative elements, and most importantly, has a large-scale trade infrastructure with free port policies at its core. The Al-Maktoum Airport is also under construction precisely as the Dubai International Airport has just been expanded, as was the case when Jebel Ali's construction coincided with Port Rashid's expansion. Furthermore, just as Sheikh Zayed Road became the second urban spine, after the creek, when the Jebel Ali Port was constructed, it seems likely that with the new DWC Airport City development and other large-scale leisure and residential projects (Dubailand, Falcon City, etc.), Emirates Road will assume this central structuring function for new development as the emirate's third urban spine, albeit *ex post facto* for the development that has already occurred along this axis.

In the face of what is being called a catastrophic contemporary crisis for Dubai, surely the Al-Maktoum International Airport will be built on the new DWC site, though it has yet to be seen what will happen with the other projected "cities" of the project. If Jebel Ali can be a reference for the contemporary DWC plan, as I argue it should, one can predict that if not now, these component developments simply have to wait until the next oil boom of the region, when another new city project will be devised to include those strategic components left out of this round of city building, along with a future ancillary elements to help package the new city.

The Legacy

Jebel Ali was originally imagined as the new capital city for the future UAE that was still being negotiated among the sheikhdoms in 1968. Ten years later, under construction, the project was drastically rethought, such that Dubai and the rest of the emirates ceded permanent capital status to Abu Dhabi. In the same way Abu Dhabi had to cede land claims in 1968 to achieve the goal of a unified UAE, Dubai acceptance of Abu Dhabi's leadership position established a relative autonomy within a looser federation structure. In the process, Jebel Ali would also lose its airport and the urban appendage that the PTCT plan had envisioned next to the massive port and industrial area. In their place, after the primacy of the port and industrial areas, the free zone was built and opened in 1985 to help enhance Jebel Ali's service profile for maritime trade. The late 1970s and early 1980s marked the first time that Dubai's post-oil development confidence was sobered by an international recession and the fall in oil prices, but these conditions helped bring Sheikh Rashid's infrastructural urban development priorities to the fore, and elucidate the patterns of Dubai's urban history from its modern origin. Indeed, almost 15 years before the DWC airport city and the Waterfront City were announced to essentially resume with plans originally laid out for Jebel Ali, in the intervening years Dubai developed the management structure (DPA, Ports, Customs and Free Zone Corporation, Dubai World) that could begin to strategically leverage the hardware infrastructure built up over the last half century. The Jebel Ali Port, Industrial Area, and Free Zone, as a cumulative expression of the infrastructural development up to 1976, would also become the model upon which the management structure's development was based.

The force and impact of Jebel Ali on Dubai's territorial organization and growth coordinates were definitive. Jebel Ali served as a growth pole, and established a growth corridor that would guide infill development through today. Accepting that outward-looking, large-scale trade infrastructural facilities—beginning with the creek (which was engineered as a project with the original dredging, and continued with its artificial extensions) and continuing with Dubai International Airport, Port Rashid, the World Trade Center, Jebel Ali, and the future Al-Maktoum International Airport—have defined Dubai's development processes, the emirate is best understood as a port geography, whose ancillary sectors and ambitions grow out of this central trade function. This was codified with the ambition and realization of Jebel Ali and all its components, and emphasized all the more by the development priorities that emerged once the project was scaled back.

Jebel Ali's legacy also includes the definitive abandonment of master planning pretentions, opting for mega-projects with autonomous spatial logics (reflecting Jebel Ali) and their own administrative bodies to regulate and govern their processes. Just as the port's free trade policies could be applied to service sectors, real estate developments, modeled on Jebel Ali Village, could eventually assume this autonomous (infrastructural) character as well. Chapter 5 will reflect further on the larger patterns of urban development in Dubai over time, but one cannot speak of these patterns without recognizing the Jebel Ali Port, Industrial Area, and Free Zone as their maximum expression to date, and the definitive project that marked a "before and after" point for the emirate.

Chapter 5
Borrowing, Replication, Amplification

> I do not regard the UAE as occupying a fatally disadvantageous position because of its status as a "late developer." Indeed, given the rising fluidity in the world economy, late developers with positive financial flows from oil and gas exports and gifted leadership able to sidestep likely and unlikely pitfalls find themselves in advantageous positions. Their "advantages to backwardness" come from being able to skip "stages" in industrialization to take advantage of the newest technology and, more important, to benefit from the experience of others. Although no country can expect to find a perfect development strategy in the history of its predecessors, it can approach that history as a repertoire of experiments, some successful others not. An understanding of what worked and why, or what didn't work and why, should be of value to the UAE policy makers charting the course of their nation into the always uncertain future (Tétreault 2000: 109, Gerschenkron 1962).

When reflecting on Dubai's urban development processes over the past century, patterns emerge in the physical evolution of the emirate's morphology and the parallel political and economic development choices and investments made by the ruling regime. In the face of urban expansion, conventional planning—which first appeared during the late 1950s with Harris's first master plan and the founding of the technocratic Dubai Municipality—has given way to a predominance of interrelated large-scale infrastructural developments with separate administrative systems, most of which are responsive to a matrix of global flows of goods, services, and capital. Since the World Trade Center, and more definitively with the Jebel Ali Port and Industrial Zone, development conforms not to an overall master plan, but rather each specific swath of development has its own internal logic and environmental character, the sum total of which appears as a yet-to-be-completed mosaic. Over the past 30 years, once a successful form for a particular type of development has arisen it has become emulated for subsequent developments of a similar kind. Within specific moments during this process of replication aspects of the model have also been amplified; motivated since the World Trade Center project by a competitive, supply-side strategy, speculative in its nature, which initially strove to outdo regional infrastructural trade capacity and eventually began to compete, within these sectors, with the entire world. Thus the creek gave rise to Port Rashid, and then to the massive Jebel Ali Port; the "ground+nine" buildings along the creek led to the Dubai World Trade Center, and now to the Burj Khalifa (which is presently the tallest building in the world); the Dubai creek airstrip became the Dubai International Airport, and will soon become the planned Al-Maktoum International Airport (world's largest planned passenger and cargo airport); the Palm Jumeirah to the proposed Palm Jebel Ali, Palm Deira, "The World" islands, and so on, across different kinds of development. Furthermore, this process of typological borrowing, replication, and amplification, once specific locational requirements have been satisfied, has allowed Dubai to closely mirror exogenous demands, remain open to present and future uncertainties, as well as to develop more or less at will, without the potential strictures of a predetermined master plan. The sum total of this urban development process has also become a kind of cumulative model, plotted diachronically and incrementally over this period through projects and strategies, to the point where the strategic clustering of investments (consolidation) and the spatial replication and amplification of projects (urban expansion) occur simultaneously and mutually intensify one another.

The last three chapters analyzed Dubai's urban history through the particular lens of infrastructural development, with the argument that the Jebel Ali Port, Industrial Area, and Free Zone marked the decisive moment in this history where the mimetic replication of imported models along with self-referential, supply-side driven replication of trade infrastructure was amplified into *something else.* Jebel Ali projects not only changed the territorial organization structure of the emirate, but once leveraged, also became the example for strategic clustering for the business models that would develop first into the Dubai Port Authority, and eventually become the Dubai World Holding Company. With these histories recounted in the previous chapters, I will now elaborate on this argument more precisely by exploring the processes of typological borrowing, replication, and amplification as a meta-narrative for the history of Dubai's urban development already laid out.

Typological Borrowing

The import of architectural and urbanism styles in foundational or equally decisive moments of nation-building is by no means a new phenomenon. Thomas Jefferson, third president of the United States and author of the United States' Declaration of Independence, was clearly involved in founding a new nation, but his famed Monticello borrowed heavily from classical Palladian architecture. Washington, DC's national architecture also looked to classical monumental style for guidance. Even modernism's best example of a new foundational capital, Brasilia, demonstrates an imported geometry and structuring axis that nods to Versailles, but also to the same kind of classical geometry represented in Washington, DC. The examples are too numerous to mention, simply because the moments of nation-building and political change rarely coincide historically with moments of architectural or urban formal innovation, at least not at their beginning. Moreover, when there is an urgency in building construction and urban development, as often is the case within a nation-building project, this kind of typological borrowing and replication demonstrates an essential pragmatism that accompanies the pretense of the modern state. If this is true for architecture and urbanism, it is even more the case for engineering, which is fundamentally functionalist in nature. The replication of the above-mentioned examples follows the kind of symbolic replication exemplified by Camillo Sitte's desire for historicism, and the need to design buildings and cities with their appropriate classically or historically defined typology to fit their functions.

Since Dubai's foundation in 1833, borrowing and imitation have been an important part of its development processes. Dubai was less influenced by historic typologies, and instead looked to functional, infrastructural typologies and strategies to replicate, motivated by a competitive streak that through some form of differential sought to outdo those from whom they borrowed. Dubai and its leadership have proven to be close followers of regional trends, from Lingah, Aden, Kuwait, Bahrain, and their UAE brethren, and took advantage of its "latecomer" status. Dubai's borrowing would take many forms, but throughout its boom period of the past half century it has been essentially incremental, reactive, strategic, and competitive in nature. Whether the result of capitalizing on an historical event or policy change within the region, as was the case with Lingah and Aden, or capacity competition with a neighboring or international infrastructural project, Dubai's investment has repeatedly sought exogenous inspiration as the measure by which to chose and then judge its own development strategies, typologies, and pace. This is not to deny the importance of local politics, for clearly courtly political positioning (albeit publically opaque) played a role in the decision-making process, along with political and financial negotiations with Abu Dhabi, but once an investment decision was made, external models were sought out and then identified as references from which to borrow.

At the beginning of the twentieth-century, Dubai was able to import the free port policies of Lingah when the Persian regime imposed punitive taxes on its merchant class (particularly affecting the Indian Banians). As a result, Dubai was able to attract trade, the trade community, and the important British steamer trade routes that Lingah had enjoyed during the late nineteenth-century. The Persian community brought their "wind tower" architectural typology to the Bastakia neighborhood located west of the creek, which is now an historic preservation theme park for Dubai tourism. Those who were considered citizens of Dubai during various waves of immigration would fluctuate during different periods, but immigration is certainly part of this importation of styles and cultures, and Dubai's cosmopolitan merchant character absorbed these kinds of disparate traits from its beginnings.

If Persia was an inspiration for Dubai in terms of immigration, commercial strength, and free port policies, Dubai borrowed even more heavily from its northern neighbors of Kuwait and Bahrain, largely because of their similar regional characteristics and historic circumstances. Kuwait and Bahrain were the "first-comers" in this development profile, which included port primacy in pre-oil urban development, oil (and sometimes natural gas) discovery, the large revenues from these natural resources, small populations and the need for immigrant labor, and patrimonial developmental governments with essentially open commercial ethos and histories of international trade (Owen 2008, Broeze 1997a). The Dubai *majlis* revolt in 1938 was inspired by similar *majlis* revolts in both Kuwait and Bahrain due to the same political economic effects of the decline of the pearling sector, though the revolts were arguably more successful for Dubai's northern neighbors. Dubai's own banking infrastructure, beginning in 1963 with the founding of its National Bank of Dubai, was specifically modeled on the National Bank of Kuwait, for which advisors from Kuwait were flown in to help set up. Oil discovery in Kuwait and Bahrain also moved gold trade southward. Gold trade continues today in Dubai, but its oil discovery also changed the emirate's dependence on bullion as the sole palliative for lost pearling between the 1930s and 1966.

The British Gulf presence during the nineteenth and twentieth-century was an important factor that linked Dubai, Kuwait, and Bahrain, through the political connections, banking institutions such as the BBME, and also through the consulting and engineering firms working in the area. Both the John Harris and Sir William Halcrow firms were working in Kuwait before accepting work in Dubai (Humaid Al Tayer 1999, Cordery 1979b), and the Kuwaiti International Development Fund offered the initial capital that helped Sheikh Rashid complete the creek dredging and widening in the late 1950s. The subsequent large presence of British CEDOs in the Gulf after oil discovery, and particularly after the 1973 oil crisis, was also an important factor in the mercurial import/export of developmental and infrastructural ideas.

If the import/export of developmental ideas arrived to Dubai from Bahrain and Kuwait as a "latecomer," it should also be underscored that part of this tendency to imitate ideas was also motivated by the Janus face of competition/cooperation that defined Dubai's complex relationships with its Gulf neighbors. Dubai's foundation began as a breaking away from Abu Dhabi, and border wars and federal brotherhood marked the complex dynamics between Dubai and its capital partner. In their relationship, Dubai assumed a more cosmopolitan, merchant-minded position in contrast to Abu Dhabi's more conservative, insular orientation. Abu Dhabi's great oil wealth, discovered before Dubai in 1958, helped to solidify its insular orientation. Nevertheless, it was Abu Dhabi, through the emirate federation, that played an important role in helping Dubai either secure or leverage funds for many of its large-scale infrastructural projects during the 1970s that helped to bolster Dubai's international profile. Dubai, to some degree, helped its northern Sharjah emirate neighbor in a similar manner until it too discovered oil in 1973, but there was a clear history of competition between the two emirates that accompanies its collaboration. From arguments through the British political agencies over airport rights and competing creek dredging for primary southern Gulf *entrêpot* status, to more recent reluctance to allow Dubai workers to live in Sharjah (though eventually revoked) to prevent emigration of Dubai workers who sought cheaper housing to the north, competition has been a strong motivational factor for each emirate's development strategy.

This is essentially the same replication competition mentioned in the previous chapter. Dubai's development strategy replicated regional trade or industrialization projects, and through either price or capacity differentiation, sought to do what its neighbors were doing, although in a more competitive way to win regional business and investment: the Dry Docks project as an expanded version of the Bahraini Arab Shipbuilding and Repair Yard (ASRY), the Dubai Aluminum Company (DUBAL) at Jebel Ali as an expanded Aluminum Bahrain (ALBA), the Jebel Ali Port and Industrial Area *vis-à-vis* Saudi's Jubail and Yanbu, and so on. Furthermore, within Dubai's own history, oil exploration and air landing rights were the initial infrastructural pursuits that tilted monetary dependency and power advantage away from the *majlis* to favor the ruler. This demonstrates both the logical advantage that Sheikh Rashid saw in continuing the infrastructural urban development with which he had secured power over the *majlis*, and also the same kind of regional competition exemplified in differential replication, displayed shrewdly at the local level.

More recently, of course, the obvious significance of borrowing is in the financial sense: the large amount of money Dubai borrowed from international sources to fund speculative local development projects and acquire international diversified assets. While Dubai World searched the globe for port management, logistics, and real estate opportunities, the investment arm of the holding company, Istithmar, went shopping. Istithmar purchased stake in Barneys of New York, Cirque du Soleil, W and Mandarin Oriental hotels, and even the Queen Elizabeth II luxury liner. Dubai raised money in international markets, borrowing high on short-term payment plans (Thomas Jr. 2009). Dubai World raised credit in both Islamic *sukuk* bond markets and the Western bond markets, heavily leveraging Dubai's foundational trade assets and services for speculative investment in real estate and finance sectors to increase its international portfolio command and diversity. Imprudent investment in volatile trophy assets would prove too heavy for the mantle. As mentioned, the conglomerate business model is itself a Southeast Asian import, and the contemporary Gulf crisis almost appears modeled on the same crisis that hit that region at the end of the previous decade. The latter, of course, was unintentional, but time will tell as to whether it can escape the current financial difficulties as some Asian countries were able to, or if it is destined to a kind of Japanese lost decade that country experienced in the 1990s.

Typological import, however, was only part of the larger development process that also included essentially modular repetition, programmatic intensification and periodic scalar amplification. These processes are best explored within the particularities of projects' territorial expressions in Dubai.

Replication/Amplification

The import of infrastructural, urban, and architectural ideas for Dubai's development borrowed specific typologies to first meet certain locational and demand requirements (though this eventually became more supply-side driven), after which the typology could then be replicated internally within Dubai in parallel with the replication of internationally-imported typologies mentioned previously. This kind of repetition parallels that infrastructural logic of repetition as an endless blanketed, prepared ground surface for development, but in this case, the infrastructural typological replication acted as both ground and modern (and modernization) monument. Typological repetition is usually understood as prototypical. While replication of typologies was prototypical during intervening periods within Dubai's development, this was accompanied by decisive moments where typologies were significantly amplified in replication, through programmatic intensification and scalar magnification, and transformed into a new, distinct typology. The product of typological amplification would then become its own new typology, which could be subsequently replicated and/or amplified further. But it is this distinction between mere prototypical or modular replication from a more complex inter-relation of typology, replication, and amplification that is important to establish.

Dubai's competitive spirit switched from demand-side planning and construction to supply-side strategies to offer a capacity differential, which again, were measured against regional or international parallel infrastructure projects. Oil revenue from Dubai's reserves, along with money borrowed from the UAE Central Bank (which was mainly funded by Abu Dhabi's immense oil wealth), enabled scalar amplification, and programmatic intensification was incorporated to central trade infrastructure through linkage and cluster development strategies. Dubai's import of certain regional typologies, and their subsequent replication, demonstrates its history as a close follower of regional trends and patterns. Sheikh Rashid developed a clustered portfolio of trade infrastructure assets that began by looking to previous regional examples of urban development in areas with similar cultural and economic profiles. The inclusion of basic infrastructure such as housing developments, banking institutions, mixed-used buildings (from those ground+nine buildings that lined the creek, to those that line Sheikh Zayed Road, to those that may spring from the new Burj Khalifa scalar typology) would indeed seem to simply be the rapid deployment of elemental structures of city-building in almost any context. In Dubai, however, this infrastructure development strategy, as the logic that fueled mimetic project replication, was combined with periodic amplification to compete with those same neighbors from who it borrowed developmental strategies and typologies. As a competitive state, Dubai sought competitive advantage in its trade sectors through either size and/or capacity differential, incorporating the latest technologies in each sector as part of its investment strategy. Spatially, Dubai amplified those typologies it imported in reaction to regional, and then global, criteria. Thus, its development was fundamentally reactive, and even Harris's flexible urban planning could not contain the mercurial dynamism of a development strategy that perpetually sought to attract international business through this borrowing/amplification process. Examples from Dubai's urban history help to illustrate this pattern.

The Creek

Sheikh Rashid first's dredging and widening of the creek in the late 1950s commissioned the British Halcrow group to carry out the large-scale engineering project. Sheikh Rashid contacted Halcrow through British political contacts in Kuwait, where Halcrow, British architect/planner John Harris, and the BBME all had previous experience. The funding for the dredging project came from the Kuwaiti International Fund. The 1960 Land Law that accompanied this project was based specifically on the recently-completed Sudanese land law after their independence from the British in 1956, and supervisors from Sudan were invited to advise the Dubai Municipality on the writing and implementation of the new land law. With planning and land regulations in place, the Dubai Municipality saw the strategic opportunity to reclaim land on the Deira side of the creek by using what was removed from the dredging project. This reclaimed land then became the corridor for office, hotel, and municipal development, which the municipality was in turn able to either lease or sell without having to buy out any existing landowner plots within Deira—one of the densest parts of the city. In 1986, Erhard Gabriel writes about the Deira development:

> During the past 20 years, about 50 high-rise buildings including hotels, banks, public services, company offices and shopping arcades were erected in the Bani Yas Road along the Creek and in the parallel road one block inland ... On the ground floors of these high-rise buildings are exclusive shops and elegant shopping arcades. Above these are two or three floors of offices, followed by up to five floors of apartments. This unusual vertical combination of residential and commercial activity within one building, together with hotels, entertainment, restaurants and offices, ensures the area remains lively night and day (1987: 12).

In effect, the southward development along the creek on this reclaimed land became the city's central business district, and the vertical programmatic diversity of the buildings reinforced a kind on interchangeability and repetition among the buildings. The land was reclaimed as an infrastructural surface on which to build this new urban corridor, and after the first building demonstrated success with vertical mixed-use, the typology was simply replicated with limited variation in form, height, and function. All in all, this development also conformed to Harris's 1960 plan, and 1965 height regulation of "ground plus nine."

The example shows several aspects of the urban development pattern in its nascent form, including the commissioning of international consultants (British, as was often the case) to carry out an ambitious engineering project. It originated from the initial request petitioned by the local *majlis* to increase trade capacity, but was imported typologically from Kuwait, which was already involved in a similar project. Excess earth from the dredging project could then be used to help reclaim and bund the two banks of the creek. Reclaimed land created new land and land value after the land law valorized this and all Dubai territory, which was

Figure 5.1 Examples of ground+nine buildings along the northeast bank of the creek. Photo also shows further creek dredging from the late 1960s

Source: Halcrow Archive

then retroactively leveraged and served as a guarantee on the Kuwaiti loan. Once the surface was established on each bank, the Deira bank, with its commercial history, was developed through typological and vertical programmatic replication, in a prototypical manner, during building construction. The new central business district was built, and the creek could thus accommodate more trade throughput, particularly in competition with Sharjah, whose creek was heavily silted but did not react as quickly. The example also demonstrates the beginnings of strategic clustering of projects, with the simultaneous physical expansion of the creek. In other words infrastructure, urbanization, and financial investments are consolidated precisely as the city and the creek are expanded.

Port Rashid

The pattern continued with the construction of Port Rashid, which expanded on the rudimentary berth and storage facilities of the creek. Again, the need for higher trade throughput prompted the commissioning of Halcrow to lead a joint

Figure 5.2 Aerial photo of Port Rashid extension, March 5, 1977
Source: Halcrow Archive

venture to engineer an amplified facility to accommodate trade demand. A second Harris master plan for the territorial organization of the city would contemplate new traffic patterns that the new port would produce. Thus Port Rashid both replicated and amplified strategic clustered development (from the creek) around a central, new large-scale trade infrastructure. It also marks a point at which the development strategy looks not only to regional or international examples for inspiration, but also begins to include self-referential examples to draw on as well, with the amplified trade vocation of the creek built as Port Rashid. The second Harris master plan amplified the scale and scope of his first. Similar to the "ground+nine" typological replication along the creek, "ground+one" villas were built and then replicated throughout Jumeirah as a new typology for housing ex-patriot consultants working on both Port Rashid construction and for the Dubai Petroleum Company only years after the city's first cement houses were constructed. Port Rashid's construction also incorporated ambitious dredging and land reclamation for approach and turn-channel facilities, which were also amplified for the construction of a container port during the Phase Two expansion at the end of the decade.

Within a very short period, Port Rashid opened in 1972 with 12 cargo berths that were immediately insufficient to handle the staggering new tonnage of imports, and it immediately had to be amplified exponentially so that by 1979 it had 37 berths. It is worth noting that Halcrow, in its 1965 report, suggested Port Rashid would require no more than four berths and dismissed Sheikh Rashid's

Figure 5.3 Aerial image of the Dry Dock and Ship Repair facility with Port Rashid and extension in background

Source: Cordery 1979b. Halcrow Archive

suggestion that at least ten should be built (Cordery 1979b). Nevertheless, it is also clear that these same engineering consultants were asked back repeatedly, project after project (even today). Though anecdotal, the example shows how Dubai's development pattern used consultant input similar to the way it sought exogenous projects or strategies as measures of its own ambitions. Supply-side motivations would then move projects and programs beyond those recommended by consultants, but their input was just that, a consultancy against which to test or develop project ideas. Some of these project ideas may have originated at the suggestion of consultants, but their realization strategies were plotted specifically along this accumulated development pattern. By this time, however, Sheikh Rashid's requests were still essentially based on demand-side numbers that could be planned and predicted. Thus Harris's second master plan could still be essentially implemented, as development in general followed predictable demand-side statistics and construction patterns that a master plan could still interpret, extrapolate, and express spatially.

World Trade Center

The break with Harris's second plan, and master planning overall, occurs after Queen Elizabeth's visit in 1972 to the international trade show at Dubai International Airport's newly-constructed terminal. The first of the ancillary facilities Sheikh Rashid decides to build in his cluster investment to expand trade—and by indivisible association, urban development—is the World Trade Center. Sheikh Rashid goes once again to John Harris, essentially his resident architect/planner, and asks Harris to design a building to be located at the mouth of the creek. By this time, the trade center could have punctuated the curtain of buildings along the Deira side of the creek and assumed a primary position as both the "leader" of these buildings and a beacon for the mouth of the creek, which was the symbolic urban origin of the city. Interestingly, when Harris presented Sheikh Rashid with a model of the proposed trade center complex, the ruler protested that the main building needed to be much taller; perhaps because of the inspiration of New York's trade center projects and its height aspirations (Humaid Al Tayer 1999). It was Harris who had both established construction height regulations of "ground+nine" for Dubai and had written the second master plan, and Sheikh Rashid was commissioning him to build a 39-storey building at the mouth of the creek, where Harris had already recommended construction of either a bridge or a tunnel to increase automobile crossing of the creek in general, and particularly for trade in and out of Deira to the new port. Surely on their own, neither of these two points would have prevented Sheikh Rashid from going ahead with these location and height choices for the trade center, but the true deterrent would come from another trade infrastructure project: the airport, and the flight pattern routes which would not allow for such a tall building in their paths. Given the choice between a more humbled, demand-side driven project at the mouth of the creek and the prospect of the tallest building in the Middle East, Sheikh Rashid, as we know, went with the latter, and accentuated the move by locating it beyond the outer limits of the city.

As a result of increased spatial demands and new technology, ports and airports throughout the world at this time were moving beyond city limits into their hinterlands for access to greater, cheaper land to be developed for trade and travel purposes (Hoyle 1996). Jebel Ali would mark this definitive move in Dubai, but the first step in this pattern began with the World Trade Center. In this regard, along with the obvious ancillary trade functions it served, the trade center also had the spatial qualities of large-scale trade infrastructure by initiating Dubai's push beyond its urban limits of the second master plan. Again, with the World Trade Center, similar to Port Rashid, Dubai incorporated a self-referential typology of "ground+nine" buildings replicated on the creek. With the supervision of an international consultant, it amplified the typology, with the difference that this amplification was no longer constricted by demand-side, market numbers, but rather competitively motivated to be the tallest building in the Middle East. In thinking back to Palan and Abbot's work on the "competitive state," the World Trade Center was both an architectural manifestation of this developmentalist shift to supply-side strategies, as well as an urban manifestation by growing the city southwestward beyond its boundaries and the dictates of Harris's second master plan.

Figure 5.4 Architect John R. Harris showing his initial model for the World Trade Center project to Sheikh Rashid

Source: John R. Harris and Partners

This point of superlative construction was discussed in Chapters 3 and 4, but it is important to consider this point historically within urban development. In the nineteenth-century, as is often quoted, the railway station became the new cathedral to modern transportation, industrialization, and capitalism, during moments of modern, formative nation-state and urban development, particularly in Europe and the United States. Once railway stations moved beyond the very basic structural functions of mere sheds to mark stopping points where the passengers and cargo would embark and disembark, their structures were understood essentially as a combination of two functions joined together: that of the "passenger building," which was considered to be the domain of the architect, and that of great "hall" or train shed, considered to be the responsibility of the engineer (Dethier 1978: 14). As the number of passengers increased rapidly throughout the century, the spatial demands on both the passenger building and the train shed also increased, requiring greater engineering muscle for extended horizontal expanse. In his seminal book *The Railroad Station: An Architectural History*, Carroll Meeks points out that similar to the race to build the tallest vertical building of the twentieth and twenty-first centuries after the Chicago skyscraper, the nineteenth-century construction race sought to build the most extensive horizontal train shed ceilings using the newest metals as they were available to engineers (1956: 65), and finer architectural design to deliver the kind of monumentality progressively associated with the new mode of transport. Thus, it is also important to underscore that though engineering consultants may have seen themselves as the rational agents modernizing the wealthy and extravagant sheikhs of the region, there is a definitive quality of engineering that, while emphasizing rational structural functionality, is equally driven by these ambitions of superlative construction hubris. The Burj Khalifa, now the tallest building in the world, is, of course, a product of this same waltz of a ruler's monarchical power and desire and the engineer's challenge to compete and outdo the abstract but irresistible challenging limits posed by global precedent.

Jebel Ali Port, Industrial Area, and Free Zone

Jebel Ali Port, Industrial Area, and Free Zone is a more dramatic example of infrastructural typological replication, whose amplification moved beyond the comparative sights of the Gulf and even the Middle East to become the largest port engineering projects in world history. Though the marine industrial development area model can be understood as an import from similar models in port cities of Japan and Europe, ambitious dredging and land reclamation were certainly not new to Dubai. Jebel Ali's industrial components drew on industries that were either oil derivatives or construction-related, similar to the industrial strategies of neighboring countries that had discovered oil before Dubai, and particularly the Saudi new industrial city projects of Jubail and Yanbu, and Umm Said in Qatar (Merlamid 1980: 474). The machinistic characteristics of the site itself amplify the inter-relation and working elements of Dubai's own National Cement Company, which was completed while Jebel Ali was under planning and construction. The port, of course, replicated Port Rashid, and is essentially the next amplification of Port Rashid's final construction of 37 berths, as Jebel Ali Port's 67 berths were originally planned to have 74 (Wilson 2006: 385, Peddle et al. 1977)—not coincidentally twice Port Rashid's size, which, at this point, was already the largest port in the Middle East. Here, as with the World Trade Center, the scalar motivation was clearly supply-side driven, with Dubai seeking to outdo both itself (doubling the Port Rashid expansion, which would be inaugurated the same day in 1979), and the entire world. The same kind of replication will occur with the future Jebel Ali Free Zone (JAFZA) South, which simply extends the Jebel Ali Free Zone beyond Sheikh Zayed road to a large inland plot.

The force of the Jebel Ali Port, Industrial Area, and Free Zone changed Dubai's territorial morphology definitively, becoming a growth pole to structure metropolitan expansion, as well as creating the second metropolitan development axis along the Dubai-Abu Dhabi road (eventually named Sheikh Zayed in honor of the Abu Dhabi ruler), which was specifically rerouted to accommodate the new port. Reflecting on the road connecting Dubai to Jebel Ali, Alexander Melamid wrote in 1980, "At present an unplanned ribbon-like strip of housing and services, mostly primitive, is developing along the highway that connects the city of Dubai … and Jebel Ali" (Melamid 1980: 473). The infill development along this new growth corridor occurred no longer under the direction of Harris's second master plan, but was essentially prototypical, with the World Trade Center serving as the replicated typology in building construction along each side of Sheikh Zayed Road (and accompanying parking garages directly behind the buildings), and the entire area of Jumeirah subdivided in a cellular manner for residential use. Following the specifications of Harris's second plan, along with the recommendations of the land law, the Jumeirah plots were all geometrically consistent, 1,000 square meters in size, and the construction essentially replicated the "ground+one" villas first built there for the expatriate community, but would eventually be inhabited by a mixed demographic of various incomes and ethnic origins. Some of the residential communities were originally designed as permanent housing for the traditionally nomadic Bedouin population of the emirate, in this similar prototypical housing block group manner, such as Saffa, Al Awir and Lisayli, which were built in the late 1970s (Gabriel 1987). As was the case with Deira, the housing settlements varied slightly in design, social composition, and size, but the striking similarity of these residential areas, again, follow prototypical designs that were replicated in many subsequent government and ex-patriot housing developments. Harris had warned of varying plot sizes as a possible obstacle to development in his second plan, and the grid logic of Jumeirah's residential development follows his recommendation to correct this. Jumeirah followed an extensive low-rise development pattern within the residential area. Though this was eventually broken by both the Burj-al-Arab and the Jumeirah Beach Hotel, it essentially retains this low-rise character today.

Figure 5.5 Saffa Villas development in Jumeirah
Source: Halcrow Archive

Jebel Ali Village

The 48 Jumeirah villas leased to DPC and Port Rashid expatriate consultants in the late 1960s were amplified into the Jebel Ali Village, which also catered to expatriate families and offered 300 villas, including community and retail facilities in the village center. The expanded Jebel Ali Village model, and the original Jumeirah villas, were not unsimilar to parallel oil company town expatriate settlements built by US and British companies throughout the mid-twentieth-century in neighboring Saudi Arabia and Iran, thereby fusing a self-referential replication/amplification of the Jumeirah villas with another imported regional model, which itself had been imported from company towns in the US and England. Emaar's "Emirate Hills" project in the late 1990s replicated the Jebel Ali Village model of modular residential units for high-end ex-patriot communities, with programmatic intensification by adding luxury golf facilities. This project amplified the income potential of the typology by pushing the UAE's legal framework and advocating non-GCC unit ownership, which would unlock financial leveraging potential and an entirely new ownership market for Dubai. "Emirate Hills" will certainly influence similar real estate models throughout the Gulf. Thus, after amplification, the typology originally imported from Britain and the US passes through Dubai, changes, and is then exported as something else, in parallel to the light assembly goods manufacturing and transshipment trade that occurs in Jebel Ali Port and Free Zone.

More recent projects, including "Jumeirah Lakes," "Business Bay," and the Palm Jumeirah also replicate the Jebel Ali Village's template of modular units, with the addition of the dredging and land reclamation to frame the real estate and increase its value. This too can be understood as yet another kind of amplification, though in fact, as we have seen, it marks the mere combining of two development strategies elaborated over time: large-scale earth/land engineering, originally executed to increase trade throughput, but which can now help create real estate value, and housing for an international professional class that must continue to be imported, for lack of local capacity, to meet Dubai's international business objectives. Again, it strategically combines two kinds of infrastructure, or infrastructure within infrastructure, to produce what can then be branded as "cities within a city."

In addition, using a similar logic of the original ex-patriot Jumeirah villas, the more conservative elements of the Dubai government are contented by isolating this international community so as to not influence local custom and practices, which this faction hopes to shield from such influence. The final effect also mirrors precisely the kind of visual preposterousness that continually fuels Dubai's marketing hyperbole to the world, but which is actually driven by clear historical development patterns that have been replicated and amplified over the past half century. This neither excuses nor justifies the deleterious environmental effects of this kind of development, nor the labor pact that makes it possible. It does demonstrate the muscular urbanism Dubai has developed over time, lead by engineering, replication, and amplification that exemplified a kind of spatial pragmatism, particularly for project delivery, and also for emirate territorial settlement in general

Nevertheless, the proliferation of off-sheet, high-end real estate projects and companies that characterized Dubai's recent boom period call to mind the same kind of Promethean projects that Konvitz used to described Swedish seventeenth-century port city planning that lead to its economic collapse. Moody's rating agency estimates Dubai's present debt at over $100 billion, of which Nakheel, the real estate company that promised the World, raised $60 billion to extend waterfront property development into the Gulf after the coast had been settled from Sharjah to Abu Dhabi. Since the 2008 market crash, Dubai property prices have reportedly fallen between 50 and 75 percent (Fattah 2009, Packard 2009). The fact that it is precisely the projects built on water that precipitated Dubai's debt crisis—the same ones that captured international attention with such bravado at the beginning of the new millennium—seems appropriate; almost Cartesian. Real-estate replication and amplification over the past decade underscores the important element of risk inherent in the development strategy: namely, that the wrong infrastructural element can be either over-replicated and/or over-amplified.

Bilateral Asymmetry

Though the project was eventually scaled back and most of the Jebel Ali New Town project was unrealized in its moment, the legacy of the dual urban system established a bilateral structure between the Dubai creek area and Jebel Ali. This essentially amplifies to emirate scale that same kind of bilateral structure centered around the creek in Harris's second plan, and further back to the morphology established on each side of the creek from its urban origins. With the projected emirate-scale structure, however, there was no pretense of symmetry between the Dubai and the Jebel Ali areas. Mirroring the doubling in size and capacity of Port Rashid with the Jebel Ali port, projected plans for the future of the southwestern area around Jebel Ali sought amplification, wherein a bilateral *asymmetry* distinguished Jebel Ali as an entirely amplified city-region, centered around the port and free zone. Within this structure, the center of the emirate is no longer symbolized by the original creek, but in an oddly appropriate way, is now marked by the first Palm Jumeirah project; as if to pay homage to the emirate's history of dredging and reclamation that were central to Dubai's infrastructural and urban development. It replaces the creek's eastward internal scope with an outward looking westward Palm, in a positive, replicated relief (with an exaggerated, megalomaniacal plastic element for good measure), thus moving the city's original cardinal-point crossing from the mouth of the creek, southwest, to the point where sea, central Palm, and the coast all meet.

The same way that Deira was the original commercial settlement and Al-Shindigah was the ruler's domain, Jebel Ali was originally understood as the industrial area, and Dubai would remain an administrative center. Modern spatial functional separation informed the Jebel New Town project, along with the port, industrial area, and free zone, and although this since changed to include the "city" suffix for branding and marketing, the spatial signifiers remain attempts at discrete spatial categorization, not unsimilar to zoning, but as mentioned in Chapter 4, without a sole agency or regulating body to coordinate these "cities."

The examples of this dual city model, projected in the Jebel Ali New Town but realized in the Jebel Ali Port, Industrial Area, and Free Zone, and with the reduced component of the Jebel Ali Village, are clearly both replicated and amplified in the future DWC airport city. This is where the Dubai International Airport, like Port Rashid, is also both replicated and amplified by the new Al-Maktoum International Airport and its associate airport city in the southwest. Though still a project that could yet be scaled back because of the current international financial crisis, the DWC plans incorporate all the elements of Jebel Ali, and turn them each into "cities."

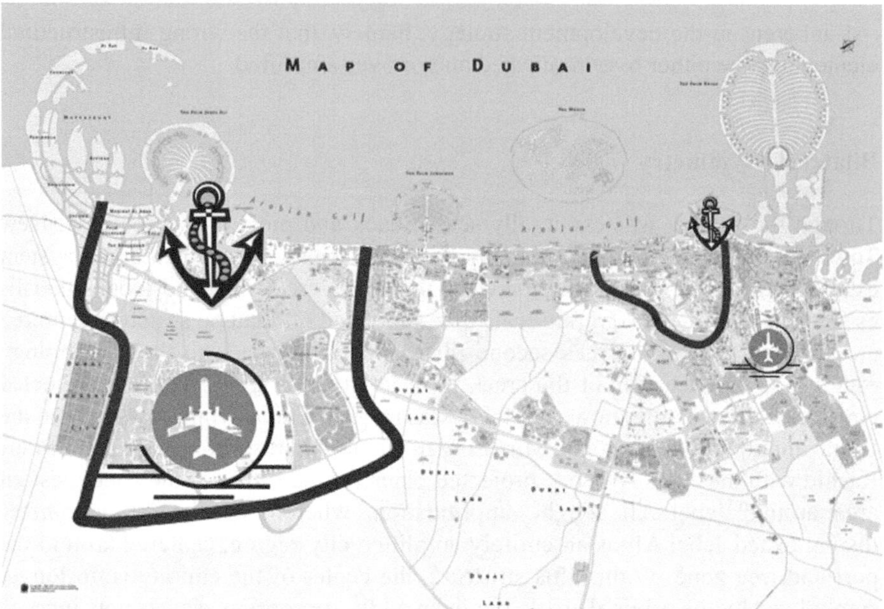

Figure 5.6 Dubai "bilateral asymmetry." Creek, Port Rashid and Dubai International Airport to the northeast and the projected Arabian Canal, Jebel Ali, and the projected Al-Maktoum International Airport to the northeast

The projected plot sizes of the southwest are also amplified, and although subdivision may occur as these plots are developed, the southwest area both amplifies and leaves behind the gridded plot uniformity of Jumeirah that was prescribed by Harris. The same is true for the "Arabian Canal," which was announced as a project to dig a creek through the southwest of Dubai, just as the original creek was also announced to be extended back to the coast in an inland "u" shape. Again, the amplified creek in the southwest was proposed at the same time the original creek was extended, just as Port Rashid was amplified while Jebel Ali was being built. Additionally, the Dubai International Airport has just completed its new facilities as Dubai is building the new Al-Maktoum International Airport. This replication/amplification strategy becomes the point where business consolidation and spatial expansion meet, and with the creek example, signify an ambitious engineering project that will serve as an infrastructure to serve specific economic objectives. While Port Rashid, Dubai International Airport, and even Jebel Ali Port and the future Al-Maktoum Airport all serve as infrastructure to increase trade and tourism throughput, the Arabian Creek was to serve as an infrastructural element to bring the coast inland, and create more waterfront property; the original creek's extension was to do the same. This continues the pattern of the original creek extension as a means to expand trade flows and ship access, and as a consequence create new land surface. Its additional function is that the canal would also create value for a sector of the new economy, namely real estate, and also serve as a future location for a second hydroelectric water desalinization plant. Thus it is yet another example of strategic clustering activities associated with large-scale engineering infrastructure projects, and by design, territorial organization.

Another legacy of the Jebel Ali New Town will be the amplification of the city it proposed southwest of the port, which is projected for development as "Waterfront City" to be designed by Rem Koolhaas. The semicircular corniche proposed in the PTCT plan has now simply been turned on its side, amplified, and become an infill island project that will wrap around the future Palm Jebel Ali. The monorail transportation system included in the PTCT plan has also been revisited, but will now ambitiously serve as part of a large-scale elevated metro system that will finally connect the southwest with the northeast in a comprehensive, emirate-wide public transit system.

End of the Line?

Waterfront City, along with planned solar electric installations, would bring Dubai development to the end of the line at the Abu Dhabi border. Waterfront City, through reclaimed land, even wraps around the planned Palm Jebel Ali into the Gulf in search of more territory, as the urban coastal development reaches its limit. The Arabian Canal and the creek extension sought to extend this coastal urban development logic to the emirate's interior, and land reclamation for more island development could also create more territory, though tidal flows and the needs for coastal maintenance and flushing could prevent this kind of reclamation from going on forever. Should these projects resume in the future, one imagines that the palms and islands may one day be all joined in a mass, unifying reclamation project, but this is probably a ways off. Clearly the DWC airport city project will also promote both territorial and economic growth, which as shown, finally merge into one development logic for Dubai, but the full realization of the DWC city may have the same fate as the Jebel Ali New Town, and require future iterations and development when financial times again allow for the scalar ambition to deliver a city "twice the size of Hong Kong" as a package.

As mentioned in Chapter 4, the Dubai World Holding Company grew specifically out of the Dubai Port Authority, adding those elements of the local development model to the larger holding company, whereby real estate development, port management, airlines, and manufacturing and logistics could combine to seek business opportunities in Dubai, the UAE, the Gulf region, and internationally. Following the incremental and exponential growth of Dubai's development, replicating typologies from Gulf neighbors and beyond, to now re-export this incrementally formed model internationally again demonstrates a kind of pragmatism and strategic thinking that produced the model over time. The different business entities work in concert (in a similar machinistic manner as the components of the National Cement Company and Jebel Ali) to identify international opportunities for the different sectors that Dubai has been able to combine strategically in its own spatial development. The result allows any number of these businesses agencies, ranging from JAFZA International to DP World to Limitless real estate development (whose name was absolutely in line with this thinking), to jointly explore international business opportunities. Jeffrey Sampler and Saeb Einger, in their book *Sand to Silicon: Achieving Rapid Growth Lessons from Dubai*, refer to this as the fourth stage of Dubai development that "closes the loop" of infrastructural asset development through "asset cross-fertilization" (2003), but with the additional caveat that this product can now be exported. The diachronic model, developed over time by combining both the strategic business consolidation of sector-specific or intersectoral clusters with spatial development of replicated typologies—originally from abroad, but later combining these with home grown typologies developed through amplification—can now be replicated in other parts of the world at any scale. The amplification itself, once bound by Dubai's territory, can now be exported as a model to be experimented with internationally, whereby the territorial elements of the model are no longer confined specifically within Dubai. The King Abdullah Economic City in Saudi Arabia described in Chapter 4 is perhaps the clearest example, but this kind of trade urbanism product exportation and delivery is also occurring in Djibouti, Vietnam, Peru, and beyond, where most projects begin with DP World acquiring a local port to manage, and essentially replicating the Jebel Ali Port, Free Trade, and residential/commercial model *in situ*. As I have argued, in the same way the Jebel Ali model influenced in the incremental agglomeration and structure of the Dubai World Holding Company, it also now informs the strategic complementarity and deployment of these business ventures within specific urban port locations around the world, so that the Dubai-Abu Dhabi border, or any other of its borders, is no longer a limitation. How the Dubai World Holding Company weathers current financial troubles will of course affect this international strategy, but if anything, it is precisely its international projects and assets that will offer a solvency and stability to counterbalance the risk fall-out from those speculative real-estate projects in Dubai built over the past decade.

This is not to say that typological experimentation has reached its limit within Dubai. During the swaggering days of 2008 Dubai development, two pieces of news were announced: first, that the Nahkeel real estate developer was going to tear down Jebel Ali Village to make way for a new, more luxurious residential development, and second, that Port Rashid would soon be phased out as a functioning industrial and commercial port—moving these functions to an expanded Jebel Ali Port that, through land reclamation, will reach further into the Gulf—and would be transitioned too as an infrastructure for tourism to receive luxury cruise line ships (Zin 2008, AMO Info News 2007). The Satwa,

Al-Wasl, and Al-Safa neighborhoods—located between Sheikh Zayed Road and the Gulf near the World Trade Center and home to much of the South Asian population—was also identified as an area for the "Jumeriah Gardens" high-rise redevelopment (Hope and Khan 2009). In addition, again within the ambitious days of 2008, preliminary renderings were being drawn to convert the creek into a commercial waterfront esplanade, which would remove current trade functions of regional imports, exports, and transships goods between Dubai and neighboring Iran, India, and the southern Gulf, and turn the creek into a kind of Harbor Place or South Street Seaport. This form of eastward orientation after development has reached its westward limits certainly has precedent elsewhere, be it once manifest destiny had reached the Pacific or when Manhattan development reached the Hudson River and decided to re-visit Alphabet City and then Brooklyn. Present economic conditions in Dubai will forestall some of this northeastward redevelopment, but sights have already been set on revisiting those infrastructural elements that were essential to forming the Dubai development pattern as a way to continue typological experimentation and amplification, and the associate business opportunities created in the process. This kind of layered development and redevelopment is given rhythm by the cycles of investment booms and busts and creates an accumulated urban history. If its past has been a proper indicator, and Dubai proceeds with this planned northeastern development, this will be carried out specifically by revisiting those large-scale infrastructural elements that have driven urban development up to this point, and proposing new catalytic, strategic projects to redevelop areas. Again, however, the fate of luxury real-estate development over the past decade will likely give pause to future developers of that particular typology.

Time

> From minimalism to Andy Warhol, from cybernetics to Robert Smithson, the main task of much late modern culture seems to have been the development of the idea of processing infinity through endless repetition (Aurelli 2008: 100).

In Chapter 3, I discuss briefly the importance of time in Dubai's development history. As a "latecomer" to both oil discovery and industrialization, and its comparatively low quantity of oil reserves (particularly in relation to Abu Dhabi), the emirate's development pace, scale, and intensity strove to compete with neighboring countries in similar circumstances, but also against time itself, with the belief that limited oil reserves offered a limited time window for development opportunities. The book has been organized chronologically to underscore specifically both the cumulative and diachronic components of what has become a model of borrowed typologies that are both replicated and amplified over time. The cumulative effect expressed itself in the planning and construction of specific projects, so that a diachronic learning process could then be temporally flattened into the different components of new projects for synchronic delivery, or the "infrastructure within infrastructure." Replication and amplification in Dubai occurs within this temporal element. The supply-side scalar ambitions of the World Trade Center were combined with the exponential amplification of Port Rashid trade facilities and its ancillary infrastructures (dry docks, logistics storage sheds, bridges and tunnels), the dredging and land reclamation that began with the creek, the machinistic qualities, components and inter-functioning of the National Cement Company, along with regional and international typologies to replicate (Jubail, Yanbu, etc.), all came together in the planning and construction of Jebel Ali Port, Industrial Area, and Free Zone. Indeed, the amplification itself seems to be the influence of combining replication of previous experiences with programmatic intensification consisting of new typologies and/or ancillary components, such that each successive infrastructural project is necessarily more ambitious in scale, intensified programmatically, and has increasing territorial impact. Thus far, the apex of this process is the King Abdullah Economic City in Saudi Arabia, which, at the scale of an entire city, flattens the Dubai urban development processes, and through phased planning and construction, can deliver an entire city based on the various components developed over time in Dubai. But this was also the logic for the Jebel Ali New Town project, as well as for the future DWC airport city, should it actually be built once the airport is complete.

This cumulative development process also occurred within a comparatively short, intense period of time, with only 25 years between the first creek dredging project and the completion of Jebel Ali. Just as economists describe the "spill-over" advantages of agglomeration economies, similar "spill-overs" occurred with the successive infrastructural projects within Dubai, for the obvious reasons: it was the same ruling regime commissioning the projects, often the same group of consultants realizing them, they were spatially located within essentially the same small territory, but also because of the fact that there was a temporal agglomeration or compression that joined the infrastructural projects and their associate urban development, which facilitated projects informing one another. This does not deny the strategic planning of Dubai's clustering infrastructural investments, but recognizes that the time element encouraged the complementarity and mutual reinforcement among the projects.

Another side of this temporal element of Dubai urbanization emerged when supply-side strategy overtook demand-side bound development. Simultaneously with the temporal flattening that occurred with projects mentioned above, projects that were overbuilt (beginning with the World Trade Center, but continuing with Jebel Ali's port and industrial capacity and subsequent large-scale real estate developments) developed forwardly over time as they gradually grew into their capacity and/or were inhabited. This of course reverses the trend mentioned above, so that synchronic development is followed by diachronic inhabitation and use. Trade re-routed through Jebel Ali during the Iran-Iraq conflict helped the massive port gradually reach an acceptable level of activity, and it also required time before the dry dock facility was profitable (Broeze 1999). In addition to meeting their economic objectives, it has also taken time for the residential "ground+one" villas of Jumeirah to be inhabited and demonstrate specific characteristics (gardens, additions, etc.) so as to become a neighborhood rather than simply a subdivision of replicated housing. This kind of temporal element was certainly also the case with new town projects throughout post-war Europe and the United States, where the delivery of a large amount of built environment within such a short period required 20 or 30 years (the span of at least two generations) to develop gradually after the shock of instant supply delivery. This supply-side driven development runs counter to demand-driven, market-oriented urban organicism in growth, but over time, these places are inhabited by other kinds of organic processes. However, as Dubai begins to consider the redevelopment projects heading back northeasterly toward the creek, and that Jebel Ali Village was scheduled to be demolished, one wonders how long Dubai redevelopment will allow the original housing stock of Jumeirah, or that of Deira, Al-Shindigah or Bur Dubai, to develop forward, even in this way, organically.

Ulrich Beck argues that the two contradictory views within modernity are expressed simultaneously in self-destructiveness and the ability to begin anew (2009), but this is from the vantage point of what he calls "reflexive modernity." Dubai's development was clearly guided by foundational modern and modernization aspirations. At least up through Jebel Ali and settlement up to the Abu Dhabi border, the expression of these aspirations in large-scale infrastructure projects was built with an awareness of a limited time window, but also within the modern pretence of timelessness for the projects themselves. The extemporal conceits of both immortality (monarchical, but also societal, as with all modern nation-state building), and infinity (as in reference to the quote at the beginning of this section, and the replication referred to) informed Dubai's development aspirations, and it is hard to imagine that Dubai could have achieved what it has over such a short time without these modern pretentions and conceits. Thus it becomes hard to imagine Dubai's future now that this confidence has been fundamentally shaken. Sheikh Mohammed's announcement that Dubai is "alright" and "will be more careful" projects a conservative tone that is absolutely counter to its developmental history of consistently trying to compete through capacity differentials. If Dubai first sought to compete with its regional neighbours and then the entire world, it's curious to see that it has become its own most formidable adversary. Time will tell, indeed.

Entrepreneurial Modernism

In simple terms, one could argue that replication and amplification throughout Dubai's urban and territorial development merely reflects the same replication of oil exploration and discovery, which brought in exponentially larger revenue as a result of the 1973 international crisis. Between 1969 and 1975 alone, Dubai's oil revue exploded from \$376,114 to an estimated \$600,000,000. With these numbers, it is no surprise that a construction boom spiked, or that the imported South Asian labor required for the boom (also part of the regional model already established by Kuwait, Saudi Arabia, and Bahrain) would triple Dubai's population during these same six years. Oil's impact on Dubai's capacity to replicate and amplify large-scale infrastructural projects, based on typological borrowing, was certainly an important factor. But precisely the fact that Dubai's oil reserves were comparatively low in relation to regional neighbors also provided a motivational incentive and a perceived time constraint for development opportunities that intensified investment, program, and scalar ambitions during this period of urban expansion.

Palan and Abbot's notion of the "competitive state" as one that promotes national (or in this case emirate) economic development through supply-side investment measures rather than relying on demand-side information, along with Porter's theory of competitive advantage developed through intensified clustered investments, together help to better understand Dubai's investment during this booming period. But, as argued in Chapter 2, much of the development pattern that Sheikh Rashid built upon for post-oil development was established before 1966. The shift from a demand-side orientation to that of competitive supply-side thinking coincided with Dubai's move away from master planning. Master planning was specifically concerned with the rational and incremental growth of the city by extrapolating previous socioeconomic patterns forward and developing accordingly. However, the changes precipitated by oil discovery, even though Harris finished the second plan after 1966, were outside the capacity of rational master planning, just as the original projections for Port Rashid recommended four berths only to have its ten berths immediately oversubscribed when the port opened in 1971. The parallel is important, because throughout Dubai's urban development, trade infrastructure has served as smaller scale urban experiments from which to learn lessons that would then inform larger territorial organization and scalar ambitions. Thus the succession of the creek, Port Rashid, and Jebel Ali along the Gulf coast, and the creek, the Dubai International Airport, and the future Al-Maktoum International Airport, all serve as mega-project generators of metropolitan form, such that Dubai's territory over the past 50 years, again, is best described as a port geography. The catalytic nature of these large-scale infrastructure projects was similar to previous mega-projects, from train stations in Paris to Rockefeller Center in New York, but with the important primary focus on trade, which is historically appropriate in the "city of merchants." Given this trade vocation, it is also appropriate that Dubai now exports this urban model, as the logical and pragmatic amplification of its own combination of consolidated business strategy, trade, and spatial replication and amplification.

The processes are easy to imagine for a growing business in an emerging market: borrow money and ideas from international banks and consultants, grow a business through strategic clustering and competitive differentials, establish a recognizable, flamboyant name-brand that projects ambition, confidence, and success that will help the company raise capital, diversify investments across assets to spread risk, and explore international opportunities to expand the asset portfolio and strengthen the brand. The difference, of course, is that it embarked on precisely this kind of private sector strategy as a state, within a compressed temporal context, under the auspices of modern nation-building and development. Dubai developed an entrepreneurial modernism, originally borrowed from other references, but eventually *sui generis*, expressed spatially and over its territory through large-scale infrastructure developments. Indeed, it is precisely because of this overarching entrepreneurial imperative that it is necessary to understand nearly all its territorial investment as infrastructure, in that it was all, in one way or another, a strategic piece within these specific national, territorial, and business projects, and the overarching development strategy that joined them all.

The back-up plan, or *bail out*, now comes from Abu Dhabi to help maintain Dubai as a feasible, solvent state. If Dubai has been able to blur and even erase the boundary between public and the private sector pursuits, for its future viability, Dubai will now need to decide which of the two—Dubai or "Dubai Inc."—is more important.

Conclusion

> The only place remotely comparable to China today is Dubai, which, thanks to our addiction to oil, has been growing by leaps and bounds in recent years. But Dubai is a tiny city-state of just over a million people. China is a hundred Dubais, with a thousand times its ambition (Campanella 2008: 15).

The quote from a recent book on China's development seeks to put its vertiginous urban expansion into a comparative international context by using Dubai—at its 2008 construction zenith—as the watermark, but perhaps its significance goes beyond the author's hyperbolic intention. The modularity and replication of Dubai within an international, developing context outside its territorial boundaries is certainly a strategic objective of the Dubai World Holding Company. The modularity is part of an infrastructural logic, which as we've seen with the case of Dubai, comes to the fore particularly during moments of urban expansion, and acutely within a developmentalist political economic framework. The quote suggests comparative and competitive aspirations, signifying scalar and symbolic intentions of a nation-state striving to both catch up and supersede an exogenous precedent—in this case, a role cast for Dubai. What is unusual about the quote is that it uses the Dubai example as precedent for an Asian urbanization boom, which reverses the trend over the past 20 years of describing Dubai as a kind of misplaced East Asian city-state geographically located in the lower Gulf (Ho 2008, Parsa et al. 2003).

Trade relations with Japan and South Korea brought companies, technology, and consultants to Dubai to help build port infrastructure based on their own postwar development model. Singapore and Hong Kong, which have become among the world's leading *entrepôt* ports thanks to the region's enormous import and export markets, are often conjured as examples on which Dubai based part of its development strategy. After Dubai's typological borrowing, it would appear that its development is now also exported. If not specifically in form or as Dubai World project, Dubai now travels in notoriety, and even infamy, within the international literature on cities and the wider media, which serves as a kind of global radar. In this regard, the use of exogenous projects and templates, particularly during moments of urban expansion, symbolically and functionally, continues in contemporary city-building. The expansion of global media connectivity and iconography, along with an increased role of global consultants, intensify the younger expression of these patterns in Dubai of the 1970s (Wu 2004).

The quote should also serve as a warning to China, for if Dubai imported Asian trade conglomerate and developmental models, it also seems to have imported a crisis precipitated by the accelerated, unregulated markets that hit Asia a decade earlier. China's size and capitalization makes it less vulnerable, but the image of China as "a hundred Dubais"—indeed amplification itself amplified—in the present context, should be enough to give any developing nation pause.

Large-scale trade infrastructure continues to act as mediators between international flows and local environmental, political, and urban networks. The protagonism of these platforms and circuitries increases not only in the developmentalist circumstances of China and the Gulf, but also in cities throughout the world. There is a growing literature on airport cities (Hoete 2003, Kasarda 1999, 2000), and as demonstrated in cities like Barcelona, the Dutch Randstad, and Los Angeles, an increasing tendency to agglomerate and network sea port and airport facilities (and their associate trade activities) for more competitive intermodal trade movement. As the programmatic components intensify, and ship and airplane technology builds increasingly larger vessels, the spatial requirements for trade platforms are periodically intensified. Because large capital investment is required to finance this trade infrastructure race, regional competition increases for central public funds to help finance these expansions, which plays out politically particularly in a large country like the United States.[1] In addition, agencies that operate these facilities are often either "black box" institutions with significant political autonomy, or are now starting to be run by third-party private international transportation facility operators (Baird 2005). The increasing spatial demands and decreasing direct political accountability of large-scale trade infrastructure pose a challenge to local governance and spaces of *civitas*. This of course was Camillo Sitte's critique of the demands of excessive urban functionalism, and time will demonstrate how cities balance the needs of these autonomous urban spheres of trade infrastructure with those of social and civic gathering.

Enseng Ho has described Dubai's ruling structure as a "'trading state' in which the ruling family, the Maktoums, combined the role of both ruler and chief merchant" (Ho 2008, Owen 2008). In the early twentieth-century, when the *majlis* played a larger role in the political decision-making process due to their pearling largess and its importance in essentially maintaining the ruler, Dubai's free port policy was certainly influenced by the trade interests of the merchant community. Once pearling fell, Sheikh Rashid continued to listen to merchant petitions, as demonstrated by the creek dredging, which merchants had petitioned since their reform movement in the 1930s. Interestingly, it was precisely the air rights landing money that came to Sheikh Said, along with oil exploration funds that solidified the ruler's position over his *majlis* with new economic autonomy. Clearly the trading spirit on which the city was founded has continued to be the philosophical and strategic center of the emirate's policies, and is manifest spatially through the large-scale trade infrastructure projects.

1 See research of METRANS Transportation Center. See: http://www.metrans.org/.

But with this, we must also consider Palan and Abbot's work on the competitive state; for clearly Dubai's economic development is guided by emirate competitiveness. In pursuit of this competitiveness, once oil revenue allowed for it, Dubai amplified its traditional demand-side investment to a far more ambitious, speculative supply-side strategy. The creek's limited trade infrastructure and services, and offshore demand cues for berthing, precipitated the construction of Port Rashid. By 1975, Port Rashid's offloading cues for its 15 berths lasted up to 60 days. Its expansion to 37 berths—becoming the largest port in the Middle East—and the parallel commission of the largest port in the world only months afterward, physically punctuated this change in strategy, as did the commissioning the ancillary dry dock and trade center facilities. Over this period, Dubai's urbanism has reflected the coastal scalar and programmatic intensification in the southwestern move from the creek to Jebel Ali, with intermittent periods of cyclical downturns that would put some project ambitions on hold until the next cyclical upswing would enable project continuation and reiteration. The maximum expression of these competitive trade aspirations was the Jebel Ali Port, Industrial Area, and Free Zone, upon which future projects, business strategies, and administrative structures were (and continue to be) modeled. Drawing on both, it is more accurate to describe the Dubai ruling structure as a *competitive trade state* that seeks to increase its international business opportunities with a diversified portfolio of interests, but all of which center around the emirate's central traditional trade vocation.

I have closely explored the development of Dubai through the lens of its trade infrastructure to better understand the multiple roles infrastructure plays within urban environments. In Dubai, infrastructure serves as an important physical element and artifact of the emirate, as exemplified by the creek, Dubai International Airport, Port Rashid, the World Trade Center, and the Jebel Ali Port, Industrial Area, and Free Zone. The creek, and then the road system also serve as a structural infrastructure to first actively guide and channel development, as intended in Harris's two plans, and then reactively as a way to connect the ambitious large-scale projects of the post-1973 boom era. After this boom, the infrastructure projects became the mechanism for territorial organization and infill settlement, which too was expressed in modular, replicated infrastructural logic. The hotel, bank, and housing infrastructure built in the 1950s and 1960s served as foundational systems for the development of more complex, advanced sectors of tourism, international finance, and real estate. The strategic clustering of these infrastructures, and their multiple layers and roles, created "cities within cities," or as I have argued, infrastructural systems both within one another and connected through linkages, in an iterative and cumulative manner that have settled Dubai's coast from the creek to the Abu Dhabi border. Indeed, the land reclamation projects, in their plasticity, certainly focus more on the ground condition than anything that could be built on them, which again stresses infrastructure and engineering over the inhabitation of those spaces.

If infrastructure is traditionally understood in spatial planning as the elemental "hardware" that undergirds urban development, the case of Dubai helps to expand the meanings of infrastructure. Infrastructure in Dubai came more as a package of objects, networks, and services that are projective in nature and can be deployed as a larger strategy for territorial settlement. In this regard, infrastructure did not simply precede a future primary programmatic or use intention, but was itself fused with this intention, cotemporally. From this package of infrastructural elements, a selection was made to decide upon which were specifically to be borrowed, replicated, and potentially amplified. Beginning in the late 1950s with creek dredging, Harris's first master plan, and the 1960 Land Law, infrastructural selection focused primarily on borrowing from regional infrastructure examples to establish communication infrastructure, similar to what Joan Busquets refers to as "colonial infrastructure." When creek trade facilities were no longer sufficient, and urban growth moved beyond the confines of Harris's layout, these infrastructural elements were amplified into Port Rashid and Harris's second plan, continuously building upon the central trade development strategy. Expatriate housing began with the 48 villas in Jumeirah to specifically house consultants for DPC and those working on Port Rashid, but as these residential developments were amplified over time, real estate itself took on a central development role. What began as a housing infrastructure to facilitate oil extraction and port construction was itself spun off into its own economic activity. The development of these kinds of ancillary programmatic elements through amplification is part of this cumulative development process.

The danger of recounting history is that its narrative can be understood as logical and organic fact. In the case of infrastructural development in Dubai, it must be underscored that these processes of borrowing, replication, and amplification involved a series of specific choices. These choices were inspired initially by traditional developmental motives to modularly grow outward, beyond the small fishing town and into the hinterland to claim and settle its territory. One is reminded of the Roman *centuriazione*, deployed both for its urban functions for furloughed centurions, but also to establish and protect Roman territory. Indeed, in the case of Jumeirah, the replication of Harris's gridded street pattern provides an enduring framework for urban settlement that has proven itself from the Rome castrum plan to Cerdà's *ensache*. In this initial development phase, Dubai looked externally to borrow urban typologies and facilities to help guide its investment. Once oil was discovered, however, Dubai competitively and reactively looked abroad to guide and measure the dimensions of its investments. The competitive motive established scale and capacity differentials in specific infrastructural trade systems and facilities that proved successful, particularly thanks to luck and geography during the conflicts of the 1980s. These investments, while admittedly a gamble, were based on the emirate's trade history, and an understanding of how to leverage this history regionally in competition with its neighbors.

More recent forays into high-end real estate development through land reclamation and the creation of artificial islands also borrows, replicates, and amplifies infrastructure from Dubai's own specific past. The "fronds" of the Palm projects bear specific resemblance to the breakwater extensions of Port Rashid and Jebel Ali, and the speckled "World" islands look like the preliminary phase of any land reclamation project. Time demonstrates which kind of infrastructural development is more resilient. The point being that within a bundled possibility of infrastructural elements from which to chose, a city can potentially chose *incorrectly*, as may end up being the case for the island experiments. The island projects provide an exaggerated example, but whether because of the dangers of temporal obsolescence, or an overemphasis placed on certain infrastructure because of an unusual fad or trend, the correct selection of enduring infrastructure continues to involve an element of risk. In this way, the same synergetic and strategic clustering linkages run both ways. The viral debt resulting from excessive risk, internationally and locally, now threatens Dubai World, specifically, as well as Dubai's overarching, agglomerated, blurred public-private governing structure. The Gordian entangling of investments, and the drastic fall of real estate price for which so much debt was risked, makes it difficult to see how this kind business and territorial management strategy can continue. The trust in this insistent clustering, in retrospect, exposes acute vulnerabilities to exactly the kind of international financial and real estate meltdown that occurred. Traditionally, infrastructure precedes construction and creates value for real estate. It undergirds the development process. In Dubai, trade infrastructure assets helped to raise international capital for speculative real estate development, which has resulted in the dramatic fall in property values.

Thinking back to the seventeenth-century port city, the Swedish examples of Gothenburg and Jönköping are useful in helping to understand Dubai's experience. Each city first incorporated pragmatic port city design strategies developed by the Dutch to prudently match physical infrastructural needs with the trade requirements of the moment. When this did not attract the power or the wealth that the new port cities hoped for, they then gambled on the Italian ideal port cities tradition of design with the hope that a more grandiose design would be more successful in conjuring maritime dominion. The gamble did not pay off. The Swedish constructed beyond their means, and this precipitated deep debt and economic collapse for the cities and the country as a whole. Dubai also began with pragmatic planning for the dredging of the creek and the first phase of Port Rashid's construction, but once oil liquidity allowed, the new city planned for Jebel Ali served as a new kind of ideal city planning for its time. This is not to try to fit the aspirations for the new industrial port city specifically into those of the Italian ideal city tradition, but if, as Konvitz points out, ideal city planners tried to relate the parts of the city to each other in a holistic, symmetrical, systematic fashion, Jebel Ali's programmatic inter-functionality certainly fulfills this criteria. For the time, the scalar amplification of the port and its requirements were certainly in the realm of the fantastic, given that the largest port in the world was built for no appreciable hinterland import nor export market that could nearly match Jebel Ali's supply, and it would take 30 years and several regional conflicts to get it near capacity. Jebel Ali was the monument to modernization, combining machinistic functionality with scalar grandeur, and thus, for a city of trade merchants, an ideal. For Dubai, the gamble paid off, but unforeseen regional conflict and enough financial means to run an infrastructural oversupply for several decades were clearly advantages that helped Jebel Ali succeed. As mentioned, Dubai's more recent "new economy" gambles in the financial and real-estate sectors have not had the same luck.

If idyllic for a merchant city, Jebel Ali continued Dubai's pattern of following regional precedents, such as Aden, Jubail, and Yanbu, and leveraging its favorable geographic location as a platform for trade and transshipment. Jebel Ali again demonstrates both the proactive and reactive nature of development and regional competition, where British withdrawal from Aden opened the need for an *entrepôt* port and industrial facility, and Yanbu and Jubail provided regional templates that involved British consulting groups, which could both be called upon to construct something similar, but greater in scale and programmatic capacity.

Dubai's relationship with the United Kingdom was an important part of its development history. British' vast nineteenth-century trade networks established far-reaching routes between India and East Asia with the UK. For Dubai, along with attracting a large portion of its trade community, the significance of the regional coup at Lingah was the attraction of British stream liner ships to its port. While the costs and benefits of Dubai's relationship to the British can be debated, it was clearly an important factor for many reasons. The network of British consultants working in the region during the 1950s was of particular importance to Dubai. Both the Halcrow engineering group and John R. Harris were working in Kuwait and were put in contact with Sheikh Rashid through the system of contacts within the British regional political agency structure. Access to this network of consultants, including those Sudanese who helped to develop the 1960 Land Law, gave Dubai a wide resource base to call upon, and provided the regional templates from which to borrow for its own development strategies. Institutions such as the British Bank of the Middle East and the Grey Mackenzie & Sons, who also had histories working the region, played important roles in helping Dubai to establish banking and port management systems. Thinking back to Alexander Gerschenkron's work, in the same way that the European continent took advantage of British technology and industrialization patterns of as "latecomers," Dubai too was a beneficiary of previous development precedents and strategies, many of which came to Dubai through the wide range of contacts of the waning British Empire. As with the case of the BBME, however, the development of autonomous institutions—an essential step for Gerschenkron's understanding of latecomer borrowing—upset the original monopoly of British institutions in Dubai. These were small problems for the British compared to their situations in Iran and South West Arabia, so Dubai's steps toward autonomy were never really contested (Davidson 2007).

The British also limited Dubai's access to certain networks and development strategies, as exemplified by the fall of the pearling industry, which some local merchant factions claimed was the fault of the British for denying them contact with other world powers who may have provided fishermen with better pearling technology to adapt to changing international competition. The need to petition external agents for the right to develop an airport also rings of a yoked circumstance and a paternalistic scenario where Dubai was not fully autonomous. These issues played out politically in Dubai from the fall of the pearling industry through the formation of the UAE, as they did to various results throughout the region during this period. Nevertheless, even after the formation of the UAE, Dubai favored British consulting firms. The role of Queen Elizabeth II, as both inspiration and inaugurator of the large-scale trade infrastructure of the 1970s, demonstrates that the relationship between Dubai and the UK remains important after independence. Today, British consulting firms continue to have a strong presence in Dubai.

Finally, throughout Dubai's history, it is important to reiterate the simple role of luck and location in Dubai's trade success. Clearly Dubai made opportunistic decisions in response to historical events in the region that fortuitously resulted to Dubai's benefit. The Persian withdrawal from trade prominence at the beginning of the twentieth-century opened an opportunity for Dubai, as did the British withdrawal from Aden, and the Iran-Iraq conflict of the 1980s. This is not to say that Dubai was not quick to respond to these events, or to pose luck as a sole causal factor for its trade success. But the coincidental nature of these factors within Dubai's specific geographic surroundings and along specific international trade, were undeniably part of its developmental trajectory. Whether or not this luck will return remains to be seen.

Dubai is presently experiencing perhaps the most difficult moment in its history. An international financial crisis has highly impacted its producer-service sector and forced the emirate to put many of its development projects on hold. At the same time, DP World is among the world's top four marine terminal operators in the world with 49 marine terminals and 12 new developments across 31 countries (Jacobs and Hall 2007),[2] and the business opportunities generated by DP World's operations are capitalized upon by the complementary services within the larger Dubai World Holding Company. The lack of financial transparency of the individual companies that make up the larger holding company interests could result in their structural and financial reshuffling, but one imagines the overall interactive, complementary strategy will remain in tact. In addition, Dubai has had to ask for financial help from Abu Dhabi through the UAE Central Bank to help it weather the current financial downturn through a $25 billion bond sale (*Economist* Briefing 2009). Thus Dubai is looking outside its territory, both through international projects and to its capital neighbor, to solidify its economic buoyancy, when, as we have seen, the success of its infrastructural development within Dubai over its history has been precisely the foundation both for its international projects, as well as for its relative autonomy from Abu Dhabi centralism.

2 DP World web site. See: http://portal.pohub.com/portal/page?_pageid=761, 248330&_dad=pogprtl&_schema=POGPRTL.

One wonders if Dubai markets will eventually pick up again. What is interesting is that, along with the competing maritime companies from Singapore, China, and Rotterdam, the intensification and increasing importance of trade infrastructure has now produced networks of ports managed under competing larger companies, in ways parallel to European colonial port and trading networks of the past, though clearly under new and different circumstances. Technology remains an important factor in this competitive race for the control of maritime sea trade, and this competition plays out between local port agencies and international operators, as was the case with Barcelona and its new port terminal concession to the Hong Kong Hutchinson Port Holdings operator (Herrero and Alarcon 2006).

The urban repercussions of port competition and development express themselves spatially in local and regional development as the result of international markets, trade routes, and their interconnectivity. As these global trade circuitries become more complex, programmatically intensified, and amplified in scale, their urban and regional spatial repercussions will both reflect these changes, and dialectically, guide them through specific projects. Dubai's development is defined by its close following of regional and international trends, and an eager willingness to accommodate the spatial needs of its central trade sector, and as such, it provides an important example for how trade intensification plays out within a specific territory. Indeed, the port remains both a cause and result of development, but in the twenty-first century this must be amended: the "superterminal" is the cause and result of multiple developments. The many roles and meanings of infrastructure in spatial development—variously employed, clustered, and rebundled through overarching, projective strategies—continue to be central mediators of this dialectical relationship between international flows and their local expressions. Nevertheless, the challenge remains for cities, within the highly functional pragmatism of infrastructural logic, how to balance international economic demands with those of local social *civitas*.

Bibliography

Al-Abed, I. 2001. Formation and Evolution of the Federation and its Institutions, in *United Arab Emirates: A New Perspective*, edited by I. Al-Abed and P. Hellyer. London: Trident Press.

Abramovitz, M. 1986. Catching Up, Forging Ahead, and Falling Behind. *The Journal of Economic History*, 46 (2), 385–406.

Ahmadjian, C.L. 2006. Japanese Business Groups: Continuity in the Face of Change, in *Business Groups in East Asia: Financial Crisis, Restructuring, and New Growth*, edited by S.J. Chang. Oxford: Oxford University Press.

Albrechts, L. and Mandelbaum, S.J. 2005. *The Network Society: A New Context for Planning*. London and New York: Routledge.

Altshuler, A. and Luberoff, D. 2003. *Mega-Projects: The Changing Politics of Urban Public Investment*. Washington, DC: Brookings Institute Press.

AMO Info News. 2007. Nakheel to Redevelop Jebel Ali. *AMO Info Online*. August 22, 2007. Available at: http://www.ameinfo.com/129686.html.

Andrés, L.A., Guasch, J.L., Haven, T. and Foster, V. 2008. *The Impact of Private Sector Participation in Infrastructure: Lights, Shadows and the Road Ahead*. Washington, DC: World Bank.

Anthony, J.D. 2002. *The United Arab Emirates: Dynamics of State Formation*. Abu Dhabi: The Emirate Center for Strategic Studies and Research.

Armstrong, C.K. 2007. *The Koreas*. New York and London: Routledge.

Aureli, P.V. 2008. Toward the Archipielago: Defining the Political and the Formal in Architecture. *Log*, 11, 91–119.

Baird, A.J. 2005. Privatization Trends at the World's Top-Hundred Container Ports, in *World Shipping and Port Development*, edited by T.W. Lee and K. Cullinane. New York: Palgrave.

Balfour-Paul, G. 1991. *The End of Empire in the Middle East: Britain's Relinquishment of Power in Her Last Three Arab Dependencies*. Cambridge: Cambridge University Press.

Ballon, H. and Jackson, K.T. 2007. *Robert Moses and the Modern City: The Transformation of New York*. New York: W.W. Norton & Co.

Bannerman, J.P. 1986. The Impact of the Early Oil Concessions in the Gulf States, in *The Gulf in the Early Twentieth Century: Foreign Institutions and Local Responses*, edited by R.I. Lawless. Durham: Centre for Middle Eastern and Islamic Studies.

Barnett, J. 1995. *The Fractured Metropolis: Improving the New City, Restoring the Old City, Reshaping the Region*. New York: Westview Press.

Beck, U. 1992. *Risk Society: Toward a New Modernity*. London: Sage.

Beck, U. 2009. Risk Society's "Cosmopolitan Moment," in *New Geographies: After Zero,* 1, edited by S.J. Ramos and N. Turan. Cambridge, MA: Harvard University Press, 24–35.

Beehler, M. 2008. Interview with the author. Beehler is Associate Vice President of California firm WATC, hired for the planning of KAEC, Spring 2008. Available at: http://www.kingabdullahcity.com/en/Home/index.html.

Bel, J.M. 1998. *Aden: Port Mythique du Yémen: The Mythical Port of Yemen.* Brusseles and Paris: Amyris.

Berman, M. 1982. *All That is Solid Melts into Air: The Experience of Modernity.* New York: Simon and Schuster.

Bird, J.H. 1963. *The Major Seaports of the United Kingdom.* London: Hutchinson.

Bouman, O., Mitra Khoubrou, M. and Koolhaas, R. 2007. *Al Manakh/Dubai Guide, Gulf Survey, Global Agenda/Moutamarat, AMO, Archis.* Netherlands: Stichting Archis.

Broeze, F. 1989. *Brides of the Sea: Port Cities of Asia from the 16th–20th Centuries.* Honolulu: University of Honolulu Press.

Broeze, F. 1997a. Kuwait Before Oil: The Dynamics and Morphology of an Arab Port City, in *Gateways of Asia: Port Cities of Asia in the 13th–20th Centuries,* edited by F. Broeze. London and New York: Kegan Paul International.

Broeze, F. 1997b. *Gateways of Asia: Port Cities of Asia in the 13th–20th Centuries.* London and New York: Kegan Paul International.

Broeze, F. 1999. Dubai: From Creek to Global Port City, in *Harbours and Havens: Essays in Port History in Honour of Gordon Jackson,* edited by L.R. Fisher and A. Jarvis. St. John: International Maritime Economic History Association.

Brown, K. 1978. Mina Jebel Ali. *Construction News Magazine,* September.

Bulmer-Thomas, V. 2003. *The Economic History of Latin America Since Independence.* New York: Cambridge University Press.

Burdett, R. and Sudjic, D. 2007. *The Endless City: The Urban Age Project by the London School of Economics and Deutsche Bank's Alfred Herrhausen Society.* London: Phaidon.

Busquets, J. et al. 1992. *Treballs Sobre Cerda i el seu Eixample a Barcelona/ Readings on Cerda and the Extension Plan.* Barcelona: Ajuntament de Barcelona: MOPT.

Busquets, J. 2005. *Barcelona: The Urban Evolution of a Compact City.* Rovereto: Nicolodi.

Butler, S.M. 1991. The Conceptual Evolution of Enterprise Zones, in *Enterprise Zones: New Directions in Economic Development,* edited by R.E. Green. London: Sage.

Calderón, C., Easterly, W. and Servén, L. 2003. Latin America's Infrastructure in the Era of Macroeconomic Crisis, in *The Limits of Stabilization: Infrastructure, Public Deficits and Growth in Latin America,* edited by W. Easterly and L. Servén. Washington, DC: Stanford University Press and World Bank.

Calderón, C. and Servén, L. 2004. *Trends in Infrastructure in Latin America 1980-2001*. World Bank Policy Research Working Paper No. 3400. Washington, DC: World Bank.

Calthorpe, P. and Fulton, W. 2001. *The Regional City: Planning for the End of Sprawl*. Washington, DC: Island Press.

Campanella, T.J. 2008. *The Concrete Dragon: China's Urban Revolution and What it Means for the World*. New York: Princeton Architectural Press.

Caro, R.A. 1974. *The Power Broker: Robert Moses and the Rise and the Fall of New York*. New York: Knopf.

Castells, M. 1983. *The City and the Grassroots: A Cross-Cultural Theory of Urban Social Movements*. Berkeley: University of California Press.

Castells, M. 1989. *The Informational City: Information Technology, Economic Restructuring, and the Urban-Regional Process*. Oxford: Blackwell.

Cau, L. 1996. Environmental Perception and Planning: The Case of Plymouth's Waterfront, in *Cityports, Coastal Zones, and Regional Change: International Perspectives on Planning and Management*, edited by B. Hoyle. Chichester: John Wiley & Son.

Cerdà, I. 1867. *Teoría General de la Urbanización y Aplicación de sus Principios y Doctrinas a la Reforma y Ensache de Barcelona*, 2 vols. Madrid.

Cevero, R. 1998. *The Transit Metropolis*. Washington, DC: Island Press.

Chanda, N. 2007. *Bound Together: How Traders, Preachers, Adventurers, and Warriors Shaped Globalization*. New Haven: Yale University Press.

Chang, S.J. 2006. Korean Business Groups: The Financial Crisis and the Restructuring of Chaebols, in *Business Groups in East Asia: Financial Crisis, Restructuring, and New Growth*, edited by S.J. Chang. Oxford: Oxford University Press.

Cherry, G.E. 1988. *Cities and Plans: The Shaping of Urban Britain in the Nineteenth and Twentieth Centuries*. London: E. Arnold.

Chiu, T.N. and Chu, D.K.Y. 1984. 10 Port Developments in the People's Republic of China: Readjustment Under Programmes of Accelerated Economic Growth, in *Seaport Systems and Spatial Change: Technology, Industry, and Development Strategies*, edited by B.S. Hoyle and D. Hilling. Chichester and New York: John Wiley & Sons.

Choay, F. 1997. *The Rule and the Model: On the Theory of Architecture and Urbanism*. Cambridge, MA; London: MIT Press.

Cisneros, H.G. 1995. *Regionalism: The New Geography of Opportunity*. Washington, DC: US Department of Housing and Urban Development.

Clemence, R.V. 1989. *Essays: On Entrepreneurs, Innovations, Business Cycles, and the Evolution of Capitalism/Joseph A. Schumpeter*. New Brunswick: Transaction Publishers.

Cordery, J. 1979a. Mina Jebel Ali: Brochure for the Inauguration, on 26 February, of Mina Jebel Ali. Produced for Halcrow International Partnership. Coxheath: John Cordery Associates Limited.

Cordery, J. 1979b. Marine Works: Docks and Harbours. Sir William Halcrow and Partners. Coxheath: John Cordery Associates Limited.

Crawford, M. 1995. *Building the Workman's Paradise: The Design of American Company Towns*. New York: Verso.

Crowder, J.R. 1983. *United Arab Emirates: Building Conditions and Materials*. Garston, Watford: Department of the Environment, Building Research Establishment, Building Research Station.

Davidson, C.M. 2005. *The United Arab Emirates: A Study in Survival*. Boulder: Lynne Rienner.

Davidson, C.M. 2007. Arab Nationalism and British Opposition in Dubai, 1920–66. *Middle Eastern Studies*, 43 (6): 879–92.

Davidson, C.M. 2008. *Dubai: The Vulnerability of Success*. New York: Columbia University Press.

Davis, M. 2006. Fear and Money in Dubai. *New Left Review*, 41, 46-68.

Dawson, A. H. 1996. Cityport Development and Regional Change: Lessons from Clyde, in *Cityports, Coastal Zones, and Regional Change: International Perspectives on Planning and Management*, edited by B. Hoyle. Chichester: John Wiley & Son.

De Langen, P.W. 2004. Analyzing the Performance of Seaport Clusters, in *Shipping and Ports in the Twenty-First Century: Globalisation, Technology, Change, and the Environment*, edited by D. Pinder and B. Slack. London: Routledge.

Dethier, J. 1978. *Le Temps des Gares*. Paris: Centre National d'Art et de Culture Georges Pompidou.

Duany, A., Plater-Zyberk, E. and Speck, J. 2000. *Suburban Nation: The Rise of Sprawl and the Decline of the American Dream*. New York: North Point Press.

Dubai Municipality. 1988. *Dubai Urban Area Plan*. Report No. 5.

Dubai Statistics Center. 2010. http://www.dsc.gov.ae/DSC/Pages/Home.aspx.

Economist Briefing: The Repercussions of Dubai. Dishdashed. 2009 *The Economist*. December 5–11, 2009, 79.

Elder, C. 1999. *China's Treaty Ports: Half Love and Half Hate*. Oxford: Oxford University Press.

Elian, A.A. 1990. Dubai Experience in Development of Large Stone Asphalt Mixtures, in *Mechanical Tests for Bituminous Mixes – Characterization, Design and Quality Control: Proceedings of the Fourth International RILEM Symposium*, edited by E. Eustacchio and H. W.Fritz. London: Routledge.

Erie, S.P. 2004. *Globalizing LA: Trade, Infrastructure, and Regional Development*. Stanford: Stanford University Press.

Escobar, A. 1995. *Encountering Development: The Making and Unmaking of the Third World*. Princeton: Princeton University Press.

Everything According to Plan: Passing on British Planning Experience to the Middle East. 1983. *Middle East Construction*, 8, 31–4.

Ewing, B., Goldfinger, S., Wackernagel, M., Stechbart, M., Rizk, S.M., Reed, A. and Kitzes, J. 2008. *The Ecological Footprint Atlas 2008*. Oakland: Global Footprint Network.

Fairservice, I. 2002. *Dubai: Gateway to the Gulf*. London: Motivate Publishing.
Fattah, Z. 2009. Deyaar's Earnings Fall 74% on Dubai Property Slump. *Bloomberg.com*, October 19, 2009. Available at: http://www.bloomberg.com/apps/news?pid=newsarchive&sid=a6cj5CyCeL8Q.
Feiocke, R.C. 2004. *Metropolitan Governance: Conflict, Competition, and Collaboration*. Washington, DC: Georgetown University Press.
Filippi, M.R. 2003. Le Procedure: Le Operazioni Preliminari, in *Misurare La Terra: Centuriazione e Coloni Nel Mundo Romano*, edited by S. Settis et al. Modena: F.C. Panini.
Firth, R. 1951. *Elements of Social Organization*. New York: Philosophical Library.
Fleming, C. 2005. *The Dubai Coastline – The Formative Years*. Swindon: Halcrow Group Ltd.
Fleming, C. 2008. Interview with author.
Frampton, K. 1983. Towards a Critical Regionalism: Six Points for an Architecture of Resistance, in *The Anti-Aesthetic: Essays on Postmodern Culture*, edited by H. Foster. Port Townsen: Bay Press.
Frieden, J.A. 2006. *Global Capitalism: Its Fall and Rise in the Twentieth Century*. New York: W.W. Norton & Co.
Friedmann, J. and Weaver, C. 1979. *Territory and Function: The Evolution of Regional Planning*. Berkeley: University of California Press.
Frug, G.E. 1999. *City Making: Building Communities Without Building Walls*. Princeton: Princeton University Press.
Gabriel, E.F. 1987. *The Dubai Handbook*. Ahrensburg: Institute for Applied Economic Geography.
Garreau, J. 1991. *Edge City: Life on the New Frontier*. New York: Doubleday.
Geddes, P. 1915. *Cities in Evolution*. London: Williams & Norgate.
Gerschenkron, A. 1962. *Economic Backwardness in Historical Perspective*. Cambridge, MA: Harvard University Press.
Ghanem, S.M.A. 1992. *Industrialization in the United Arab Emirates*. Aldershot: Avebury.
Gordon, P. and Richardson, H.W. 1997. Are Compact Cities a Desirable Planning Goal? *Journal of the American Planning Association*, 63 (1), 95-105.
Gottmann, J. 1961. *Megalopolis: The Urbanized Northeastern Seaboard of the United States*. New York: Twentieth Century Foundation.
Graham, S. and Marvin, S. 2001. *Splintering Urbanism: Networked Infrastructures, Technological Mobilities and the Urban Condition*. London; New York: Routledge.
Green, T. 1973. *The World of Gold Today*. New York: Walker and Company.
Gulf to Avoid Aviation Infrastructure Crisis. 2007. *Middle Eastern Airport Exchange*, 17.
Al-Gurg, E.S. 1998. *The Wells of Memory*. London: John Murray.
Gurr, T.R. and King, D.S. 1987. *The State and the City*. Chicago: University of Chicago Press.

Hall, P. 1991. The British Enterprise Zone, in *Enterprise Zones: New Directions in Economic Development*, edited by R. Green. London: Sage.

Hamade, R. and Sharif, A. 2009. Dubai "Not Worried" About Maturing Debt, Ruler Says. *Bloomberg.com*, September 8, 2009. Available at: http://www.bloomberg.com/apps/news?pid=newsarchive&sid=auIRXyNS4gwE. Accessed September 26, 2009.

Hamza, K. 1968. *Dubai: The Pearl of the Coast*. Beiruit: *Al-Massaref* Magazine.

Hanappe, P. and Savy, M. 1981. Industrial Port Areas and the Kondratieff Cycle, in *Cityport Industrialization and Regional Development: Spatial Analysis and Planning Strategies*, edited by B.S. Hoyle and D.A. Pinter. Oxford: Pergamon.

Hanley, R.E. 2004. *Moving People, Goods and Information: The Cutting-Edge Infrastructures of Networked Cities*. London: Routledge.

Harcourt, F. 1997. British Oceanic Mail Contracts in the Age of Steam, 1838–1914, in *The World of Shipping*, edited by D.M. Williams. Aldershot: Ashgate.

Harris, J.R. 1994. Dubai Development Plan May 1971, in *Development Plans of the GCC States 1962–1995*. London: Archive Editions.

Hasegawa, K. 2004. *Constructing Civil Society in Japan: Voices of Environmental Movements*. Melbourne and Portland: Trans Pacific.

Hawley, D. 1970. *The Trucial States*. London: George Allen and Unwin.

Hayami, Y. 1997. *Development Economics: From the Poverty to Wealth of Nations*. Oxford: Clarendon Press.

Heard-Bey, F. 1982. *From Trucial States to United Arab Emirates*. London and New York: Longman.

Henning, M. 2010. Sea-Land History 1956–1996. Available at: http://www.mgar.net/sealand2.htm. Accessed February 26, 2010.

Herrero, I. and Jose Alarcon, J. 2006. Hutchison Port Holdings Leads Barcelona Port Push. *Hong Kong Trade Development Council (HKTDC) Online*, October 10, 2006. Available at: http://www.hktdc.com/info/mi/a/imn/en/1X00A75A/1/International-Market-News/Hutchison-Port-Holdings-Leads-Barcelona-Port-Push.htm.

Hirschman, A.O. 1958. *The Strategy if Economic Development*. New Haven: Yale University Press.

Ho, D.K.H. 1996. *The Seaport Economy: A Study of the Singapore Experience*. Singapore: Singapore University Press.

Ho, E. 2008. Dubai and Singapore: Inter-Asian Connections Through Indian Ocean Port Cities. Paper presented to SSRC Conference on Inter-Asian Connections, Dubai School of Government, Dubai. February 2008.

Hoete, A. 2003. *R.O.M.E.: Reader on the Aesthetics of Mobility*. New York: Black Dog.

Holston, J. 1989. *The Modernist City: An Anthropological Critique of Brasilia*. Chicago: University of Chicago Press.

Hope, B. and Khan, S. 2009. Evicted Jumeira Gardens Residents Return Home. *The National Online*, January 7, 2009. Available at: http://www.thenational.ae/apps/pbcs.dll/article?AID=/20090107/BUSINESS/599826714.

Howard, E. 1898. *Tomorrow: A Peaceful Path to Real Reform*. London: S. Sonnenschein.

Hoyle, B.S. and Pinder, D.A. 1981. *Cityport Industrialization and Regional Development: Spatial Analysis and Planning Strategies*. Oxford: Pergamon.

Hoyle, B.S. and Hilling, D. 1984. *Seaport Systems and Spatial Change: Technology, Industry, and Development Strategies*. Chichester and New York: John Wiley & Sons.

Hoyle, B.S. 1989. Maritime Perspectives on Ports and Port Systems: The Case of East Africa, in *Brides of the Sea: Port Cities of Asia from the 16th–20th Centuries*, edited by F. Broeze. Honolulu: University of Honolulu Press.

Hoyle, B.S. 1996. *Cityports, Coastal Zones, and Regional Change: International Perspectives on Planning and Management*. Chichester: John Wiley & Son.

Huff, W.G. 1995. *Growth and Planning in an Asian NIC: Singapore Considered*. Centre for Development Studies Occasional Paper No. 13. Glasgow: University of Glasgow.

Humaid Al Tayer, O. 1999. Dubai World Trade Centre: 20 Years of Success. Sponsored supplement of *Gulf Business*. Dubai: Motivate Publishing.

Hvidt, M. 2007. *The Dubai Model: An Outline of Key Components of the Development Process in Dubai*. Working Paper No. 12. Centre for Contemporary Middle East Studies, University of Southern Denmark.

Jacobs, J. 1961. *The Death and Life of Great American Cities*. New York: Random House.

Jacobs, W. 2005. *Empire Along a Creek: Territorial Competition and Dubai Ports*. Working Paper No. 1. Institute of Urban and Regional Planning and Development. American University of Sharjah.

Jacobs, W. and Hall, P.V. 2007. What Conditions Supply Chain Strategies of Ports? The Case of Dubai. *GeoJournal*, 68, 327–42.

Jebel Ali Village. Sir William Halcrow and Partners promotional publication. Date not specified.

Jones, G. 1987. *Banking and Oil: The History of the British Bank of the Middle East Volume 2*. London: Cambridge University Press.

Jones, S. 1986. *Two Centuries of Overseas Trading: The Origins and Growth of the Inchcape Group*. London: MacMillan Press.

Josselyn, C. and Borel, P. 2009. Asset Class: Defining Infrastructure and Why it Matters. *Infrastructure Investor*, Issue 4.

Kasarda, J.D. 1999. *New Logistics Technologies and Infrastructure for the Digitized Economy*. Online Working Paper. Kenan Institute of Private Enterprise, Kenan-Flagler Business School, University of North Carolina.

Kasarda, J.D. 2000. *Aerotropolis: Airport-Driven Urban Development in Cities in the 21st Century*. Washington, DC: Urban Land Institute.

Kassar, K. 2007. *1000 Numbers and Reasons Why Dubai*. 2nd Edition. Beirut: BISC Group.

King, A.D. 1984. *The Bungalow: The Production of Global Culture*. London: Routledge and Kegan Paul.

King, G.R. 1997. The History of the UAE: The Eve of Islam and Islam Period, in *Perspectives on the United Arab Emirates*, edited by E. Ghareeb and I. Al-Abed. Abu Dhabi: Trident Press.

Kinzer, S. 2003. *All the Shah's Men: An American Coup and the Roots of Middle East Terror*. Hoboken, NJ: John Wiley & Sons.

Knight, F.W. and Liss, P.K. 1991. *Atlantic Port Cities: Economy, Culture, and Society in the Atlantic World, 1650–1850*. Knoxville, TN: University of Tennessee Press.

Koolhaas, R. 1978. *Delirious New York: A Retroactive Manifesto for Manhattan*. New York: Oxford University Press.

Koolhaas, R. and Mau, B. 1995. *Small, Medium, Large, Extra-Large*. New York: Monacelli Press.

Konvitz, J.W. 1978. *Cities and the Sea: Port City Planning in Early Modern Europe*. Baltimore: Johns Hopkins University Press.

Korea Development Institute. 1980. *Manpower Development Master Plan for Jubail and Yanbu*. Royal Commission for Jubail and Yanbu. Kingdom of Saudi Arabia; Seoul.

Krieger, A., Cobb, D. and Turner, A. 1999. *Mapping Boston*. Cambridge, MA: MIT Press.

Al-Kuwari, A.K. 1978. *Oil Revenue in the Gulf Emirates: Patterns and Allocations and Impact on Economic Development*. Boulder: Westview Press.

Kyung-Sup, C. 1999. Compressed Modernity and its Discontents: South Korean Society in Transition. *Economy and Society*, 28 (1), 30–55.

Ledger, D. 1983. *Shifting Sands: The British in South Arabia*. London: Peninsular Publishing.

Levinson, M. 2006. *The Box: How the Shipping Container Made the World Smaller and the World Economy Bigger*. Princeton: Princeton University Press.

Longhurst, H. 1959. *Adventures in Oil: The Story of British Petroleum*. London: Sidgwick and Jackson.

Lorimer, J.G. 1970. *Gazetteer of the Persian Gulf, Oman, and Central Arabia*. London: Gregg International Publishers.

Lovering, J. 1993. Theory Led by Policy: The Inadequacies of the 'New Regionalism' (Illustrated from the Case of Wales). *International Journal of Urban and Regional Research*, 23, 379–95.

Lui, P.C. and Tan, T.S. 2001. Building Integrated Large-Scale Urban Infrastructures: Singapore's Experience. *Journal of Urban Technology*, 8 (1), 49–68.

Mackenzie, R.D. National Cement Co. Ltd. Promotional Pamphlet. National Printing Press. Date unspecified.

El-Mallakh, R. 1981. *The Economic Development of the United Arab Emirates*. London: Croom Helm Ltd.

Maraqa, M.A., Ali, A., Imran, H.D., Hamza, W. and Al-Awadi, S. 2008. Simulation of the Hydrodynamic Regime of Jebel Ali Harbor, Dubai, United Arab Emirates. *Aquatic Ecosystem Health and Management*, 11 (1), 105–15.

Marcuse, P. and van Kempen, R. 2000. *Globalizing Cities: A New Spatial Order?* Malden: Blackwell.

Marshall, R. 2001. *Waterfronts in Post-Industrial Cities*. London; New York: Spon.

Mcafee, A.P., Ooms-Walls, K. and Al Aqasimi, L. 2003. Dubai Ports Authority (A). Harvard Business School Case Study. 9-603-061. Boston: Harvard Business School Publishing.

McCalla, R.J. 2004. From 'Anyport' to 'Superterminal': Conceptual Perspectives on Containerization and Port Infrastructure, in *Shipping and Ports in the Twenty-First Century: Globalisation, Technology, Change, and the Environment*, edited by D. Pinder and B. Slack. London: Routledge.

Meeks, C.L.V. 1956. *The Railroad Station: An Architectural History*. New Haven: Yale University Press.

Melamid, A. 1980. Urban Planning in Eastern Arabia. *Geographical Review*, 70 (4), 473–7.

Melamid, A. 1989. Dubai City. *Geographical Review*, 79 (3), 345–7.

Meller, H. 1997. *Towns, Plans and Society in Modern Britain*. Cambridge: Cambridge University Press.

Meyer, H. 1999. *City and Port: Urban Planning as a Cultural Venture in London, Barcelona, New York and Rotterdam: Changing Relations Between Public Urban Space and Large-scale Infrastructure*. Utrecht: International Books.

The Middle East/Congressional Quarterly, Inc. 10th edition. 2005. Washington, DC: CQ Press.

Mina Jebel Ali. Project Information Packet for internal use. Halcrow International Partnership. Date unspecified.

Mitchell, W.J. 1995. *City of Bits: Space, Place and the Infobahn*. Cambridge: MIT Press.

Morgan, D. 1979. Fiscal Policy in Oil Exporting Countries, 1972–1978. *Finance & Development*, December, 14-17.

Morris, A.E.J. 1979. *History of Urban Form: Before the Industrial Revolutions*. 2nd Edition. New York: John Wiley & Son.

Mostafavi, M. and Najle, C. 2003. *Landscape Urbanism: A Manual for the Machinic Landscape*. London: Architectural Association.

Mumford, L. 1961. *The City in History: Its Origins, its Transformations, and its Prospects*. New York: Harcourt Brace Jovanovich.

Nawwab, I.I., Speers, P.C. and Hoye, P.F. 1980. *Aramco and its World: Arabia and the Middle East*. Dhahran, Saudi Arabia: Aramco.

Nugée, J. and Subacchi, P. 2008. *The Gulf Region: A New Hub of Global Financial Power*. London: Chatham House.

Nyrop, R.F. 1977. *Area Handbook for the Persian Gulf States*. Washington, DC: American University.

Onley, J. 2007. *The Arabian Frontier of the British Raj: Merchants, Rulers, and the British in the Nineteenth Century Gulf.* Oxford and New York: Oxford University Press.

Al-Otaiba, M.S. 1977. *Petroleum and the Economy of the United Arab Emirates.* London: Croom Helm.

Olds, K. and Yeung, H.W.C. 2004. Pathways to Global City Formation: A View from the Developmental City-State of Singapore. *Review of International Political Economy,* 11 (3), 489–521.

Ostwald, J.H. 1948. *Otto Wagner, Ein Beitrag Zum Verständnis Seines Baukünstlerischen Schaffens.* Baden: Verlag Buchdr.

Owen, P.G. 1978. Survey of Middle East Ports. *Dock and Harbour Authority*, 59 (695), 164–8.

Owen, R. 2008. *Cities of the Persian Gulf: Past, Present and Future*. Lecture delivered at the University of Nicosia, Nicosia, Cyprus, October, 14 2008.

Pacione, M. 2005. City Profile: Dubai. *Cities*, 22 (3), 255–65.

Packard, S. Dubai House Prices Plunge 47% as Speculators Flee. *Bloomberg.com*, September 10, 2009. Available at: http://www.bloomberg.com/apps/news?pid =newsarchive&sid=aU.I.vUJkPJo.

Palan, R., Abbott, J. and Deans, P. 1996. *State Strategies in the Global Political Economy*. London: Pinter.

Pampanini, A.H. 1997. *Cities from the Arabian Desert: The Building of Jubail and Yanbu in Saudi Arabia.* Westport: Praeger.

Parsa, A. et al. 2003. *Emerging Global Cities: Comparisons of Singapore and the Cities of United Arab Emirates.* Sharjah, London and Singapore: RICS Foundation.

Peck, M.C. 1986. *The United Arab Emirates: A Venture in Unity*. Boulder: Westview Press.

Peddle, Thorp, Chapman, and Taylor, in conjunction with Roger Tym & Associates. 1977. *Jebel Ali New Town.* London: Photoprinters.

Peterson, T.T. 2006. *The Decline of the Anglo-American Middle East: A Willing Retreat.* Brighton and Portland: Sussex Academic Press.

Pinder, D. and Slack, B. 2004. *Shipping and Ports in the Twenty-First Century: Globalisation, Technology, Change, and the Environment*. London: Routledge.

Planhol, X. 1964. Abadan: Morphologie et Fonction du Tissu Urbain. *Revue Géographique de l'Est*, 4, 338–85.

Pollock, E.E. 1981. Free Ports, Free Trade Zones, Export Processing Zones and Economic Development, in *Cityport Industrialization and Regional Development: Spatial Analysis and Planning Strategies*, edited by B.S. Hoyle and D.A. Pinter. Oxford: Pergamon.

Pope, A. 2008. We are all bridge-and-tunnel people... *Log*, 12, 41–58.
Porter, M.E. 2000. Location, Competition, and Economic Development: Local Clusters in a Global Economy. *Economic Development Quarterly*, 14 (1), 15–34.
Pounds, N.J.G. 1981. *Success in Economic Geography*. London: John Murray Ltd.
Rammin, T. 1999. *The Ensemble of Port Development Factors in the Mediterranean Region: 1815–1999*. Doctoral Dissertation. Harvard University Graduate School of Design.
Ramos, S.J. 2008. *Sinews of Growth: Generative Infrastructural Urbanism in Dubai.* Policy Brief No. 4. Dubai School of Government
Ramos, S.J. and Turan, N. 2009. *New Geographies: After Zero*. Vol. 1. Cambridge, MA: Harvard University Press.
Richardson, H.W. 1978. *Regional and Urban Economics*. Harmondsworth: Penguin.
Rimmer, P.J. 1984. Japanese Seaports: Economic Development and State Intervention, in *Seaport Systems and Spatial Change: Technology, Industry, and Development Strategies*, edited by B.S. Hoyle and D. Hilling. Chichester and New York: John Wiley & Sons.
Rimmer, P. and Taniuchi, T. 1989. Japan's Seaports and Regional Developments During the Era of High-Speed Growth, 1960–75, in *Brides of the Sea: Port Cities of Asia from The 16th–20th Centuries*, edited by F. Broeze. Honolulu: University of Honolulu Press.
Rist, G. 1997. *The History of Development: From Western Origins to Global Faith*. London: Zed Books.
Roberts, M.H.P. 1979. *An Urban Profile of the Middle East*. London: Croom Helm.
Rodrigue, J.P. 2004. Appropriate Models of Port Governance: Lessons from the Port Authority of New York and New Jersey, in *Shipping and Ports in the Twenty-First Century: Globalisation, Technology, Change, and the Environment*, edited by D. Pinder and B. Slack. London: Routledge.
Rosenberg, M.T. 2009. Cheng Ho: The Famous Chinese Eunuch Admiral-Explorer of the 15th Century. *About.com: Geography*. Available at: http://geography.about.com/od/historyofgeography/a/chengho_2.htm.
Rostow, W.W. 1959. The Stages of Economic Growth. *The Economic History Review*, 12 (1), 1–16.
Rovira, J.M. 2005. *Sert, 1928-1979: Complete Work, Half a Century of Architecture*. Barcelona: Fundació Joan Miró.
Rowe, P.G. 1991. *Making the Middle Landscape*. Cambridge, MA: MIT Press.
Rowe, P.G. and Pasini, R. 2004. *Urban Territorialization in Areas of Romagna Italy/Il Processo di Territorializzazione in area Romagnola.* Cambridge, MA: Harvard University, Graduate School of Design; Bologna: Universita di Bologna.

Rowe, P.G. 2005. *East Asia Modern: Shaping the Contemporary City*. London: Reaktion.

Rusk, D. 1993. *Cities Without Suburbs*. Washington, DC: Woodrow Wilson Center Press.

Salama, V. and Hall, C. 2009. Dubai Seeks to Dispel Gloom, Lure Skeptics to Metro. *Bloomberg.com*, September 8, 2009. Available at: http://www.bloomberg.com/apps/news?pid=newsarchive&sid=atFY5THHVy8g. Accessed on September 26, 2009.

Salem, F. and Jarrar, Y. 2009. *Cross-Agency Collaboration in the UAE Government: The Role of Trust and the Impact of Technology.* DSG Report. Dubai: Dubai School of Government.

Sampler, J. and Einger, S. 2003. *Sand to Silicon: Achieving Rapid Growth Lessons from Dubai.* London: Profile Books.

Sargent, A.J. 1938. *Seaports and Hinterlands*. London: Adam and Charles Black.

Sarkis, H. and Abulhasan, N. 2005. Dubai: The City of Many Cities, in *The Arab City: Amman, Beirut, and Dubai*, edited by G. Arbid. Beirut: ESCWA Publications.

Sassen, S. 1991. *The Global City: New York, London, Tokyo.* Princeton: Princeton University Press.

Sassen, S. 2002. *Global Networks, Linked Cities.* New York: Routledge.

Al-Sayegh, F. 1998. Merchants' Role in a Changing Society: The Case of Dubai, 1900–90. *Middle Eastern Studies*, 34 (1), 87–102.

Schorske, C.E. 1961. *Fin-de-Siècle Vienna: Politics and Culture.* New York: Random House.

Scott, A.J. 2001. *Global City-Regions: Trends, Theory, Policy*. Oxford: Oxford University Press.

Seccombe, I. and Lawless, R. 1987. *Work Camps and Company Towns: Settlement Patterns and the Gulf Oil Industry*. Durham: University of Durham, Centre for Middle Eastern and Islamic Studies.

Sen, A.K. 1983. Development: Which Way Now? *Economic Journal*, 93 (372), 745–62.

Settis, S. et al. 2003. *Misurare La Terra: Centuriazione e Coloni Nel Mundo Romano*. Modena: F.C. Panini.

Al-Shamsi, F. 1999. Industrial Strategies and Change in the UAE During the 1980s, in *Change and Development in the Gulf*, edited by A. Abdelkarim. New York: St. Martin's Press.

Shannon, K. and Smets, M. 2010. *The Landscape of Contemporary Infrastructure.* Rotterdam: NAi Publishers.

Simmonds, R. and Hack, G. 2000. *Global City Regions: Their Emerging Forms*. London: Spon.

Sitte, S. 1909. *Der Städtebau Nach Seinen künstlerischen Grundsätzen* [The Art of Building Cities: City Building According to its Artistic Fundamentals]. Wien: K. Graeser.

Smith, S. 2004. *Britain's Revival and Fall in the Gulf: Kuwait, Bahrain, Qatar, and the Trucial States, 1950–71*. London; New York: Routledge Curzon.

Soja, E.W. 2000. *Postmetropolis: Critical Studies of Cities and Regions*. Oxford; Malden, MA: Blackwell.

Solà-Morales i Rubió, M. and Gómez Ordoñez, J.L. 1977. Crecimiento Urbano como Inversión de Capital Fijo: El Caso de Barcelona (1840–1975). *Ciudad y Territorio*, 2, 53–62.

Solà-Morales i Rubió, M. 1997. *Las Formas de Crecimiento Urbano*. Barcelona: UPC.

Sorensen, A. 2002. *The Making of Urban Japan: Cities and Planning from Edo to the Twenty-First Century*. London; New York: Routledge.

Stanford Research Institute. 1971. *Area Handbook for the Peripheral States of the Arabian Peninsula*. Washington, DC: American University.

Stanley, B. 2001. "Going Global" and Wannabe World Cities: (Re)conceptualizing Regionalism in the Middle East. *GaWC Research Bulletin 45*. Loughborough: Globalization and World Cities Study Group and Network.

Sucharov, L. 1977. Port Construction, A MEED Special Report. *Middle East Economic Digest*, 25, V-IX.

Sutherland, H. 1989. Eastern Emporium and Company Town: Trade and Society in Eighteenth-Century Makassar, in *Brides of the Sea: Port Cities of Asia from The 16th–20th Centuries*, edited by F. Broeze. Honolulu: University of Honolulu Press, 1989.

Symposium on Contracting and Implementing Down-Stream Petroleum Projects: Abu Dhabi, November 7–9, 1981. 1982. Kuwait: Organization of Arab Petroleum Exporting Countries.

Tétreault, M.A. 2000. The Economics of National Autonomy in the UAE, in *A Century in Thirty Years: Shaykh Zayed and the United Arab Emirates*, edited by J.A. Kechichian. Washington, DC: Middle East Policy Council.

Thomas Jr, L. 2009. A Dubai Investment Arm Struggles With Debt Load. *New York Times*. September 14, 2009. Available at: http://www.nytimes.com/2009/09/15/business/global/15dubai.html?_r=1&scp=1&sq=istithmar&st=cse.

Tohmo, T., Littunen, H. and Tanninen, H. 2006. Backward and Forward Linkages, Specialization and Concentration in Finnish Manufacturing in the Period 1995–1999. *European Journal of Spatial Development*, 19. Online journal.

Trench, R. 1994. *Arab Gulf Cities: Doha, Abu Dhabi, Dubai, Sharjah, Ras Al Khaimah*. Oxford: Archive Editions.

Tsui-Auch, L.S. 2006. Singaporean Business Groups: The Role of the State and Capital in Singapore Inc., in *Business Groups in East Asia: Financial Crisis, Restructuring, and New Growth*, edited by S.J. Chang. Oxford: Oxford University Press.

Turner, A. and Smulian, J. 1974. New Cities in Venezuela, in *The City in the Third World*, edited by D.J. Dwyer. New York: Barnes & Noble Books.

Vigarié, A. 1981. Maritime Industrial Development Areas: Structural Evolution and Implications for Regional Development, in *Cityport Industrialization and Regional Development: Spatial Analysis and Planning Strategies*, edited by B.S. Hoyle and D.A. Pinter. Oxford: Pergamon.

Ward, S.V. 1992. *The Garden City: Past, Present and Future*. London; New York: E & FN Spon.

Ward, S.V. 2006. "Cities are Fun!": Inventing and Spreading the Baltimore Model of Cultural Urbanism, in *Culture, Urbanism, and Planning*, edited by J. Monclus and M. Guardia. Hampshire; Burlington: Ashgate.

Waldheim, C. 2006. *The Landscape Urbanism Reader*. New York: Princeton Architectural Press.

Walker, A.R. 1984. Oil-Dependent Economies and Port Development, in *Seaport Systems and Spatial Change Technology, Industry, and Development Strategies*, edited by B.S. Hoyle and D. Hilling. Chichester: John Wiley & Son.

Wang, M. 2005. The Rise of Container Transport in East Asia, in *World Shipping and Port Development*, edited by T.W. Lee and K. Cullinane. New York, Palgrave.

Weber, M. 1958. *Protestantische Ethik und der Geist des Kapitalismus* [*The Protestant Ethic and the Spirit of Capitalism*]. New York: Scribner.

Williams, D.M. 1997. *The World of Shipping*. Aldershot: Ashgate.

Wilson, G. 1999. *Father of Dubai: Sheikh Rashid bin Saeed Al Maktoum*. Dubai: Media Prima.

Wilson, G. 2006. *Rashid's Legacy: The Genesis of the Maktoum Family and the History of Dubai*. Dubai: Media Prima.

Wilson, R. 1987. *Gulf Trade and Finance: Trends and Market Prospects*. London: Graham & Trotman.

Wirth, L. 1925. A Bibliography of the Urban Community, in *The City*, edited by R.E. Park, E.W. Burgess and R.D. McKenzie. Chicago: The University of Chicago Press.

Wray, W.D. 1984. *Mitsubishi and the N.Y.K., 1870–1914: Business Strategy in the Japanese Shipping Industry*. Cambridge, MA: Council on East Asian Studies.

Wu, F. 2004. Transplanting Cityscapes: The Use of Imagined Globalization in Housing Commodification in Beijing. *Area*, 36 (3), 227–34.

Yergin, D. 1991. *The Prize: The Epic Quest for Oil, Money, and Power.* New York: Simon & Schuster.

Yuen, B. 1998. *Planning Singapore: From Plan to Implementation.* Singapore: Singapore Institute of Planners.

Zahalan, A.B. 1984. *The Arab Construction Industry*. New York: St. Martin's Press.

Zin, C.T. 2008. Port Rashid Ends Cargo Handling Operations. *PortWorld Online.* January 21, 2008. Available at: http://www.portworld.com/news/2008/jan/70441.

Index

Note: Page numbers in **bold** refer to figures and tables